WC

Wood Technology
for the Junior Certificate

General Editor: Bill Gaughran

Co-operating Authors: Bill Gaughran

Sean O'Broin

Liam Quirke

Jim O'Farrell

David Anderson

Rory O'Toole

John Fitzgibbons

GILL AND MACMILLAN

Published in Ireland by
Gill and Macmillan Ltd
Goldenbridge
Dublin 8
with associated companies throughout the world
© Bill Gaughran, Sean O'Broin, Liam Quirke, Jim O'Farrell,
David Anderson, Rory O'Toole, John Fitzgibbons 1992

0 7171 1962 9

Artwork: Jim O'Farrell
O'Shea Computing
Bill Gaughran

Design: The Unlimited Design Company, Dublin

Photography: Melvyn Burton

Print origination: Seton Music Graphics Ltd,
Bantry, Co. Cork

Photocopying
prohibited
by law

Contents

Locating Assignments and Activities

Preface

While this textbook is tailored to suit the course for Materials Technology (Wood) in the Junior Certificate it is also seen as beneficial to any technology based course. Its approach is intended not just to deal with the technical information associated with Wood and other technologies but to do so in an interesting and stimulating fashion.

The textbook covers all aspects of the course thoroughly and enjoyably. The authors have co-operated in producing a comprehensive and exciting textbook. Throughout the book there are hundreds of activities and projects to suit all levels of experience and ability.

The chapters on electronics (chapter 21) and on mechanisms (chapter 23) are included to broaden the pupil's approach to project activity.

Bill Gaughran
July 1992

Acknowledgments

For assistance in the preparation of this book, grateful acknowledgment is made to the following:

Murt Flanagan, Seamus O'Shea, Donal Lynch.
Niall O Muirgheasa, Chief Forester, Forestry and Wildlife Services.
Pat Coakley, Timber Research Unit, Eolas.
John McLoughlin, Coillte.
Martina Wilkins, Coillte.
Margaret Murphy, Medite Europe.
Pat O'Connor.
John Madden.
Woodgrey, Coolock, Dublin.
McQuillans Tools, Capel St, Dublin.
Engineering Equipment, Santry, Dublin.
Parkway Tools and D.I.Y., Limerick.
Dodds, Mary St, Dublin.
R.S. Gough, Little Mary St, Dublin.
Post Primary School, Rathangan.
Army Apprentice School, Naas.
Thomond College, Limerick.

For permission to reproduce additional photographs and illustrations, grateful acknowledgment is made to the following: Gillian Beckett, Office of Public Works, Sean O'Broin, Coillte, Stanley Tools, Record Holdings Plc.

Introducing wood technology

There is no doubt that trees have been one of our greatest natural resources since people first came to be on earth. People have used trees for fuel, food, shelter, in bridges, buildings, tools, furniture, transport, art, toys, sportsgoods and for many other uses. Its unique properties and intricate beauty make wood a very valuable resource. However, unlike many other natural resources which are also rapidly diminishing, trees are renewable. Forests may be replanted to go on producing trees indefinitely. Many species of trees live for hundreds of years and some for even thousands. Yet a great oak tree may be felled in minutes. Few other plants can compare with the beauty of a mature tree fully arrayed with leaves and its flowers or fruit.

Leaf and section

A mature tree: weeping ash

Trees are a vital part of the earth's ecosystem. The human race, however, often treats its forests with disdain. The Romans devastated the forests of North Africa 2,000 years ago. Today the devastation is even greater, particularly of the rainforests in the Southern Hemisphere. There people denude the forests in greedy pursuit of oil or minerals or to claim the land for other uses. This not only affects the climate but displaces ancient tribes and places many species of plant and animal in danger of extinction.

Tropical rain forest

In many places acid rain falling on the delicately designed leaves or saturating surrounding terrain is sounding the deathknell of many forests. For example, many trees are dying in the beautiful Black Forest in Germany because of acid rain, a result of heavy industry. We can all do our part to help by replacing at least some of the wood we use. If each of us were to plant just one hardwood and one softwood tree we would be making a positive contribution. Later in the text it will be explained how to go about cultivating trees, even from seedlings.

Hardwood table

Hardwoods are generally much slower to grow than softwoods and are much scarcer. They should therefore be used only where softwoods would not be suitable. As you learn more about their characteristics and uses you will be in a position to know which material to choose. Most good-quality furniture is made from hardwood such as mahogany or oak. Thin slices of hardwood known as veneers are glued to a cheaper softwood or composite board base to provide a quality surface. This not only saves expensive hardwood but gives the full beauty and characteristics of the wood and is usually more stable on large panels. It also provides the opportunity to create patterns and designs.

Marquetry panels

Craftspeople and designers have developed many ways of enhancing and embellishing wood down through the centuries. Turning and carving are examples, and for these hardwoods are generally used. Carving may go beyond embellishment to being an artform in itself. Patience, skill and knowledge are required to produce most worthwhile artifacts in wood, and of course the correct tools for the task on hand.

The craft and technique associated with working wood have developed over thousands of years. Hand tools have changed very little down through the centuries. The materials and design may improve but the basic design changes little.

Turned artifacts

Carved panel

Hand tools

The selection of tools which are appropriate to a process or task is very important. So too is their care and maintenance. Unless tools are kept quite sharp you cannot pare, cut or shape wood with any degree of success.

Most of the improvements in tooling have been in power tools. The wear and tear and constant sharpening associated with machining wood, particularly hardwoods, are much reduced by improved steel technology. Tungsten carbide cutters or tipped saws produce a far better finish and last much longer. The extra cost of such tools is therefore recouped in a short time. Advances in the technology of glues and adhesives have provided new possibilities in

Tungsten-tipped saw-end cutters

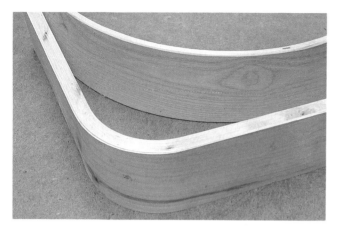
Examples of laminated Bentwood

Risk of danger sign

designing using wood, as well as reducing waste. Lamination, for example, gives greater flexibility in furniture and building.

Computer technology has also had an impact in the wood and furniture industries. For accurate reproduction of turned elements or routing and moulding of panels or for some decorative work CNC (computer numerically controlled) machines are becoming more common. Some CAD (computer aided design) programmes may be interfaced (i.e. used in conjunction with) CNC machines. This allows the lathe or router, for example, to be remotely controlled from a computer workstation. In industry this can improve productivity and maintain constant standards. Many schools now have CNC machines.

Whenever you are using hand or electrically or otherwise powered tools safety standards must be closely adhered to. Using tools according to established safety practices not alone prevents accidents but usually produces higher quality results. Always adhere closely to specified safety standards and manufacturers' instructions for hand and powered tools. Throughout this book safety will be stressed. When in doubt seek advice from your teacher or somebody with the necessary experience.

When designing or making any object choice of materials will have a major influence on the finished product. The materials chosen will be influenced by safety, function, appearance, cost, availability, etc. Where, for example, wood is not most suited to a particular project other materials should be used in conjunction with or instead of wood. Therefore it is necessary to appreciate the properties and uses of other materials such as plastics and metals. Then you

CNC router

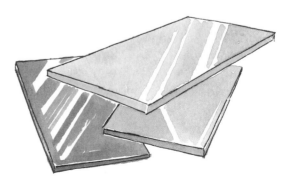
Sheet plastics

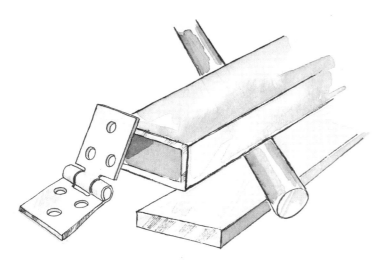

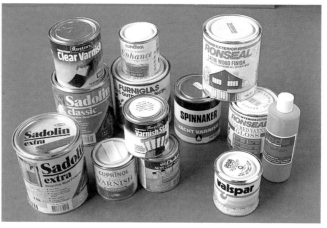

Some furniture materials

Metals

can make an informed choice as to which material is best suited for a particular purpose. As you develop the variety of skills associated with working materials this will provide greater insight into their properties and characteristics.

Most articles which are made will require something more than a surface finish. Applied finishes used appropriately will enhance the appearance of an article and probably extend its durability. So, like the variety of woods and other materials, surface finishes need to be considered for their properties and characteristics. The variety of surface finishes is constantly expanding. They must be appropriate to the material on which they are being applied as well as its use and its environment. A carefully chosen and skilfully applied finish highlights the beauty of wood or can add colour and durability to any material. Some surface finishes are toxic and should be used with care.

Each material has its own finish

Polished mahogany unit

5

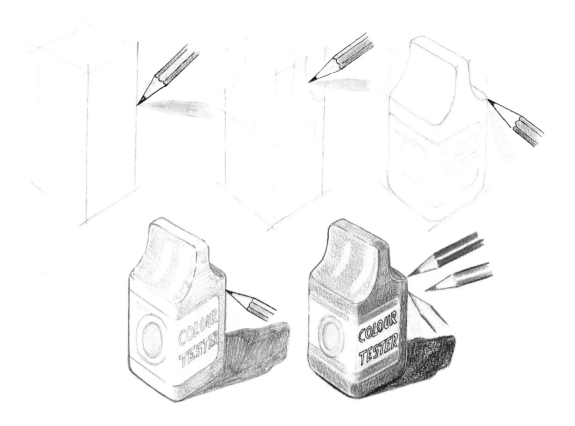

Freehand sketching

Whether you are making something designed by yourself or another it is very important to be able to interpret and communicate design information. Drawings are the best way of communicating design ideas and details. It is therefore essential to be able to sketch and draw with reasonable accuracy. Some working drawings may be well-proportioned freehand sketches. Others, especially the more complex projects, will need measured working drawings.

Computers are becoming increasingly common in schools and industry. There are a variety of good computer aided design (CAD) software packages available. Linking the computer with electronically controlled printers or plotters allows one to produce very high-quality drawings. However, CAD packages can only be used with efficiency when the user understands the principles of projection and the conventions and standards which apply to communicating design information graphically. Having produced the drawing on the computer they may be used to provide hardcopy (printouts) or interfaced with a CNC machine.

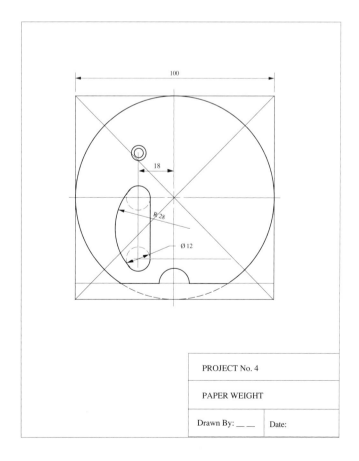

Basic working drawing

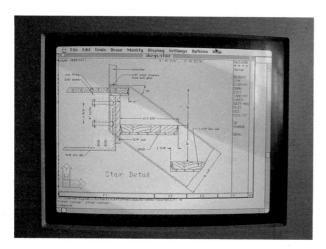
Computer with CAD drawing

Whether you are designing an occasional table or a woodcarving or a child's toy you will find that the greatest satisfaction comes from the realisation of the project. The feeling of accomplishment is worth all the effort. The degree of success will depend on your desire to develop and improve upon all the skills associated with designing and making, as well as an appreciation of the materials you work with.

Any making or designing task needs to be approached in a systematic manner. The need or the project has to be investigated. Various options will need to be considered and an appropriate solution chosen. Sketches and notes expressing ideas are an essential part of the process, as is consideration of materials and resources, including your own skills. While there are a variety of ways of designing all include: investigating the task or problem; deciding on a solution; making the item; and evaluating its effectiveness. This is known as the process of designing and is shown graphically in the diagram.

Wood carving

Wooden furniture

Pull-along toys

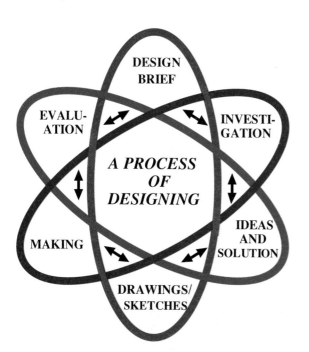

DESIGN BRIEF

EVALU-ATION

INVESTI-GATION

A PROCESS OF DESIGNING

MAKING

IDEAS AND SOLUTION

DRAWINGS/ SKETCHES

The story of our trees

Ireland is a beautiful country. It has a great variation of scenery, from unspoilt areas of mountain and bogland in the west to rich rolling pastureland in the centre and east.

Forestry plantation

layers or strata of plants laid down to form bogland

pollen from the earliest trees

Testing the substrata

Our boglands hold the secrets of our past. The last Ice Age receded about 10,000 years ago. The climate became wetter and warmer and therefore bogs grew and covered large areas of the country. Bogs preserve plant material. Layer after layer of plant life was laid down and compressed. Whole trees are often found preserved in our bogs.

The pollen from the different trees and plants lies stored in our bogs.

Scientists use a special auger bit to bore down through the bog and extract a sample, and with powerful microscopes they analyse the pollen grains. From this information they are able to produce a pollen chart to show what trees came to Ireland first, and then what trees came later. So from our boglands we can get a history of our trees and plants going back about 10,000 years.

Telling how old a tree is

Scientists use two methods for dating trees found in bogs.

1. Radio Carbon Dating, also called C-14 dating. By measuring the amount of carbon 14 in a sample scientists can tell reasonably accurately how old a tree specimen is.

2. Tree Ring Dating or Dendrochronology. This is the study of the growth ring pattern of trees. Scientists match up the growth ring patterns of trees of different ages and so can build up a tree ring profile. A tree ring chronology can be plotted for Irish trees going back 7,500 years.

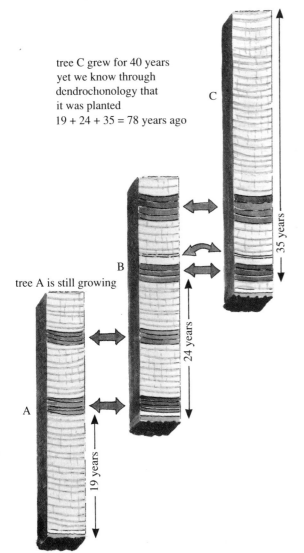

tree C grew for 40 years yet we know through dendrochonology that it was planted 19 + 24 + 35 = 78 years ago

C

B

tree A is still growing

A

35 years

24 years

19 years

Tree ring dating

Bristlecone pine

The world of trees

Trees are the tallest plants on earth. Some also survive to a great age.

The Bristlecone pines growing in the White Mountains in California are about 5,000 years old.

Trees of that age are not found growing in Ireland. However bog oak and bog deal found preserved deep in our bogs can be up to 5,000 years old.

Our first trees

After the Ice Age the climate became warmer and trees could grow. The hardy trees that could survive in cold conditions colonised first. Pollen records show that these were the **juniper**, **willow** and **birch**.

These were followed by **hazel** and **pine** and later by **oak**, **alder**, **elm**, **ash** and **poplar**.

The coming of humans

The Stone-age people found before them a densely wooded land. They travelled mainly along the river estuaries. They must have found travel very difficult. They cut and slashed their way through the dense forests using sharp stone axes.

It is very hard for us to imagine these ancient primeval forests. They were huge, silent and majestic, and very few people inhabited this country in those times.

The Bronze-age people followed the Stone-age people. They had better implements with which to fell the trees to make way for animals.

The arrival of the Celts

Iron displaced bronze about 2,500 years ago with the arrival of the Celts. Pollen counts from this period indicate great changes. The Celts began cutting the existing forests to make way for tillage. They introduced the plough and were able to till the land. They lived in raths or forts and in crannógs. Over 3,000 such forts exist throughout the country.

They used timber widely. They drove larch stakes into the ground and used clay and wattle to give a secure outer ring to the crannóg.

Inside the rath the dwellings were also of wood.

Early crannóg

Wood was also used for carts, for furniture and for fuel.

By 300 AD pine had almost completely vanished from the pollen count of that era. Some trees were already becoming scarce at this time. According to a legal tract from 800 AD, under the Brehon Laws, two milch cows was the penalty for unlawfully cutting a valuable tree such as oak, and a sheep the penalty for cutting a less valuable tree or bush. These may well have been the first attempts to conserve trees.

The Normans and the Tudors

The destruction of the Irish woods is closely linked to the political turmoil of the following centuries.

When the Normans came in 1169 about 50 per cent of the country was still wooded. By 1600 woodland cover had been reduced to 12.5 per cent.

The Battle of Kinsale in 1601 marks a turning point for the native Irish. English and Scottish settlers took over the lands and devastated the woodlands. Oak for wine casks, for ships and for building was exported in huge quantities.

By 1698 Ireland had to import wood for the first time. By 1800 only 2 per cent of the country was wooded.

Much of the wood was used to fuel the charcoal-burning iron-ore smelting plants which were numerous throughout the country.

The walled estates 1700–1845

The eighteenth century was more peaceful than the seventeenth. The landlords had consolidated their estates by building high stone walls around the perimeter. Rents were high and many landlords were well off.

In 1735 the Dublin Society, later the Royal Dublin Society, offered its first grants for tree planting. There was vigorous planting within the walled estates, and landlords took great pride in their tree planting. They imported seeds of exotic species from all over the world, and the prizes for planting estates given by the RDS were highly valued.

Walled estate

The famine and our forests

The huge starving population roamed the countryside in search of fuel and food. They cut down the trees and devasted the hedgerows as they tried to keep their starving bodies warm. In contrast, the walled demesnes were densely wooded. Prof. Mitchell (in *Shell Guide to Reading the Irish Landscape*) describes the scene:

'There were walled demesnes with their trees, the oases in the desert. And then there was nothing, not a tree, not a bush to break the view of a bare landscape dotted over with cabins and endless potato patches.'

The landlords had to protect their woodlands with firearms and often planted man traps inside the wall to deter invaders. Outside, the country was laid bare of trees by eight million starving peasants.

Post-famine forests

In 1881 Gladstone, the British Prime Minister, restricted the power of the landlord. The government gave money to the landlords as compensation and the tenants could purchase their lands. This signalled the decline of the landlords, and they lost confidence in the future. They brought over sawmillers from England who cut down the woods within the walled demesnes. Much of this was exported.

State forestry 1904–50

By 1900 the country had lost most of its woodlands. Less than half of one per cent was wooded. It presented a bleak picture. In 1903 the State got involved. It purchased the former home of Charles Stewart Parnell at Avondale, Co. Wicklow, and established a school for the training of foresters there in 1904.

In 1908 a Departmental Committee recommended that the State purchase land and establish forests.

Avondale

What trees to plant

The landlords of the previous century had introduced walnut, beech, sycamore and horse chestnut.

However, these were slow-growing species.

It was decided to import softwood species from countries with the same climate as Ireland. Seeds were imported from western coast of North America and Canada and from

Vancouver Island. Over 100 plots of these new trees were laid out at Avondale and their growth observed. Progress in forestry planting was very slow at the beginning of the 1900s. All the work of draining, fencing and planting had to be done by hand. Between 1906 and 1930 about 10,000 hectares were planted. Nowadays that amount is planted in less than one year.

There was little tradition of softwood plantation planting in this country. At first Scots pine and Douglas fir were planted but these require fairly good soils. When planted on poor soils they made very little progress. Much of the land available to afforestation was the poor blanket bogland of the west coast. The search was on for tree species that could grow in this poor soil.

Two of the imported species showed remarkable growth rates. Sitka spruce and lodgepole pine grew faster than any other species and these two trees are still the mainstay of tree plantations. They thrived with very little care in the damp deep bogs of the west and grew faster than any other species.

Lodgepole pine

Sitka spruce

Activities

1. Ireland is a beautiful country. Discuss.

2. Why are bogs so important in coming to an understanding of our past?

3. What is meant by a pollen chart and how is it of value?

4. Why do you think Scots Pine was favoured by the Celts?

5. Why did certain trees colonise Ireland first?

6. Collect their leaves and write a note about their characteristics.

7. Show with the aid of notes and sketches how early humans used trees.

8. What effect did the coming of the Celts have on the tree cover in Ireland?

9. Many succeeding generations used the wood but forgot to plant treees. Discuss.

10. From the woods a continuous stream of timber flowed out. Discuss.

11. Ship building and the production of barrel staves made inroads on the oakwoods throughout the seventeenth century. Discuss.

12. Landlords planted woods, landlords cut woods. Discuss.

13. Discuss the effects of the Famine on Ireland's woodlands.

14. In 1850 BC Ireland was densely wooded. By 1850 AD Ireland was almost bare of bush. Discuss.

15. Discuss the State's early efforts in tree planting with particular reference to Avondale.

16. Early foresters set an example to follow. How did future generations succeed?

17. Good land was not seen as suitable planting land. Why was this so?

18. The planting of the poorer lands had its own difficulties. Discuss.

19. A proper planting programme is essential to the economic development of a country. Discuss.

Post-war planting

The area of land being planted up to World War II was still inadequate to meet our needs, but by 1960 the target of planting 10,000 hectares per annum had been achieved. Two factors greatly helped this:

- the introduction of machinery to drain the land and thus speed up the planting process.

- sitka spruce and lodgepole pine had proved themselves as hardy fast-growing species.

Prior to 1960 the rate of planting was small. However, from the mid-1980s onwards there was a huge increase in afforestation. Nowadays an area of about the size of Co. Louth is being planted every four years.

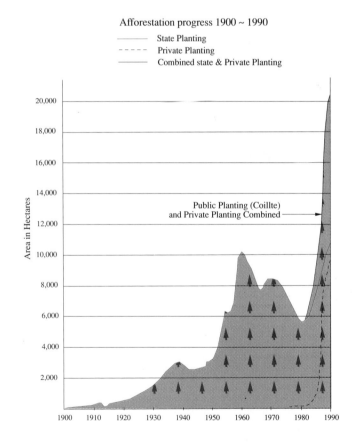

Afforestation progress 1900 ~ 1990

State Planting
Private Planting
Combined state & Private Planting

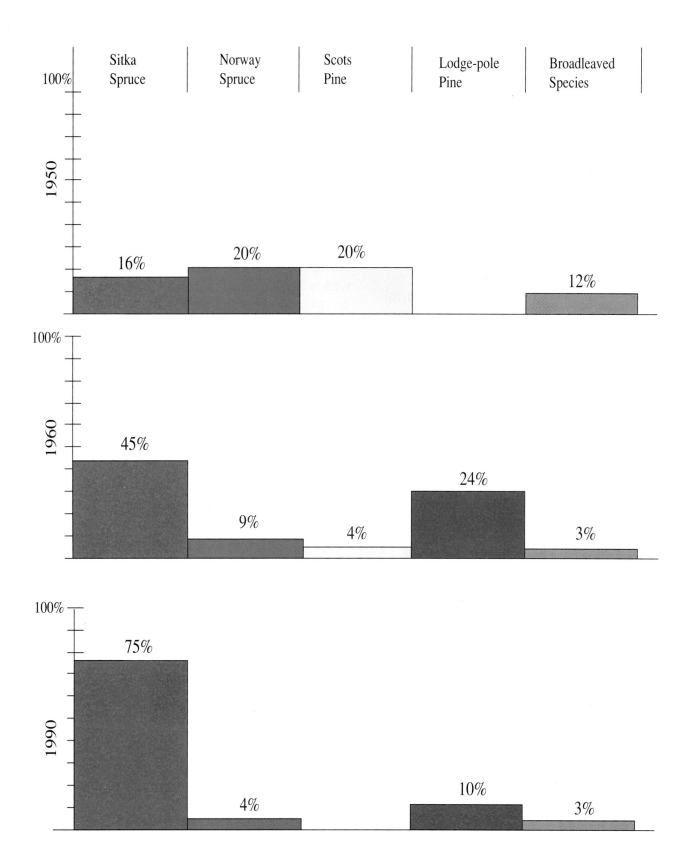

Bar chart of tree species planted by the State Forestry Service in 1950, 1960 and 1990.

EC grant aid for afforestation

From 1984 onwards there was a dramatic rise in the area being planted each year. This was a result of EC grants under the Western Package. Planting was funded on a 70 per cent EC/30 per cent State basis, in what has become known as the Western Package.

Most of the planting under the Western Package was done by private contractors, whereas until 1981 virtually all planting was done by the State-owned Forestry and Wildlife Service.

Coillte teoranta

Coillte teoranta was established as a limited company in 1988 and has taken over the duties of the Forestry and Wildlife Service. It has a commercial mandate to establish and maintain forestry on a fully commercial basis.

The forest premium scheme 1990

There is a huge depopulation of rural Ireland: 35 per cent of the population now live in the greater Dublin area. There are severe EC restrictions on over-production in the agricultural sector. In an effort to encourage farmers to plant the better lands the EC offered in 1990 generous grants for planting, in addition to annual grant income for the first 15 years.

It is hoped to encourage farmers to plant some of their better land and to manage the plantation themselves, thus deriving an income from the land and remaining on the land themselves. This is a welcome advance as it encourages farmers to get involved and hopefully to plant more broadleaved trees on their better land, and it also encourages the development of farm forestry with smaller plantations and fewer of the environmental problems associated with large-scale coniferous plantations.

Afforestation policy: some issues

- We import 10,000 cubic metres of tropical hardwoods per year. Yet the tropical forests are being cut down at an alarming rate. The supply will soon become very scarce and very dear.

- Most broadleaved trees are slow growing but our climate favours the growth of certain species. In the colder climates further north they would not grow at all.

- Certain species such as ash, cherry and sycamore grow almost as quickly as the conifers. Coillte teo. is currently planting more broadleaved trees in an effort to redress the balance. Yet the percentage of broadleaves being planted remains very low, less than 2 per cent of the total area.

- Broadleaved plantations provide ideal habitats for a wide range of insect, animal and bird life.

- Birch and alder can grow on poor soils and can be planted in irregular stands throughout coniferous plantations.

- Future generations of woodworkers will enjoy a wider variety of native hardwoods than we currently do, but only if we plant them now.

- Unlike the uniform green of conifers, broadleaves change colour and are visually more attractive.

Broadleaved plantations

- Broadleaved trees need more care than conifers especially at the early stages. Rabbits, hares and deer can eat the foliage and bark and kill the saplings. Cages are often placed around the trees in the early stages.

- Fences have to be animal proof.

- They require richer and drier soils.

- Broadleaved saplings require longer time in the nursery than do conifers.

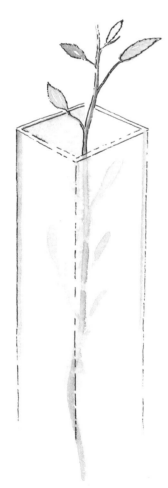

Broadleaved plantation

Forestry and the environment

We all share the environment both physical and visual of this country. Huge numbers of visitors visit Ireland each year to appreciate its beauty, bringing in almost £1,000 million each year. Sometimes we can all take this for granted.

Forest parks

Coillte manages 12 forest parks for leisure and recreational facilities, and 180 amenity sites where people can enjoy beautiful views, rest and relax in the surroundings of a forest. These sites are indicated by the international sign.

PLEASE HELP KEEP OUR FORESTS CLEAN

BRING HOME ALL LITTER

A forest park amenity

Forestry and employment

Over 2,000 people are directly employed in forestry and an estimated 13,000 more employed in forestry or forestry-related enterprises.

Protective cage to growing broadleaved tree

A conifer nursery

Controversial issues

Visual impact of forests

When forests were planted by hand, planting was slow and made little impact on the visual environment. Nowadays things are different. Huge machines on tracks can travel virtually anywhere and quickly drain and plant vast areas.

Large-scale plantations have a tremendous visual impact on the countryside, and are a controversial issue.

In 1971 Eileen McCracken in her book, *Irish Woods since Tudor Times*, commented:

'The future landscape of Ireland lies in the hands of the forest planners. Have they a plan or is the land being acquired and planted piecemeal, regardless of its site?'

'If afforestation continues at its present rate, does this mean that in time the hills will be one vast coniferous plantation and if so is that what the taxpayer wants? Are the mountain roads from which at present one can see miles over the open hills going to turn into long dark tunnels bounded by parallel lines of sitka spruce or *pinus contorta*? Will the flat boglands with their changing colours be sheets of dark green that know no seasons?'

Much of the planting to date has been in the most beautiful areas of the west and south. Great care will have to be taken when setting new plantations that these new areas are not scarred by the patchwork-type planting which does not take account of the natural contour of the land. Our boglands hold the secrets of our past; not all are worth conserving, but some are, as they are the natural habitat for endangered species such as golden plover, merlin and Greenland white-fronted geese. Some of the heathers, grasses and sedges will only grow in those wet bogs. Once drained its structure is changed forever and these delicate birds and plants vanish.

Areas of scientific interest (ASIs)

The Wildlife Service designates areas of scientific interest, which are those that contain archeological sites such as ring forts, and areas that have unique habitats with rare plants. Many of the ASIs are peatlands and there is always pressure to plant on these as they are available in large blocks and often at cheap prices.

Peatlands

Acidification of soil and water

There is some evidence to suggest that there is higher soil and water acidity in areas of intense conifer plantation. This can affect fish life which is very sensitive to changes in acid levels in water.

Modern planting procedures ensure that trees are planted back from rivers and streams allowing light to penetrate through. Birch and aspen are planted nearest the banks to neutralise the acid effect.

There is an interdependence between all living things, including trees. To plant only conifers can have an adverse effect on water quality, aquatic life, wildlife and the visual environment generally.

It takes longer to obtain an economic return from broadleaved plantations. However, as the world supply of hardwoods gets scarcer, native-grown hardwoods will be vitally necessary. The long-term benefits to the ecosystem repay fully, but only if humans acknowledge that they can live in harmony with the rest of creation.

Glendalough

Activities

1. Discuss the factors that influenced Ireland's forestry policy since 1950.

2. Give reasons why conifers were mainly planted.

3. There is a growing awareness of the importance of planting broadleaved plantations. List some of the factors leading to this awareness.

4. Why do broadleaved plantations require more care than conifer plantations?

5. 'The better the land, the better the trees.' Discuss.

6. Outline some of the schemes available to encourage the planting of trees.

7. What is meant by the term 'farm forestry'?

8. Discuss grant-aid policy to encourage farmers to plant forestry plantations.

9. Study the graph of Irish forestry plantations. Discuss *a*) the low level of plantation before 1945; *b*) the increase in level of plantations especially since 1984.

10. Discuss the visual impact of conifer plantations on Ireland's countryside.

11. Suggest means of improving the visual impact of forests.

12. You are asked to write a guideline for the sensitive location of plantation forests. Outline your proposals.

13. Discuss the effects of large-scale managed coniferous plantations on the environment.

14. Draw a map and show the location of the native hardwood forests.

15. Explain the term 'ASI' and state why they are important.

Some trees of Ireland

Oak (Quercus robor and petraea)

The tree

The majestic oak is known as the 'king of the forest'. In ancient Ireland much of the land was covered with oak, but now the last of the great oak woods are confined to the lowlands around Abbeyleix, Co. Leix, near Glendalough, Co. Wicklow, Glenveagh, Co. Donegal, in the Glens of Antrim, and, best of all, in Killarney, Co. Kerry.

Over 1,600 placenames contain '*doire*', showing how widespread oak woods were once. Many of the great oak woods were cut down for building the great sailing ships, barrel staves, roofing churches and general joinery. There are two types of oak native to Ireland and they are easily distinguished.

a) The Sessile Oak (*Quercus petraea*). Sessile means stalkless and the acorns grow directly on the woody stem. It is seen at its purest in the Killarney oak woods. However, these trees are not very large as they grow on poor soil. The lands around Killarney have been covered with oak woods since the end of the last Ice Age.

b) The Pendunculate Oak (*Quercus robor*). This is distinguished by the long stalks on its female flowers and on the acorns that follow. It thrives on the better soils of the lowlands. It grows to a larger size than the sessile oak and has a larger crown.

It has been estimated that over 240 insect species can thrive on a mature oak tree. It is therefore a very important tree for all types of wildlife.

The majestic oak

Oak leaves in fruit

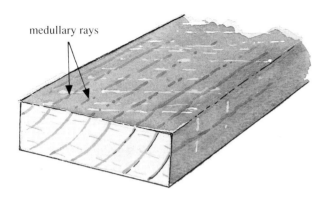

medullary rays

Oak board

The wood

There are a number of different types: American oak, Japanese oak, European oak.

Their characteristics vary with their conditions of growth. Oak has a straight grain, coarse texture with a conspicuous growth ring figure. When quarter cut it has distinct silver flecks.

Uses

Oak has always been the symbol of strength and durability and was used in the roofing of churches, cathedrals, castles. Huge spans of Irish oak were used in the roof of Westminster Hall. It was also the wood used to build the great sailing ships of the English and Spanish navies.

It was used in lock gates in canals, for railway sleepers, for the spokes in wooden cartwheels, and for wine and sherry casks.

Tannic acid was extracted from the bark of oak and used by tanners. (This corrodes steel if used outside; use brass or stainless steel for external use.)

Today oak is widely used for furniture making, most of it being imported. It is used for wall panelling in public buildings. It has a high resistance to weathering and is often used for gate posts and fencing poles.

Ash (Fraxinus excelsior)

The tree

Ash is also a very important tree. In ancient times it grew mixed with oak in the great natural forests that covered the country. Nowadays it grows in the hedgerows all over the country. It is a hardy tree and grows on most soils but grows best in deep clay soils. In winter the tree is easily recognised by its black buds. In summer it has a distinctive leaf, composed of a number of leaflets arranged on either side of the main stem. Its seeds have wings which enable them to be dispersed by the wind. These winged seeds can be collected while still green on the tree and planted directly or they can be stratified for 18 months and then sown. Ash reaches maturity in less than 60 years, and is a very important tree in hardwood replacement.

Ash tree

20

Ash leaves

The wood

Ash is white in colour with a pale pinkish tint. It has a distinct growth ring figure when flat sawn. It is easily worked with machine and hand tools. The wood has large pores easily seen in the end grain. These are surrounded by a band of very tough summerwood which gives the wood its strength, and enables it to withstand hard blows.

Uses

It is used for the making of hurleys, and ash is specially grown for this purpose. The hurley is obtained from the root buttress and stem, giving the curved grain necessary for the bos or flat of the hurley. About 20,000 trees per year are needed for this. Because of its elasticity it is also widely used for handles of all types of tools, hammers, axes, garden forks, etc. It is used for sports goods such as tennis racquets, golf clubs and hockey sticks. Because of its grain pattern it is widely used in furniture making, e.g. tables, chairs and stools. It steams well and can be bent easily.

Ash table

Ash leaf and seeds

21

Mountain ash or rowan (Sorbus aucuparia)

This is a very familiar tree having distinctive red and orange berries. It is often cultivated as an ornamental tree in small gardens and its red berries provide a useful food supply to birds during the cold winter months. It is a hardy species and will grow in most types of soils and is ideal for the small garden. Because the tree is small its wood is of little importance to the furniture industry.

Mountain ash

Mountain ash leaves in fruit

Beech (Fagus sylvatica)

The tree

Beech is not a native of Ireland and was introduced in the early eighteenth century. It now forms one of the most important trees of the Irish countryside. It is most noticeable in autumn with its smooth grey bark and russet-coloured leaves. In good soil it is a magnificent tree. It is a shade bearer and can be grown with more light-demanding species like oak and ash. In the Middle Ages the beech masts or nuts were used to fatten pigs.

It is a slow-growing tree and can be grown as a hedge as it stands clipping very well. It holds on to its russet brown leaves right throughout the winter and gives shelter as well as colour to the winter scene, and is frequently planted and clipped as a hedge around dwelling houses.

Beech tree

Beech leaves

Uses

It is an outstanding wood for furniture making, especially for the turned and bent members of chairs. It is used for kitchen utensils and tool handles. Because of its close grain and even texture it is quite wear resistant and is often used in tool making. It is used in the marking gauge because it wears evenly. It also makes a hard-wearing attractive domestic floor. Unless it is treated with preservative it is not suitable for outdoor use.

Birch (Betula)

The tree

The birch is easily recognised by its gleaming white bark which often lends colour to an otherwise bare winter scene. The white bark is not seen in young trees but develops as the tree ages. The white bark means that it loses less heat through radiation in winter yet reflects back the scorching summer sun. This temperature control by the bark means that birch can grow further north and higher up the mountains than any other broadleaved tree. It can be seen growing, alone amongst the broadleaved trees, in the mountainous areas of Scandinavia, Russia and Canada. It grows on poor land and was one of the first trees to colonise Ireland. Its bark was peeled off and used to make light canoes by the early French Canadian explorers, and the Lapps used its bark to make baskets, belts, plates and waterproof roofs for their huts. In renewing our hardwood supplies birch should be considered for plantation planting as it is fast growing, hardy and gives a useful wood.

Birch grows widely in Ireland and is often used to border coniferous plantation, its silver bark and delicate foliage giving a lively contrast to the monotonous green of the conifers.

Sometimes a parasite growth, commonly called witch's broom, which resembles a bird's nest, develops on its branches. Birch is widely grown in urban gardens for ornamental purposes but needs to be lopped occasionally.

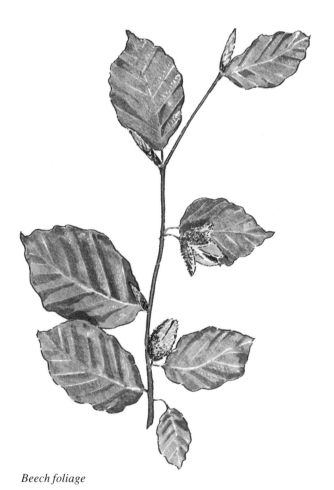

Beech foliage

The wood

Beech is white to pale brown in colour with a distinct fleck due to its medium-sized rays. It is straight grained with a fine even texture. The wood is strong, works well, takes a good finish and can easily be turned. It can be steam bent.

Birch tree

The wood

Almost white, straight grained with little figure. It compares with ash for toughness. It can be worked well by hand or machine. It turns well, but as the tree does not grow to large diameter, wide boards are unavailable. Unless well treated with preservatives it should not be used externally.

Uses

It can be rotary peeled easily and is widely used for plywood construction. The mosquito aircraft of World War II was made from birch ply. Sometimes veneers of spruce are faced with birch in plywood manufacture.

It is used for furniture making especially in the Scandinavian countries and for broom heads and handles. It is often used in the carcass of upholstered chairs and is an important pulp wood for paper making.

Elm (Ulmus montana and campestris)

The tree

The wych elm, *ulmus montana*, is a native of Ireland and was one of the first trees to grow in Ireland after the Ice Age. Its English counterpart (*ulmus campestris*) is widely planted in parklands, hedgerows and avenues. The elm is a tall magnificent tree and likes good deep rich soils.

In recent years elm trees have been devastated by Dutch elm disease, so called because it was first observed in Holland. This disease is caused by a fungus which is carried from tree to tree by a small beetle which breeds below the bark. The fungus blocks the food supply to the leaves. The foliage of the affected tree quickly wilts and the whole tree dies. The diseased trees were cut down in an effort to arrest its spread, so elm stocks have become severely depleted. Some trees have appeared resistant to the disease and it is hoped to cultivate those.

The wood

The wood is pale brown in colour with a prominent growth ring figure, showing an attractive coarse texture and irregular grain. It has a long life in waterlogged conditions, and is noted for its strength. It cuts and finishes well but needs a very sharp cutting edge for both hand and machine tools.

Elm foliage

Elm chair

Uses

Elm has a very decorative grain and is widely used in furniture making for display cabinets. It resists splitting and was used for the seats of chairs, especially the Windsor chair. It makes attractive bowls when turned. It was formerly used in the hub of wooden wheels when the oak spokes could be driven into it without splitting it. It has great structural strength and was used for dock work and piling. It was widely used for coffins.

It was used in old-fashioned water pumps, and with the centre hollowed out it was even used as pipes in town water supplies.

Sycamore (Acer pseudo-platanus)

The tree

Sycamore is not a native of Ireland but it really grows well here. It is one of a large family of trees called maples (see below). The sycamore has a greyish brown bark and a distinctive leaf pattern. Its helicopter seeds travel easily in the wind so it can be widely dispersed. It will grow in a wide variety of soils, produces lots of seeds and quickly colonises waste patches of ground.

It grows quickly and is quite tall so it should not be planted in small gardens where it could interfere with overhead wires and cables.

Sycamore tree

25

Sycamore foliage

Sycamore carving

The wood

It is a pale cream coloured wood and it has an attractive grain pattern. It is widely used as a veneer where the veneers are cut to show up a wavy grain pattern.

Uses

It is extremely hardwearing and is widely used for flooring and for making wooden rollers. It is popular for turning, carving and general furniture making. It is often used for the back, sides and stock of violins and other stringed instruments, though the soundboard is made from the more resonant spruce.

The maples (Acer)

The trees

These have the distinctive leaf featured in the national flag of Canada. Not much maple is grown in Ireland though it is planted for ornamental purposes. Its green leaves turn to shades of scarlet, rust, gold and orange before being swept away by the winter winds. A group of maples called Japanese Maples (*acer mono*) are used in small gardens and do not grow to great heights, but display vivid and varied autumn shades.

Sycamore foliage and seeds

Maple tree

Maple foliage

The wood

There are two types of maple: rock maple or hard maple (*acer saccharum*) and soft maple.

Rock maple sometimes produces a bird's eye figure which is much sought after in veneer form: small circular blotches in the grain resembling a bird's eye.

Uses

Rock maple is very hard and resistant to wear and is widely used in floors for ballrooms, sports halls, restaurants, houses etc. This maple is imported mainly from America, Canada and Japan.

The soft maples are not much used in Ireland. They are occasionally used for making musical instruments.

Horse chestnut (Aesculus hippocastanum)

The tree

The horse chestnut tree can easily be distinguished at a glance by its distinct leaf pattern, the leaflets spreading out like the fingers of a hand (palmate), having five to seven leaflets. The flowers are beautiful, upright clusters like candles. The tree demands light and is often grown in parks. In autumn its fruit is the nut known as the 'conker'.

The wood

Not widely used as it is usually in short supply, it is a soft pale whitish wood with naturally straight grain. It is soft and brittle, and tools need to be kept very sharp to get a clean cut.

Horse chestnut

Horse chestnut foliage

Uses

Suitable for turned items like brush heads and handles and kitchen utensils, floors, wood pulp and occasionally in cabinet making.

Cherry (Prunus avium)

The tree

There are two kinds of cherry which grow in Ireland: the wild cherry or gean (*prunus avium*) and the bird cherry (*prunus padus*).

There is an American or black cherry but it is not planted here as it is host to an aphid carrier of a sugar beet virus. Only the wild cherry or gean grows to a height suitable for producing wood as the bird cherry rarely grows much taller than a shrub.

The cherry is one of the most beautiful trees in flower with a delicate pink or white foliage and is widely grown in parks, avenues and housing estates. Under favourable conditions (fertile, deep, well-drained soil) it is quite fast growing, reaching 20 metres height and 600mm breast height diameter in 50–60 years. Coillte teo., the Irish forestry board, is investigating the possibility of planting cherry in an effort to replenish our dwindling native

hardwood supply. Its quick growth and excellent timber means that this gives a quick return of investment. However, its uniform green makes a dull plantation and it should be planted with other broadleaved species. But in flower it is very striking and should be sensitively planted, especially on conspicuous hillsides. Planting with larch or ash would help its visual appearance.

The wood

It is a fine-textured, straight-grained wood, pale pinkish-brown in colour when first cut but darkens to an almost mahogany red. It works very well with both hand and machine tools to an excellent finish.

Uses

It is in very limited supply now and is used in high-class joinery and furniture making and high-class cabinet making. It is also used in veneer form for cabinet making. It turns well on a lathe.

Cherry in blossom

Home-grown softwoods

Scots Pine (Pinus sylvestris)

Scots pine grew widely in Ireland about 9,000 years ago. Many trees of Scots pine have been found preserved in our bogs and this is commonly known as **bog deal.**

However, as the climate became milder and wetter the pine began to die out. These mild wet conditions favoured the growth of peatland and peat eventually covered the pines. The Scots pine almost completely died out and was reintroduced from Scotland in the seventeenth century and grown from seed. It grows from Spain right across Europe into Russia and up into Siberia. When the State forestry first began, Scots pine was widely planted and in 1958 it comprised 21 per cent of the total State forests.

However, it is not now favoured by the foresters as faster grown species are now planted. Unfortunately in recent years it is not planted at all because it is a slow-growing conifer.

The tree

The tree is hardy and grows well in all but waterlogged soils. It withstands winds and cold very well. The tree is a tall graceful conifer with a distinct brown-orange trunk. The leaves are in pairs in a brown sheath. It usually has a clear bole with a well-developed crown.

The wood

The wood is commonly known by the trade name **red deal.** The wood is a creamy brown colour with distinct red stripes running through it, giving it its name. It is strong and durable and takes preservatives very well. It works very well with both hand and machine tools.

Uses

Red deal is the most widely used softwood for both joinery and cabinet making. It is the wood most often used in the Materials Technology Wood Room. Most wood benches are made from red deal, as often are softwood windows, doors, pine kitchens, tables, chairs and dressers.

It takes preservations well and when properly treated can last as long as most hardwoods in external conditions.

Scots pine

Close up of Scots pine

Sitka spruce (Picea sitchensis)

Sitka spruce is now the most widely used tree in Ireland, and it forms 75 per cent of all the trees planted each year in Ireland. It is a native of the coastal regions of Western Canada and the USA, having climatic conditions similar to Ireland. It now occupies over 30 per cent of the area of State forests. It thrives on high rainfall and humid conditions and grows exceptionally quickly in the wet boglands of the west and south-west of Ireland. It reaches maturity in about 40 years. Most of the seed for planting is imported from the Queen Charlotte Islands in British Colombia but existing forests are now a source of seed.

The wood

The wood is fine in texture, whitish in colour, reasonably strong and straight grained.

Spruce needles

Sitka spruce

Uses

It is widely used in the construction industry for rafters, flooring joists, flooring boards.

It is now being stress graded to meet specifications in the manufacture of roof trusses and other weight- bearing members. It is difficult to impregnate with preservatives and is not used externally. It is also used in furniture making but is soft and easily marked. Much of the thinnings are used in the pulp industries for manufacturing chipboard and medium-density fibreboard.

Lodgepole pine (Pinus contorta)

The tree

This is the second most popular tree planted in Irish forestry plantations, comprising 10 per cent of species planted in 1989, and about 25 per cent of existing forests. It grows best in acidic conditions, in poor soils with excess moisture. It grows in bleak conditions where no other tree would survive. It takes root easily and develops a bright green crown. Its leaves are carried in pairs and are very densely set. The bark of the tree is rugged and develops cracks. The cones are carried in clusters, pointing down the stem. The tree has a wild and bushy appearance. It is a native of the west coast of North America and was first planted in Ireland in 1884.

It suffers from storm damage, being easily uprooted in high winds.

Pine needles

The wood

Even though the tree grows quickly its wood is strong and dense. It has an attractive appearance with parallel stripes of red to brown running through the wood. However, unless the young trees are pruned regularly the wood tends to be very knotty and difficult to work.

The tree trunk is often distorted and long straight lengths are difficult to obtain.

Uses

Selected boards are used for all types of internal joinery and for ceiling and wall panelling, since its knotty grain can have an attractive appearance. However, trees grown on poor soil generally produce poor wood and its wood is mainly used for pulpwood, paper pulp, hardboard, chipboard and MDF (medium-density fibreboard).

Lodgepole pine

Table in lodgepole pine

31

Norway spruce (Picea abies)

The tree

Norway spruce constitutes about 4 per cent of the conifers planted annually. It grows in Norway, across Northern Europe and Russia. It is the familiar Christmas tree. It is easily recognised as its leaves are soft and not prickly like those of sitka spruce. The leaves form a dense mat on top of the branches.

It is not as fast growing as the sitka spruce and may need five years in the nursery before it is planted out. However, it is a frost-hardy tree but will not grow on very poor soils.

The wood

The wood is marketed under the name **white deal**. It is white in colour and is easy to work.

Foliage and cones of Norway spruce

Uses

It is used extensively for internal joinery, flooring boards, skirting boards, machine-panelled deal furniture, box and pallet construction, pulpwood and plywood. Selected boards of spruce from Eastern Europe are used for the soundboards of musical instruments because of its exceptionally resonant qualities.

Douglas fir (Pseudotsuga Douglasii)

A Scottish botanist, David Douglas, discovered the tree in 1827, hence its name.

It is native to the western coast of North America from New Mexico north to Vancouver Island. The imported timber from this tree is known as Oregon pine from the state of Oregon.

In England it is known as Columbian pine. It is more choosy in location than sitka spruce and dislikes lime soils. It doesn't grow well on exposed sites and huge winds can damage its crown.

Native Douglas fir is now in short supply as it has been much sought after as a wood for joinery. In ideal sheltered conditions it grows into a majestic tall tree. Side branches need to be pruned to give a clear bole.

Norway spruce

Douglas fir

The wood

It has a very attractive appearance with a light reddish-brown heartwood and a slightly lighter sapwood. It has a prominent growth ring figure. It works well with both hand and power tools, but has a blunting effect on tools.

Uses

Its straight boles, impregnated with creosote, are widely used as telegraph poles. Its large baulks were used for heavy construction work, dock and harbour work, railway sleepers, ship building, roof trusses. It was used in furniture making, selected logs being sliced for decorative veneers and it is widely used for plywood.

It is highly prized for internal joinery because of its attractive colourings.

Foliage and cones of Douglas fir

A walk through a forest

We are privileged that in Ireland we have both broadleaved trees and coniferous trees. This is because we have a mild climate. Broadleaved trees cannot survive in cold conditions and coniferous trees do not grow in the tropics. We are in between these two regions so we have both types of trees.

A conifer forest

Trees have different shapes – can you recognise the tree from its shape?

The oak has a different shape to the poplar.

Sketch the outline or shape of the different trees. Take a clear look at the tree. Can you identify it from the shape of its leaf? Sketch the leaf. Place it on a piece of paper and trace its outline. Some trees have distinctive leaf shapes: oak, ash, horse chestnut.

Take a walk

If there is a wood near you go for a walk through it. You should be able to recognise the broadleaved and coniferous trees growing in Ireland. Coniferous forests are managed. They usually contain only one or two species of tree.

You need   • a notebook or sketchpad;

        • a pencil and pen;

        • a bag for collecting leaves and twigs;

        • a camera.

Broadleaved trees are deciduous – they lose their leaves in winter in temperate climates.

Tree profiles differ

Some trees have leaves that look alike. Can you identify the leaf of the sycamore and maple? How would you tell them apart?

Make your own leaf press.

Dry the leaves under weight between paper. When the moisture is dried out the leaf will not decay. Make up a scrapbook of the different leaves. Describe. Use modelling clay to get a leaf profile. Make your own tiles with leaf pattern.

Nature provides you with great variation in size, shape and colour.

Collect and sketch the seed: acorns, beech nuts, conkers, hazel nuts. Which nuts are safe to eat and which are not?

Simple leaf press

Storing the leaves

To make a leaf tile

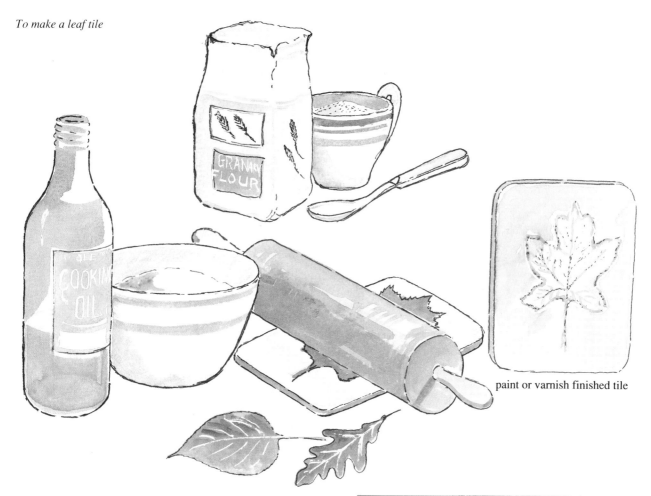

paint or varnish finished tile

– mix two cups plain flour, one cup salt, one cup water and
  two tablespoons of cooking oil
– roll to 20mm thick
– press leaf veins down on tile
– bake for two hours at 250°C

Grow your own trees from seeds

We need to plant many more deciduous trees:

• to replace trees cut down or damaged through disease, storm and old age;

• to make our surroundings more attractive;

• to create a healthier place to live;

• to provide a home for birds and wildlife;

• to provide shade, shelter and colour.

Trees improve the environment

Trees provide shelter and beauty

Which trees to plant

This really depends on where you are living. However, it is best to plant trees that are native to this country as they give food and shelter to birds and animals.

Small urban garden

Trees help to soften the harshness of concrete in an urban area. They also add visual interest with their changing shade of foliage, berry and bark.

Choose smaller trees that look attractive. These include maple, ash, mountain ash, birch, flowering cherry, flowering crab, holly, beech, hawthorn, hornbeam, etc.

Rural planting

Plant trees that grow widely in your area. You have a wide variety to choose from: oak, ash, beech, birch, elm, sycamore, hazel, lime, horse chestnut.

You can plant around your house or in a field.

Planting trees around your house provides shelter. Deciduous trees reduce the wind speeds by filtering the wind through their leaves and branches. They also help to make a house blend with the landscape, a house without trees surrounding it can look very obtrusive in a rural setting.

Trees in a city garden

Planting field corners

Beech can be trimmed as a hedge. It retains its rust-coloured leaves throughout the winter and looks very attractive.

If you are planting in a field plant trees in clumps, say, at the corner of a field.

This makes it easier for machinery to work and creates a better habitat for wildlife than lone individual trees.

Collecting seeds from trees

Growing from seeds is easy. However, there are a few points you must note.

1. Identify the trees. Keep a record of the tree you collected seed from, in your notebook.

2. Each seed contains the characteristics, both good and bad, of the parent tree. Therefore collect seeds only from the best trees.

3. Identify the healthy tree.

A healthy tree. Note the evenly spread branches of crown and the strong, straight erect bole.

4. Do not collect seeds from trees growing in isolation as they may be self pollinating and produce poor trees and have poor germination.

5. Make sure that the seeds are not damaged by weather or insects.

When to collect

Collect seeds only when they are ripe. Most seeds ripen in late summer and autumn, usually late July, August and September.

How a seed germinates

In the natural cycle of growth most seeds ripen in late summer or early autumn. They fall to the ground and get covered with leaves and grass.

Dormancy in seeds

A seed will not begin to grow as soon as it falls on the ground. It has a natural dormancy period which prevents it germinating during the cold winter months.

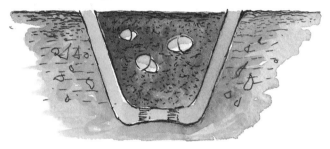

Seeds dormant

The dormancy period of various seeds differs. It can vary from a few weeks to two years.

Therefore you must know the dormancy period if you wish to collect and sow seeds.

Stratification of seeds

The cold storage of seed is called stratification. You must store seeds in moist, cold conditions, similar to the natural winter conditions, before you can sow your seeds.

This is easy enough to do.

Firstly, keep different type seeds separate.

Method 1

Mix the seeds with moist sand in sealed polythene bags and store outside or in a cold area over winter.

Storing seeds (method 1)

Note: do not overmoisten the sand as the seeds will decay.

Check occasionally to make sure that the sand is moist. Label the bags clearly.

Method 2

Mix the seeds with moist sand in unglazed pots and bury in the garden.

Storing seeds (method 2)

Sowing the stratified seed

Sow in March when the chitting stage occurs. This is when the young root tip breaks through the seed coat.

How to sow

Place the seed and some of the sand in a holed carton or pot in moist potting compost. You could sow into soil but the compost is sterile and there is less chance of disease attacking your plants.

A guide to the stratification of seeds

Ash

If you collect the seed while still green you can sow it immediately. However, germination may be poor so you can offset this by sowing large numbers of seeds.

Alternatively you can wait and collect fully ripe keys in October. Stratify for 18 months and sow in the second spring after collection. Date bags with tag or indelible ink when storing.

Oak, Beech, Horse chestnut, Sweet chestnut

These are large seeds and can be sown directly into the ground in autumn. Make a 50mm hole in the soil, insert the seed and close the hole.

Alternatively the seed can be stratified in moist sand over the winter and sown in the following spring.

Large seeds of hardwoods

Birch

Collect the seeds when they are still green enough to hold together in the catkin in August–September. Separate the tiny seeds from the catkins.

Dry the seeds and store them in a sealed container and sow in the first spring.

Hazel

Collect the nuts when browning begins in the autumn. Stratify in moist sand and sow in the second spring.

Sycamore and Field Maple

Collect the winged seeds in October–November from the trees if possible. Sow the seeds immediately. Alternatively dry the seeds, store them dry over winter, stratify in moist sand for six weeks before sowing in the first spring.

Holly

Gather the seeds in winter or early spring. This can be done over the Christmas holidays. The seeds have a long dormancy period. Stratify and sow in the second spring.

Rowan or Mountain Ash

Collect the ripe berries in August–September. Stratify and sow in the first spring.

Blackthorn, Hawthorn, Whitebeam and Flowering Crab Apple

These belong to the rose family and need a long period of stratification. Collect the berries when ripe in October, stratify and sow in the second spring.

Alder

Cut the twigs which bear the cones in autumn and allow to dry. Shake the seeds from the cones, dry them and store the dried seeds in a sealed container; sow the following spring.

Scots Pine

A beautiful native coniferous tree. Collect the cones in January. Cones open in warm dry conditions to release seeds. Collect the dry seeds, store in a sealed container and sow in April or May when soil becomes warm.

Larch

Loses its leaves in winter but has seeds in cones. Collect the cones in September, dry to obtain seeds, store in sealed envelope or container and sow in spring.

Vegetative propagation

It is truly amazing but some stems can grow their own roots and grow to maturity. These stems are called cuttings. The following can be grown from cuttings:

Poplar, willow, plane, alder, elder, some hollies, forsythia, deutzia, spirea, buddleia, fuschia.

Taking a cutting

Take a side shoot rather than a terminal shoot. Take the cuttings as soon as possible after leaf fall as the stem contains a high proportion of stored food.

(1) September
cuttings about 200mm long,
straight or angled cut below a bud,
angled cut above
store in moist
sand until March

A cutting

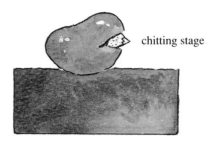

chitting stage

(2) March

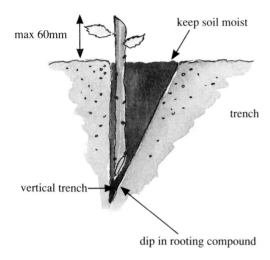

max 60mm

keep soil moist

trench

vertical trench

dip in rooting compound

(3) transplant cutting to final position in September

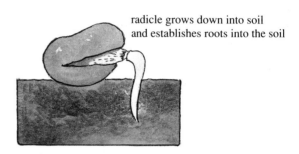

radicle grows down into soil
and establishes roots into the soil

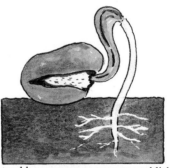

seed leaves emerge as roots establish

How does a tree grow?

1. The seed rests on or in the ground over winter and starts growing in spring.

2. Using its own foodstore to get started it sends down a young root, called a radicle, into the soil to get water and minerals.

3. It sends up a shoot which breaks through the ground and two seed leaves open out. There is a small bud between the leaves.

4. The seed leaves fall off, the bud opens out and the first true leaves appear. The tree is now established and with luck will continue to grow.

seed leaves disappear and are
replaced by first true leaves

Sowing large numbers of seeds

If you are sowing large numbers of seeds you can make a seed tray or box rather than putting each seed into an individual pot.

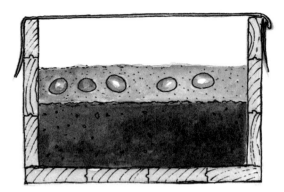

Seed box

Place the seeds on a layer of moist potting compost and cover the seeds with a light layer of sand.

To aid germination and prevent evaporation cover the box with polythene and place outside.

Pricking out

When the seedlings are large enough, usually when they have lost their first seed leaves and developed their true leaves, they can be moved into a ground bed or frame or placed into individual pots. This process is called *pricking out*.

Pricking out

Place the pots on a layer of moist sand. The roots will absorb the moisture as they need it and not become waterlogged. Keep under polythene, either in a box or tunnel until May–June to prevent frost attack.

Polythene tunnel

By mid-June the seedlings should be 50–100 mm high.

Remove the polythene, leave the pots in moist sand until mid-July.

Transplanting

Young seedlings are very susceptible to damage by rabbits and hares and to competition from weeds and grasses. They should therefore be kept for up to three years in a securely fenced area until they are strong enough to survive, or in a plastic container. By mid-July the young seedlings are ready for transplanting into the ground from the pots, or into larger pots if you prefer. Make sure to water the young plants regularly.

A tree nursery

It is best to keep young trees in a tree nursery for the first three years before planting in their final position.

42

This should be a securely wired in area kept free from weeds and well watered.

In the autumn of each year replant the young trees to give them more space and food supply which they need as they grow.

How to prepare and manage a tree nursery

Select an area that you can easily fence in and that is near a water supply.

An area 3m x 3m will enable you to grow 100 seedlings per year on a three-year rotation.

Firstly, fence in the area with rabbit-proof wire mesh. You will need to properly dig and rake the soil.

Select an area for a seed bed

Make sure this area is well dug, levelled and finely raked. Cover the seeds with a layer of coarse sand.

Do not cover with soil as the soil compacts easily when wet and the fragile young seedlings will be unable to push up through the compacted layer, and losses will be high.

Cover the seedlings with clear polythene during the cold months to prevent frost damage. Water regularly but do not saturate as they are susceptible to 'dampening off', a fungus attack which kills the stem at ground level.

Transplanting

Transplant during autumn when they are not growing, to give the plants more room and food.

Planting out

When to plant:

a) Trees in pots can be planted at any time of year.

b) Bare root trees not in a pot should be planted when they are dormant, i.e. after the leaves have fallen and before the first bud opens, i.e. between November and March.

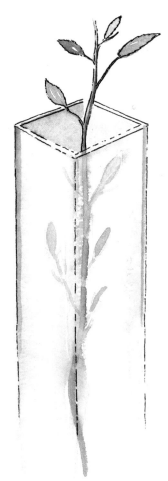

Protected plant

Tree nursery

43

Evergreens are best planted in September and late April.

How to plant:

1. Preparation of soil. Dig the hole wider and deeper than the root system. Break up the soil at the bottom of the hole to allow air and root penetration.

2. Drive a treated stake into the hole. The stake should help to anchor the roots, it should not be used to hold the stem tight as this weakens the stem. It should not be more than 300mm above ground.

3. Place your tree in the pit, backfill with soil. Firm the soil layer by layer.

4. Water the roots well.

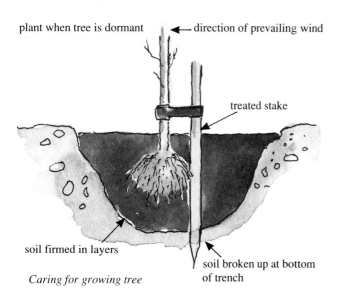

plant when tree is dormant — direction of prevailing wind

treated stake

soil firmed in layers

soil broken up at bottom of trench

Caring for growing tree

Watering

Regular watering is very important especially during a dry summer. Use 50 litres (5 gallons) at each watering. This is to make sure that water penetrates to the deep roots. If it doesn't your tree will develop a shallow rooting system.

Competition from weeds

Keep an area one metre all round your tree free from weeds.

Water regularly

Use felt or black polythene to keep area clear of vegetation.

Experiments have shown that your tree will grow much faster if it has no competition for moisture and nutrients from grass and weeds.

Bark mulch can also be used to keep down weeds.

Care of your growing tree

Your young tree still needs your care to help it get established in its final position.

Classification of trees

Any system of classification is based on who is doing it and for what purposes. Biologists divide all plants on earth into five great divisions. Trees are placed in two of these five divisions: **angiosperms** and **gymnosperms**. Foresters are mainly concerned with trees and they divide trees into two broad groups: **coniferous** trees and **broadleaved** trees.

Wood is divided into two divisions: **hardwoods** and **softwoods**.

This grouping has nothing to do with the hardness or softness of the wood. It is based solely on the structure of the wood.

Some wood is in fact very soft, e.g. balsa but because of its cell structure it is classified as a hardwood.

Some wood is very hard, e.g. pitch pine but because of its cell structure it is classified as a softwood. Therefore there are distinct differences between the cellular structure of softwoods and hardwoods. So we can only say for certain whether a particular wood is a hardwood or softwood by looking at its cell structure under a microscope.

Coniferous trees

1. They bear their seeds in cones, hence the name coniferous.

2. Coniferous trees have narrow needle-shaped leaves.

3. Most coniferous trees are evergreen, i.e. they do not drop all their leaves at once in the autumn, therefore the trees look green all year round, e.g. pines, spruces.

   Exception: Larch: it bears its seeds in cones therefore it is coniferous but it loses its needle leaves in winter.

4. The trunk is usually straight and cylindrical with an even taper.

5. They have a crown which is narrow and pointed allowing the snow to fall off. Coniferous trees are thus better adapted to grow in the colder climate of the Northern Hemisphere.

6. The wood from coniferous trees is usually soft, e.g. deals and pines. *Be warned*: yew is a coniferous tree but its wood is very hard.

Seed-bearing cones

Snow-laden conifers. Snow does not build up on downward sloping branches. Wider branches are at the bottom to get sunlight.

Broadleaved trees

1. They have covered seed, e.g. berries, acorns, stoned fruits, etc.

2. They have broad leaves, e.g. oak, sycamore, horse chestnut, hence the name.

Oak leaves with acorns

3. Most broadleaved trees are deciduous, i.e. they shed their leaves in winter in temperate climates. Thus they avoid the damage caused by frost in winter, e.g. oak, beech, ash, sycamore.

   Exception: Holly: it has broad leaves but it is not deciduous.

4. They have an irregular, less cylindrical trunk which often has little taper.

5. Most of the wood from the deciduous trees is hard, e.g. oak, beech, elm, but again *be warned*: horse chestnut is quite a soft wood but the tree is deciduous.

Broadleaved tree with large crown to hold large leaves out to the light.

The cell structure of wood

The terms hardwood and softwood refer to structural differences between the woods and not to the hardness or softness of the wood itself.

All wood is formed of tube-like cells. They differ in appearance according to their functions.

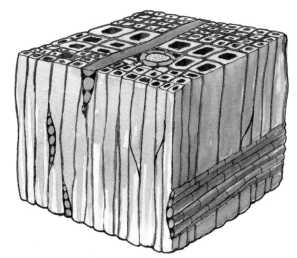

Cell structure of softwood

Cells perform three main functions in a tree:

- Some cells conduct water from the roots to the leaves. On a hot summer's day a large tree may take up 100 gallons of water from its roots and lose 90 per cent of it through evaporation from its leaves.

- Other cells give a tree its strength. These cells enable the tree trunk to support the crown, the branches to support its leaves and the whole tree to withstand strong winds.

- Other cells store the food of the tree, giving this tree its bulk or size.

Softwoods

Softwoods have a simple cell structure with only two types of cells:

1. Tracheids.

2. Parenchyma.

Tracheids

These cells are arranged parallel to the trunk and branches. They are so arranged that their taped ends interlock, giving the tree its strength.

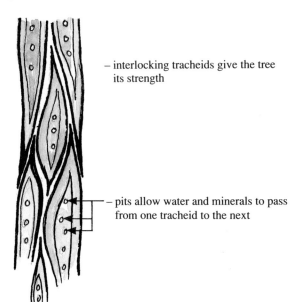

– interlocking tracheids give the tree its strength

– pits allow water and minerals to pass from one tracheid to the next

Interlocking tracheids

Water and minerals are conveyed up the trunk through the tracheids. These pass from one tracheid to the next through small holes in the tracheid walls called **pits**.

When you look at the end of a log you see distinct circular lines called growth rings. These are the tracheids. In spring when growth is fast they are light coloured, in autumn when growth is slow they are thick walled and darker in colour. This difference in colour gives the distinct growth rings.

Parenchyma cells

These cells are not very prominent in softwoods and make up the rest of the wood tissue. They are rectangular bricklike cells and they are the food storage cells of the tree.

parenchymas: brick-like cells which store the food

Softwood cells

Resin ducts

Many softwoods such as spruce, larch, Douglas fir have resin ducts which store resin and and sometimes exude it.

Cell structure of hardwoods

Hardwoods have a more complex arrangement of cells than softwoods. They have three types of cells:

1. Vessels or pores;
2. Fibres;
3. Parenchyma.

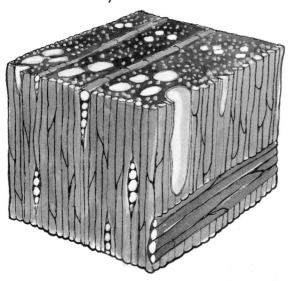

Cell structure of hardwoods

Vessels or pores

If you plane the end grain of hardwood and look at it through a hand lens you see tiny pores or little holes. These are the vessels. Softwoods do not have these pores. The absence of pores in softwood and the presence of pores in hardwoods is the major difference between the woods. Hardwood is therefore called **pored wood** and softwood is called **non-pored wood**.

Vessels are long cylindrical tubes joined end to end and running vertically in the tree. They convey water and minerals from the roots to the leaves.

Fibres

These give the tree its mechanical strength, in this way they correspond to the tracheids in the softwoods. They are long, tapered, thick-walled cells of small diameter. They form the bulk of the wood tissue surrounding the vessels.

Parenchyma cells

These are the soft tissue which surrounds the the vessels and can easily be seen with a hand lens. They are small rectangular cells and they store food.

Medullary rays

These are very like the parenchyma cells in that they store food. They run horizontally in the tree and radiate from the centre of the tree. They are very visible in some wood, like oak, and appear as decorative blotches known as silver grain, especially if the plant is quarter cut.

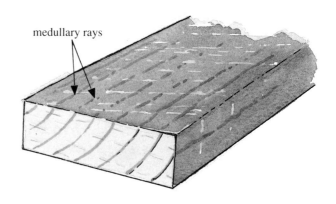

Polished oak

A tree

When we look at a tree it looks motionless and still. However, there is continuous movement day and night both inside and outside its bark.

On its bark there is a constant movement up and down of ants, slugs, beetles, spiders, caterpillars and weevils, as they make their way up to feed on the leaves and fruit and return to the soil again.

Inside the bark there is a constant movement of water and minerals, in defiance of gravity, from the roots to the leaves.

In the leaves they are converted to food for the growing cells and travel downwards again.

crown

trunk or bole

roots

The growing tree

Parts of a growing tree

The roots

These anchor the tree in the ground.

They also absorb water and minerals from the soil. Some trees have shallow rooting systems while others have deep rooting systems.

The trunk or bole

The water and minerals are conveyed through the trunk to the leaves and back down to feed the growing cells.

The trunk provides most of the wood that we use.

The crown

Consists of the branches and the leaves. The branches hold the leaves out to the sunlight which is necessary for food manufacture. The tips of the branches extend to allow the tree to grow in height.

The growth of a tree

A tree needs food to grow. This food, called **sap**, is manufactured in the leaves. If a tree did not have leaves it could not grow.

We know a tree is dead when it fails to produce leaves.

The leaves are the food factory of the tree where food for the growing cells are manufactured.

How food is manufactured

Water and minerals (raw sap) are absorbed from the soil by the roots and travel up through the sapwood to the leaves.

How does raw sap travel vertically upwards?

The sun evaporates water from the leaves. This creates a pull and more water rushes up to replace lost water. This sets up a constant upward movement. Also, the cells transporting the water are very narrow. Because they are so narrow water clings to their sides and rises upwards. This is called **capillary attraction**.

Both the transpiration pull and capillary attraction help transport water and minerals vertically within the trunk.

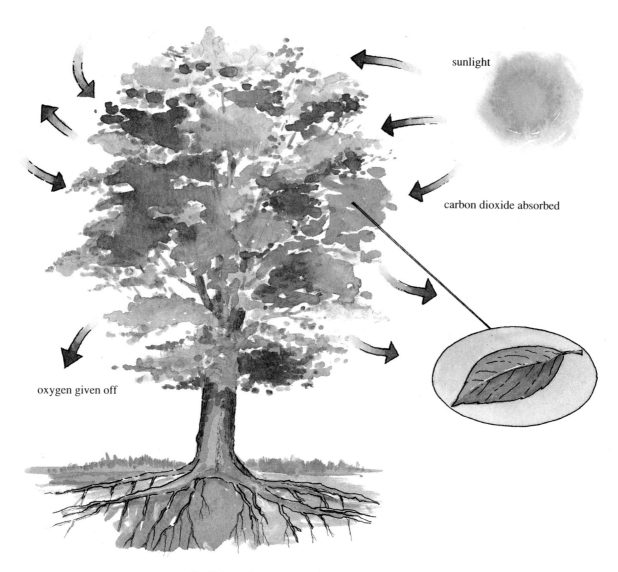

sunlight

carbon dioxide absorbed

oxygen given off

Sunlight and water are vital to the growing tree

Photosynthesis

Photo = light.

Synthesis = building.

A complex chemical reaction takes place in the leaves of a tree. This is called photosynthesis. Sunlight is absorbed by the green substance in the leaf called **chlorophyll.**

During this process carbon dioxide is absorbed and oxygen is released.

The carbon dioxide combines with the raw sap to form a sugar called **glucose.** The glucose is the food the cells need for growth.

Photosynthesis only occurs in daylight. Oxygen is given back into the atmosphere by the tree. When we breathe we take in oxygen and give back carbon dioxide. Thus a balance in nature is preserved. Such relationships are said to be symbiotic: we need oxygen, the tree needs carbon dioxide so the actions of one are beneficial to the other.

Where does the sap go?

The enriched sap can flow freely through the leaf veins and pass down the trunk to feed the growing cells.

If you strip a layer of bark off a tree you can feel and see the enriched sap. Early man peeled off a ring of bark right around the tree. The enriched sap then evaporated and the tree eventually died.

Cross section of a tree trunk

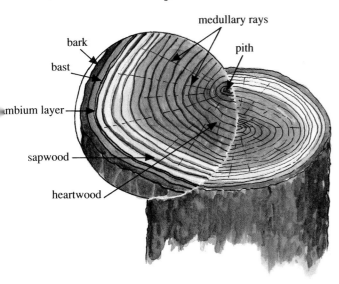

Tree cross-section

The bark

This is a layer of cork which protects the tree against external damage and prevents the sap from being evaporated. As the tree expands, the bark grows.

The bast or phloem

Also known as the inner bark. It is the moist area inside the bark. The outer layers of the bast progressively die off and form new layers of bark.

The cambium layer

This is a thin layer of living cells inside the bast. It consists of two different cell types:

1. Xylem cells

These are the 'wood cells' of the tree. They are the new sapwood cells.

New layers of xylem cells increase the diameter of the tree each year.

2. Phloem cells

These are the cells that transport the enriched sap downwards from the leaves. They bring the food supply to the xylem cells, without which they could not grow.

Sapwood

It is the newly formed outer layer of growing cells. It carries the water and minerals from the roots to the leaves. It contains foodstuffs and is soft. It therefore is susceptible to insect and fungi attacks unless it is treated with preservatives.

It can also distort and cup during drying because of its high moisture content.

Heartwood

This is the mature wood of the tree and forms the strong backbone of the tree. It is formed as a result of the tree forming new sapwood cells, thus depriving the inner sapwood of oxygen and food. In many woods it is darker than the sapwood. It is the part of the tree that supplies the woodworker with most of his/her wood.

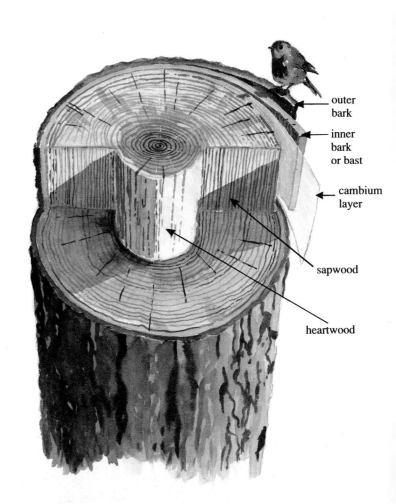

The tree bole

Annual rings or growth rings

In temperate climates such as Ireland growth takes place during spring and summer, and an annual growth ring is thus formed. This ring shows the amount the tree has expanded in diameter during the growing season. There is often a darker colour in the late summer wood. By counting these growth rings the age of the tree can be determined.

Growth rings

summer growth: thick walled dark cells

spring growth: fast-growing, thin-walled, lighter-coloured cells

one year's growth

In tropical countries with continuous high rainfall and temperatures the tree grows all the year round, and it is sometimes impossible to distinguish between each year's growth. For this reason there would be no obvious growth rings.

Medullary rays

These food storage cells radiate horizontally from the centre, giving some woods a distinctive silver fleck.

Pith

Also known as the medulla. It is the first growth of the tree and often decays as the tree grows older.

Activities

1. Many trees have an easily recognised outline. Take photographs of some trees and identify them from their outline. Describe how their outline aids identification.

2. Sketch the outline of some broadleaved trees *a)* in summer; *b)* in winter.

3. Some trees have distinctive winter buds. Collect some of these and sketch their different shapes.

4. Why do some trees lose their leaves in winter?

5. How do other trees maintain their leaves in winter?

6. Draw a sketch of a growing tree and list its parts.

7. List the functions of the roots of a tree.

8. What is meant by deep-root and shallow-root systems?

9. Discuss the effects of *a)* wind; *b)* drought; *c)* frost on shallow-root systems.

10. List the functions of the trunk or bole.

11. Of what importance is the trunk of a tree to woodworkers?

12. Using diagrams show how raw sap travels to the leaves and refined sap travels downwards.

13. Describe what factors enable sap to travel upwards against the force of gravity.

14. Discuss the functions of the leaves in a tree.

15. Large-leaved trees have a large crown. Why is this so?

16. What is meant by the term 'photosynthesis'?

17. With the aid of diagram and arrows show what happens during this chemical reaction.

18. What is meant by the term 'balance of nature'?

19. 'Mankind could not survive on earth without trees.' Discuss.

20. Draw a cross-section of a tree and label all its parts clearly.

21. What is the function of the bark? How can damage to the bark damage the tree?

22. a) Where does growth in height occur in a tree? Use a sketch to illustrate your answer.
b) How does growth in width or girth take place in a tree? List the functions of the cambium layer.

23. With the aid of sketches show where the sapwood and heartwood occur in a tree.

24. What are the characteristics of heartwood and sapwood? Which is most valued by the woodworker and why?

25. Heartwood and sapwood often differ visually. Describe the differences.

26. Sometimes when trees are felled the pith is decayed. How does this decay occur?

World distribution of timber

Two great bands of forest circle the globe.

a) The boreal or great coniferous forest belt.

b) The tropical rainforests.

The great coniferous forest belt

This great forest belt stretches across the land masses of the Northern Hemisphere between latitude 55°N and the Arctic Circle to within about 3,200 km (2,000 miles) of the North Pole.

North of this line the temperatures are too cold to allow tree growth and the forests give way to treeless tundra.

If there were land at the appropriate latitude in the Southern Hemisphere the boreal forests would have a counterpart in the Southern Hemisphere. However, the zone where this should occur lies in the vast Southern Ocean.

The boreal forests stretch from Siberia across Northern Russia and Northern Europe to Scandinavia and occur again at the same latitude in Canada and Alaska.

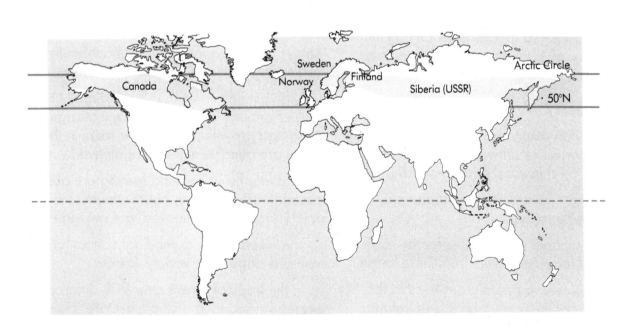

Boreal forests of the world

Features of the boreal forests

1. They are largely coniferous, the waxed needle leaves of the conifers being specially adapted to survive the cold.

2. They consist of pines, spruces, firs and larch.

   Along the eastern slope of the Sierra Nevada mountains in the west coast of the USA the giant redwoods flourish.

3. There are few tree species (just two or three species per hectare) and the undergrowth is usually sparse.

4. By keeping their hard waxy leaves during winter the conifers can resume growth in early spring and not waste a moment of the short summer growing season.

   Larches lose their leaves in winter and can survive the bleak cold climate of eastern Siberia where even the tough conifer needles cannot withstand the cold.

   Their delicate green needles return with a slight increase in temperature.

   There is no absolute line where the coniferous forest belt begins and ends.

   At the northern margins it diminishes into tundra and at the southern margins birch, ash and other broadleaved species grow among the conifers, producing a mixed forest which is richer in wildlife owing to the greater variety of trees.

Produce of boreal forests

The Scandinavian countries, Russia and Canada are world exporters of softwoods and associated products such as chipwood and plywood.

Many of these forests are now managed, with forests being replanted.

Much of the paper pulp supplies for the huge world demand for paper comes from these forests.

Growth is slower for coniferous trees in the colder climates of the north than it is in Ireland, with a cycle of 80 years being usual as compared to 40–50 years in Ireland.

American redwood

The tropical rainforests

This distinctive belt of forests runs around the equator. It occurs in South America (mainly Brazil) West, Central and East Africa, and from Malaysia and Indonesia throughout South East Asia to Papua New Guinea.

High temperatures and high rainfall (1,500 mm per annum) all year round encourage a dense lush growth of forest. The trees in these forests are almost entirely broadleaved.

Leaf fall, flowering and fruiting are not seasonal, as in Ireland, but continuous, thus the forests, though broadleaved, are evergreen.

The forest belt is exceedingly beautiful, having a staggering variety of trees.

In the tropical forests over 200 different tree species are found in a single hectare. How many tree species would you find in a hectare of forest in Ireland?

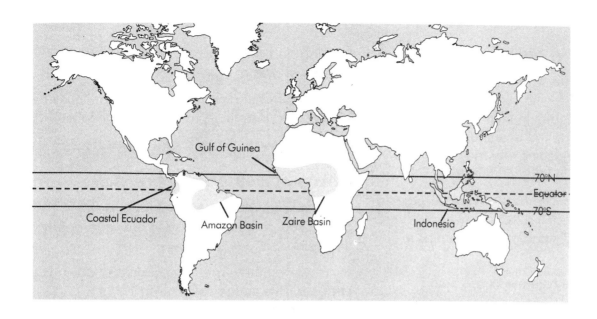

Gulf of Guinea

70°N
Equator
70°S

Coastal Ecuador

Amazon Basin

Zaire Basin

Indonesia

Tropical rain forests are rapidly diminishing

Trees are often up to 30 metres tall with long clear boles of up to 20 metres before the first branches.

Biological diversity

Tropical rainforests have existed in much the same way for thousands of years. They have developed an extraordinary biological diversity. For example, up to 200 different tree species can be found growing in just one hectare.

Madagascar, off the coast of Africa, has over 2,000 tree species whereas Canada and the USA have a combined total of 700 species.

But it is not only valuable trees like mahogany, teak, greenheart, ebony, rosewood, etc. that the tropical forests contain. They contain an extraordinary range of plants and animals. About one in four medicines contain compounds from rainforest plants.

A recently discovered drug, vinchristine, extracted from the rosy periwinkle plant found only in the Madagascar rainforests, offers a 90 per cent chance of remission in cases of lymphatic leukemia. Before this wonderdrug was discovered there was very little chance of recovery. However, only a tiny proportion of the plants have yet been assessed for use in medicine.

Tropical rain forest

55

The destruction of the rainforests

Europeans' love affair with tropical hardwoods began in the late sixteenth century when the Spanish used mahogany in their sailing ships. British Honduras supplied beautiful mahogany to Europe. However, felling was slow. It took a team of men a day to fell a mature tree.

After 1940 when chainsaws were introduced it took ten minutes to fell a tree. Nowadays huge machines can turn a standing tree to chips in one minute.

How much of the rainforests are being destroyed?

The rainforests cover about 7 per cent of the earth's surface.

It has been estimated that 100 acres per minute is being either burned or cut down, or approximately 1–2 per cent of the original area is being devastated every year.

Of the rainforests being destroyed each year almost half is being burned to make way for farming and only 8 per cent is used in the country of origin.

If the present rate of destruction continues the world could lose all its rainforests in the next 30 years.

Effects of rainforest destruction

The effects on all the world of the possible destruction of the rainforests is not yet properly understood.

However, there are immediate and obvious effects for the countries involved.

Burning of the forests

Since 1960 25 per cent of Central America's rainforests have been burned to clear land for farming. A huge pall of smoke has hung over Brazil so vast that it can be seen from outer space. Huge quantities of carbon monoxide have been ejected into the atmosphere with severe effects on the health of the people.

Destruction of tropical rain forest

Flooding

Much of the flooding that is often thought of as natural flooding is not natural but is caused directly by the destruction of the rainforests. When the protective canopy of trees is removed the heavy rains wash away huge quantities of soil. For example, flooding in Bangladesh is caused by the destruction of Nepal's rain forests. The soil was washed down into the Ganges river, causing the water level to rise.

The river cannot then discharge the water and flooding follows, resulting in huge loss of life.

Half of Nepal's rainforests have been cut down since 1950.

Massive soil erosion has been recorded in the Ivory Coast with the removal of the rainforests.

Forests and people

Tribal people have a harmonious relationship with the forests. They have deep-rooted cultural ties with the forest which give meaning to their lives and cohesion to their cultures. They have used the wood for houses, tools, for traditional medicines, and the fibres and dyes for their clothes.

They are already amongst the poorest people and the destruction of the forests spells physical and social doom. Many succumb to disease and drift into the sprawling slums of impoverished cities.

There are perilous social problems within some of these Third World countries. In Brazil 42 per cent of the cultivated land is owned by 1 per cent of the population. This means dispossession for the poor. There are huge and expanding populations and they continue burning to get more land as the erosion destroys their own.

Climate and rainforests

An area the size of West Germany is being deforested every year. Scientists believe that this will have a severe effect on world climate. The rainforests moderate the climate of the world, keeping the tropics cool through vast transpiration. With the disappearance of these forests there could be an increase in global warming, aiding the greenhouse effect.

Ireland and the rainforests

Ireland imports about 1,000 tons of tropical hardwoods each week, mainly from The Ivory Coast, Ghana and Brazil. It has been calculated that this amounts to ten hectares (25 acres approx.) of tropical forest per day being cut to supply our needs.

We are The Ivory Coast's best customer for ioroko but already 90 per cent of its forests have been cut down.

What can we do?

It has been argued that the demands of joinery and woodwork account for only 10 per cent of tropical forest felling. The rest is burned, used for fuel, etc. However, there is a huge problem, and individually we must act now.

- We can grow more broadleaved species to reduce our dependency on imported species.

- We can use manufactured boards for joinery that is to be painted, e.g. shopfronts.

- We can use veneers where possible of scarce wood.

- We will have to pay more so that poorer people will have to cut less.

- The EC is trying to develop a policy of importing hardwoods only from countries with a reafforestation policy. We must support this.

There are no simple answers to complex problems. Trees have a lifespan and cannot last for ever. We can only preserve trees for their natural lifespan. However, forests can be properly managed and new trees planted to replace those felled. The developed world will have to help poorer countries to manage their forest for all our benefit.

Forests and their products

The forest plantation

There are two types of forests:

a) natural forests, which contain different tree species and of different ages, e.g. the native oak forests, the tropical forests;

b) managed forests, which are the manmade forests, usually of one or two tree types and in which all the trees are the same age.

Stages in a managed forest

1. Draining the land and fencing

2. Planting of young trees

These trees are grown in a nursery for three years and are then transplanted. The young trees are planted close together. As they grow their branches form a mat which excludes the light. This prevents the growth of branches lower down the tree.

3. Thinning

From 15 years onwards the young conifers are thinned. This gives more space and light to the remaining trees and allows them more food. Thinning is the cutting of the smaller trees to allow the stronger trees grow to full maturity.

4. Harvesting

Conifers grow very fast in the mild moist climate of Ireland and are ready for harvesting between 30 and 50 years old. All the trees are the same age so they are **clear felled**, i.e. all the trees are cut down at the same time.

Thinning trees in a forestry plantation

Thinnings prepared for use

Clear felling

5. Second rotation

When all the trees are removed the ground is replanted, usually with the same species, and a new plantation is established.

6. Transportation

The tree is cut to length and the branches removed. It is then known as a log. Logs are transported in specially adapted lorries.

Transporting logs

Uses

Thinnings are used mainly for pulpwood, and are used by Finsa Forest Products, Scariff, Co. Clare to make chipboard and by Medite Europe at Clonmel, Co. Tipperary to make medium-density fibreboard. Ireland supplies all its own pulpwood needs and most of the manufactured boards are exported.

Thinnings are also used to make pallets and are treated with preservative and used as fencing poles.

Debarked thinnings treated with preservatives and used as fencing posts

Large saw logs. The conifers in a forestry plantation reach maturity after about 50 years. These trees provide the wood that is used in the roofing, partitions and floors of our houses. They are usually transported to the sawmill with the branches removed but with the bark on. However, modern machines can fell and debark the log in the forest. In the sawmill the log is cut into different sizes depending on its use. The **bark mulch** is separated and used by gardeners to control weeds.

Large saw logs before conversion

Sawdust being collected for further use

Debarking machine at Woodfab, Aughrim, Co. Wicklow

Methods of conversion

There are a number of methods, depending on what wood is being used and where it is going to be used. The sawdust obtained when a log is being cut is collected and used in the manufacture of chipboard and heatlogs.

1. Through and through sawing

Also known as plain sawing or slash sawing. This is the simplest method of converting a log to a plank and it is also the most commonly used method in Ireland. The log is placed on moving rollers and is cut through and through, usually by a large bandsaw.

Through and through board sawing

Conversion of timber

'Conversion' is the name given to the process of cutting a log in various pieces of regular shape, e.g. into boards or into planks, depending on where it is going to be used.

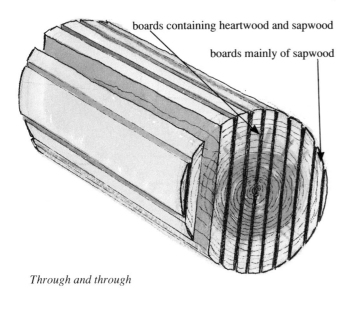
boards containing heartwood and sapwood
boards mainly of sapwood

Through and through

2. Quarter sawing

Almost all our hardwoods are imported. Some of these are quarter sawn to show distinct medullary ray marking, especially in oak known as silver grain. 'Wavy grain' and 'fiddle back' grain figures are also got by quarter sawing certain woods.

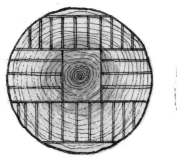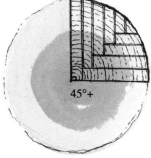
45°+

Quarter-sawn log

Advantages

- quick and easy as the log doesn't have to be turned;
- maximum width of planks obtained from log;
- little wastage;
- reveals attractive grain pattern, especially in softwoods.

Disadvantages

- some of the outer boards are almost all sapwood and therefore weaker;
- boards tend to warp when drying.

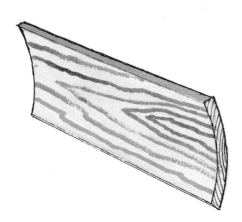

Tangential shrinkage

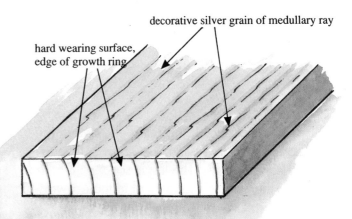
decorative silver grain of medullary ray
hard wearing surface, edge of growth ring

Quarter-sawn board

Advantages

- it shows up certain grain patterns in some hardwoods;
- the growth rings meet the face of the board at an angle of not less than 45°. This means that the growth rings are short and there is little distortion of the board during drying;
- a hard-wearing surface is exposed for hardwood floors as the edges of the growth rings wear evenly without splitting.

Disadvantages

- expensive, the log has to be first quartered and then turned after every cut;
- because the log is quartered and then cut again narrower boards are produced.

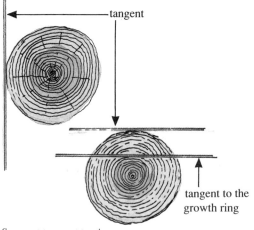

Sawn at tangent to rings

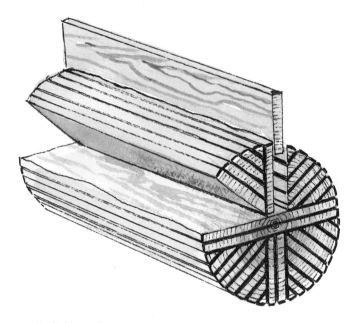

Radial-sawn log

3. Tangent sawing

This method of converting is widely used in the USA and Canada. We import some softwood from these countries. The log is sawn so that the width of the board is tangential to the growth rings.

Advantages

- boards of hardwood and sapwood are easily separated;
- knots appear circular on the face of a tangent-sawn board and are less of a structural defect;
- if the pith is decayed it can easily be 'boxed' around and the sound wood converted;
- tangent-sawn boards are structurally strong and suitable for floor joists or where weight is being supported.

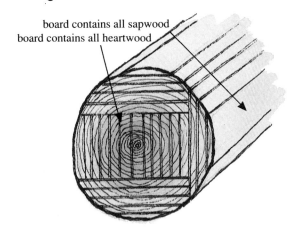

Tangentially sawn log

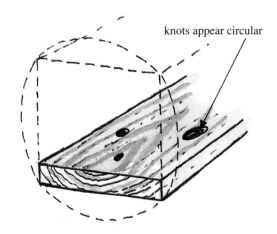

Tangential board with knots

Disadvantages

Again the log has to be turned during cutting so it is a more expensive method. However, with automation of cutting this is not as expensive as it used to be.

Wood-based materials

Wood contains an abundance of raw materials. Early man extracted gum and resins from the bark and bast of certain trees. Tannic acid was extracted from oak and used to convert raw hide into leather. Early man hollowed out the centre of large trees and used them as boats.

The Indians slit the bark of the birch, peeled it off and used it as a natural waterproof covering for their canoes. The French Canadians used the same technique for their boats and opened up the Canadian continent.

Wood was also extensively used in boat building. The Vikings built fine sailing ships of wood.

The Galway hooker, used for travel between the Aran Islands and Galway, is a wooden sailing boat.

birch bark canoe

Bark used on canoes

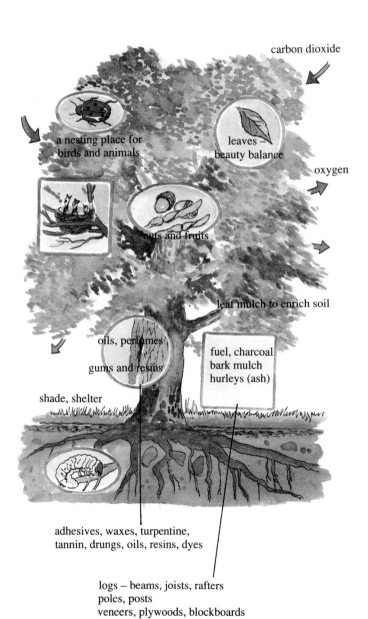

What a tree does for us

Fruits of the tree

carbon dioxide

a nesting place for birds and animals

leaves – beauty balance

oxygen

nuts and fruits

leaf mulch to enrich soil

oils, perfumes gums and resins

fuel, charcoal bark mulch hurleys (ash)

shade, shelter

adhesives, waxes, turpentine, tannin, drungs, oils, resins, dyes

logs – beams, joists, rafters
poles, posts
veneers, plywoods, blockboards
paper, pulp, chipboards, fibreboards (MDF, HDF)
flooring, furniture, musical instruments

63

Modern wood-based products

Today we have different materials with which to cover our canoes but we have found other uses for wood.

Paper is a mat of interwoven fibres. By far the most important source of these fibres is woodpulp. Huge quantities of woodpulp are used each year to make paper.

There is also a wide variety of sheet materials which use wood pulp as their base material. Hardboard, chipboard, medium-density fibreboard, are but some of these.

Woodpulp

The woody substance of a tree consists of 65–85 per cent fibre bound together with 15–35 per cent lignin.

Wood is pulped for the purpose of separating the fibres. The fibres are then reintegrated, mixed with various glues to form new substances, eg. paper, chipboard, fibreboard.

These are two methods used for separating the fibres of wood:

a) *mechanical.* The log is reduced to chips and the chips are passed between grinding wheels which tear the fibres apart;

b) *chemical.* The log is first reduced to chips mechanically. Chemicals are then used to dissolve the lignin which holds the fibres together. The fibre yield is reduced by this method but the pulp has a finer texture and is used in paper making.

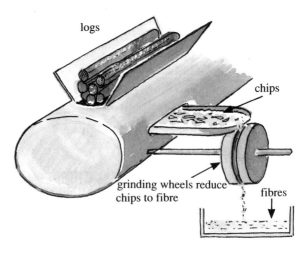

Logs reduced to chips

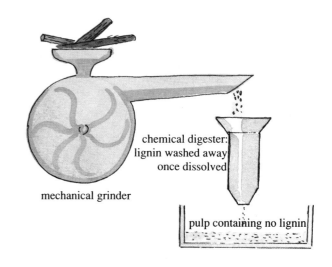

Chemical treatment to make pulp

64

Manmade sheet materials

Natural wood has certain restrictions. It is not available in large boards, the width of the board depending on the diameter of the tree.

In the late 1800s the **rotary peeler** was developed. The log was first softened by peeling and then mounted on the rotary peeler. This machine could peel off a continuous thin layer of wood from the log. This layer of wood is called a **veneer**.

These layers were then glued together to form plywood. But the the earlier glues failed under moist conditions, resulting in the layer coming apart, called **delamination**.

However, a huge advance in plywood construction was made in the 1930s with the development of moisture-resistant adhesives. These chemical adhesives were the by-product of the oil industry and new adhesives are still being developed regularly.

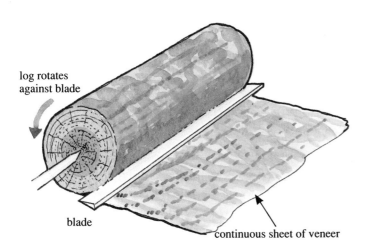

Slicing veneer

In the 1960s came the development of new materials using woodpulp. Chipboard was made by compressing and gluing chips of wood together. This development meant that wood thinnings and branches, which were formely wasted, could now be used.

The 1970s saw the development of fibreboards using smaller chips, and now not only chips but sawdust could be used. Thus all this material which would otherwise be wasted can now be used to make sheet materials.

The Woodfab company in Co. Wicklow sells its sawdust to the Finsa chipboard factory in Co. Clare.

Heatlogs are also made by compressing sawdust. These can be used as an alternative to coal.

Debarking machines strip the bark off the trunk before it is converted into logs. This bark is now widely used in gardening to cover the ground around plants, thus excluding the light and preventing grass and weed growth close to the plants.

Small thinnings and branches are debarked and impregnated under pressure with preservatives, and are used as fencing poles. The preservatives greatly extend their life, as they are treated against insect and fungal attack.

So nowadays there is almost no waste in a sawmill.

Thus the most economical use is made of one of nature's greatest resources: our trees.

Wood-based sheet materials: manufactured boards

Manufactured boards are classified into three groups:

1. laminated boards;

2. particle boards;

3. fibreboards.

1. Laminated boards

A lamina is a thin sheet and laminated boards are made by gluing together thin sheets of wood. The most important laminated board is **plywood**. It is manufactured from rotary cut veneers, bonded together with their grain alternately at right angles to one another. An odd number of veneers glued in this way prevents a structural imbalance in the ply.

There are three grades of plywood manufactured:

- Interior. The glues are not waterproof. Used mainly in furniture manufacture.

- Exterior (WBP). The glues used to bond laminates are weather- and boilproof (WBP) and are highly resistant to weather, micro-organisms, water, steam and heat. There are various grades of exterior plywood depending on the quality of the veneers.

- Marine. Made from selected veneers and glued with weather- and boilproof glue. Suitable for areas where the plywood will be saturated for long periods, e.g. boat building.

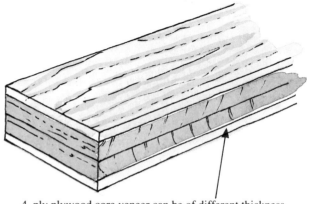

4–ply plywood core veneer can be of different thickness

4–ply plywood

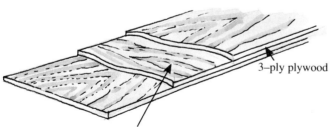

core veneer has grain direction at right angles to face and back veneer. This gives strength in length and width.

3–ply plywood

3–ply plywood

Woods used in plywood manufacture. A wide variety of woods are used, depending on the country of origin. Finnish and Russian plywoods are based on birch veneers, Canadian and American plywoods are of softwood veneers, plywood from the Far East is based on hardwood veneers. Ireland has no plywood manufacturing plant.

Uses

1. Furniture. Often a selected hardwood veneer is used as a face veneer.

2. It is widely used where large strong sheets are required: industrial flooring, concrete formwork, panels, vehicle body parts, crates, packages, ship and boat building.

Advantages of plywood

- it is available in large sheets;

- it shrinks and swells very little owing to the bonding with waterproof glues;

- alternate direction of veneers ensures that it is strong both in length and width;

- it is available generally in thickness from 4–25mm but special thicknesses are also available;

- thin sheets of plywood can be bent to form curved work;
- modern roofing materials often use plywood with insulation between.

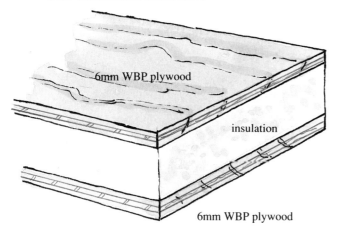

6mm WBP plywood

insulation

6mm WBP plywood

Ply sandwiched insulation

Strip core boards

Blockboard. Strips of wood from 12–25mm are glued together and covered front and back with a veneer. It was widely used in furniture making, shelving, worktops and as a core for veneering. It is expensive but makes an excellent ground for veneering in furniture manufacture.

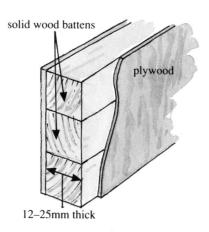

solid wood battens

plywood

12–25mm thick

Blockboard

Laminboard. Similar in construction to blockboard but the core strips are narrower: less than 12mm. It is more expensive to manufacture than blockboard. The core is less likely to show through the veneers and it was often used as a core for veneering for furniture, and for cupboard doors where no framing was necessary. Blockboard and laminboard are really plywood substitutes, but they are expensive as their production is difficult to automate. Their use has declined in recent years owing to competition from other particle boards.

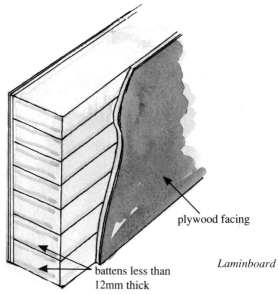

plywood facing

battens less than 12mm thick

Laminboard

2. Particle boards

Wood particle boards are made from small chips of wood glued together under pressure. The particles vary in size and the glues used to bond them also vary.

Chipboard is made from a mat of wood chips. Logs are first debarked and then reduced to chips mechanically. These logs are usually forestry thinnings. The chips are then screened and dried. The graded chips are then mixed with resin and formed into boards in a heated press.

There are two basic ways of laying up the chips for pressing, giving two different types of boards:

a) Single layer. Made from a mat of similar-sized chips evenly distributed. The sheet has a relatively coarse finish. Was widely used in the past for built-in furniture and where large panels were necessary. Not so popular nowadays except for billboards, temporary partitions, etc.

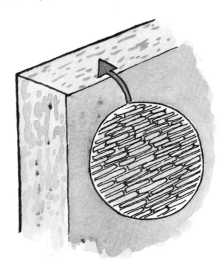

Single layer chipboard

Triple layer chipboard

b) Triple layer. The chips are graded for size with larger chips in the centre and smaller chips at the surface with a high proportion of resin. This gives a smooth finish and is suitable for painting. It also provides a suitable ground for veneering. It is widely used in furniture making where natural veneers are glued.

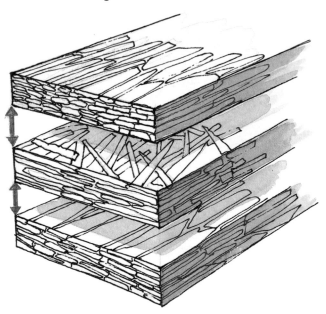

Triple-layer – note larger chips in middle

Moisture-resistant furniture-grade chipboard is clearly recognised by its green colour. It is bonded with a moisture-resistant glue and is suitable for use in areas where it is exposed to dampness or condensation, e.g. bathrooms, kitchen presses.

Melamine-faced chipboard is manufactured by covering three-layer furniture-grade chipboard with a special cellulose paper impregnated with a melamine resin. This allows for a range of colours in the finished board. The edges are also preveneered with the same cellulose paper, often to a contrasting colour. These boards have wide application in kitchen and bedroom furniture and shop-fitting, shelving, etc.

Flooring grade chipboard is a three-layered board able to withstand heavy loads. It is manufactured in 18mm and 22mm thickness. It is tongued and grooved to give it added stability and is widely used in suspended floors. There is also a moisture-resistant flooring-grade chipboard available.

Edge treatment of chipboard. When you look at a sheet of chipboard you can see the fibres along the edges. This looks unsightly and must be covered.

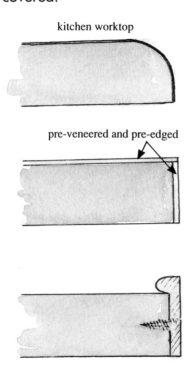

Edge treatment of chipboard

There are various ways in which the edges may be treated:

a) some chipboard panels come from the factory with the edges preveneered. This covers the unsightly fibres;

b) aluminium strips can be fitted to the edges to conceal the fibres. This method is widely used for kitchen worktops;

c) preglued strips of melamine or wood veneer can be heated with an iron and stuck on. Only satisfactory for small areas as they tend to lift off;

d) a variety of natural wood strips can be fixed to the edges.

There is a factory in Scariff, Co. Clare which manufactures chipboard for the Irish market and for export.

Iron-on veneer

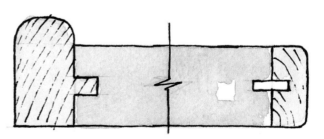

Hardwood edging

3. Fibreboards

Wood is reduced to its basic fibre elements and reconstituted to make a stable sheet material. Boards of varying density are produced depending on

(*a*) the adhesives used;

(*b*) the pressure applied.

Hardboards are high-density fibreboards produced from wet fibres at high pressure and temperature. No glues are used. The natural resins in the wood bond the fibres together. After the removal of much of the water the fibres are deposited on a wire mesh carrier. They are oil impregnated to give them water-resistant properties. The front face is then smooth with a fine mesh pattern on the back. Duo-faced hardboards are also available with both faces smooth.

Types

Hardboard in recent times has been treated to give it greater versatility. These include duo-faced (smooth both sides), sealed, primed, painted, surface laminated with melamines, PVC, paper, metal, foils and fabrics. It can also be moulded (as in modern interior door construction), embossed and perforated, i.e. peg board.

Uses

Depending on the type, hardboard has a wide variety of uses: backs of kitchen presses, drawer bottoms, partitions, panelling, caravan interiors, underlay for flooring materials and flush door construction.

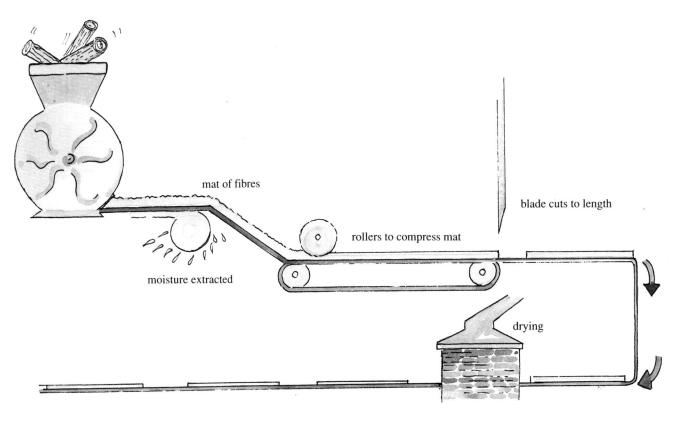

mat of fibres

moisture extracted

rollers to compress mat

blade cuts to length

drying

Hardboard production

Hardboard-faced door

Thickness

Thicknesses of hardboard range from 1.3–12.7mm but the most popular thicknesses are 2.0–6.4mm.

Softboards are medium-density boards which are manufactured by a similar wet process to hardboard but the press stage is omitted. They are mainly used as insulating boards and sometimes they are bitumen impregnated to enable other materials to stick to them, e.g. felt.

Medium-density Fibreboard (MDF). A relative newcomer to the ranks of fibreboard. It was developed in the 1970s and it is regarded as intermediate between hardboard and chipboard, in that it is manufactured from fibres like hardboard and its high internal strength is obtained by adding synthetic resin adhesive as is done in chipboard manufacture.

Properties of MDF

It has a fine structure of densely packed fibres, giving a smooth finish on its face. These fine fibres also provide an edge that can be easily machined to intricate shapes. It therefore does not need the same edge treatment as chipboard.

Medite HD Fibreboard is marketed in Ireland under the trade name 'Medite'. Medite HD is a high-density fibreboard where greater strength is required.

Medite 313 is a moisture-resistant fibreboard which can be used in humid interior areas, e.g. kitchens and bathrooms. There is also an exterior grade.

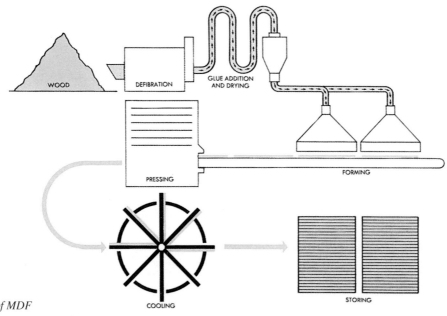

Production process of MDF

71

Woodfibres from MDF

MDF is easily moulded

MDF mat awaiting compression

Interior Medite is used in kitchen and bedroom furniture, dining tables, moulded architrave and skirting. Its smooth finish makes it an ideal base for veneering and it can also be purchased preveneered.

Veneered MDF saves on valuable hardwood

Uses

It combines the advantages of sheet materials with the distinct property that the edges can be machine profiled to almost any shape. This has led to a great variety of uses. The exterior grade can be used for decorative shop fronts, especially where they are to be painted. Its use for this purpose could help arrest the importation of scarce hardwoods from the tropical forests. It can be used in nameplates, signs in fascia and soffite boards externally.

Sizes

Thicknesses range from 4–35mm; the common sheet size is 1220–2440mm. Special sheet sizes are available at extra cost.

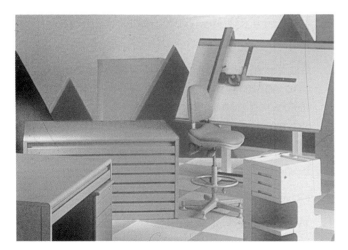
MDF in office furniture

Machining MDF

Hand tools are of little use when machining MDF, except where small items are required. Machine tools, router, planer, saw, etc. should have tungsten carbide tipped blades. Traditional wood screws are of little use. Screws with a parallel core and shallow pitch are available for use with both chipboard and MDF.

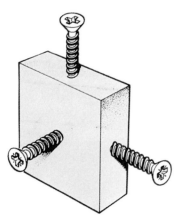
Use the correct screws

MDF dust control

The dust generated when machining MDF is very fine, and proper dust extraction systems should be fitted to all machines. Always use a face mask when working MDF by hand.

Ireland and MDF manufacture

A plant which manufacture MDF is situated at Clonmel, Co. Tipperary and trades under the name Medite Europe. It employs over 150 people, uses only homegrown softwoods, supplies the home market and exports 90 per cent of its output to Europe.

Dust extractor

Activities

1. What is meant by the terms *a)* managed forest *b)* natural forest?

2. List the procedures a forester follows in establishing a forestry plantation.

3. Why are trees planted so close together in a managed forest?

4. What is thinning? When does thinning take place and why?

5. What uses are made of thinnings?

6. What is meant by 'clear felling'?

7. When is a forest clear felled?

8. Conifers grow faster in Ireland than in most countries. List the factors that encourage fast tree growth.

9. List some of the advantages and disadvantages of of fast tree growth.

10. What is meant by the term 'conversion of timber'?

11. With the aid of sketches show and name three methods of converting timber.

12. Why is through-and-through sawing most widely used in Ireland?

13. List three advantages and disadvantages of quarter sawing.

14. How does quarter sawing enhance the *a*) visual *b*) wearing characteristics of some hardwoods?

15. What is meant by the term 'manufactured boards'?

16. Why in some circumstances, are manufactured boards more suitable than natural boards?

17. When might you use natural boards in preference to manufactured boards?

18. List the main manufactured boards.

19. Why is plywood stronger than other manufactured boards?

20. List the advantages and disadvantages of plywood.

21. With the aid of sketches, show how plywood is manufactured.

22. What do the initials 'WBP' stand for?

23. What are the greatest plywood manufacturing countries of the world?

24. List three uses for plywood and describe its advantages in each case.

25. List the main strip core boards. Compare and contrast them with plywood under the following headings: manufacture, advantages, disadvantages, uses.

26. What is meant by the term 'particle boards'?

27. How are the particles formed?

28. With the aid of sketches show how chipboard is manufactured.

29. Where is Ireland's chipboard manufactured?

30. Prepare wall charts illustrating chipboard manufacture and uses.

31. List the main grades of chipboard and describe their uses. Show how the edges of chipboard may be treated when used in furniture and fittings.

32. List the main grades of fibreboards and give their uses.

33. Describe with sketches the manufacture of hardboard.

34. List its main advantages and uses.

35. What are softboards and where are they mainly used?

36. What do the initials 'MDF' and 'HDF' stand for?

37. Describe with sketches their manufacture.

38. 'Medite' has major advantages over other manufactured boards. Discuss.

39. The use of fibreboards can help prevent the wasteful use of hardwoods. Discuss.

40. Write a note on safety precautions when using fibreboards *a*) by hand; *b*) by machine.

41. Give an account of the manufacture of fibreboards in Ireland.

Seasoning of timber

Seasoning refers to the reduction of the moisture content in wood. The word 'seasoning' probably comes from the seasons of the year when natural drying of the wood could be carried out.

When a tree is felled it contains a lot of moisture. It could be compared to a wet sponge just taken out of water. This freshly felled timber is called **green timber**.

The saturated sponge is soft and weak. Freshly felled wood is like this.

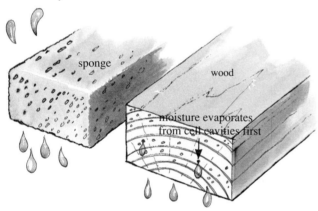

Freshly felled wood can be like a sponge

Wood contains moisture in the form of

- free moisture in the cell cavities;
- bound moisture in the cell walls.

When you squeeze the sponge it loses most of its moisture but it is still damp and weak. As soon as a tree is felled it begins losing its moisture through drying. It loses moisture from the cell cavities first. At this stage no change in dimensions occurs. However, just like the sponge the wood feels damp to touch because it still contains moisture in its cell walls.

Moisture content (MC) of wood

If we leave our sponge to dry the rest of the moisture will evaporate. The sponge will shrink, become rigid and dry to touch; likewise with wood.

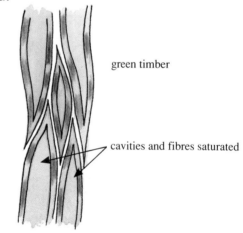

Saturated wood

When the free moisture in the cell cavities has evaporated the cell walls are still saturated. This is known as **fibre saturation point** (FSP). The wood at this stage has a MC of about 30 per cent and has reduced in weight but not in dimensions. Below an MC of 30 per cent water evaporates from the cell walls. The cell walls shrink and come closer together, and like our sponge, the wood will shrink, become rigid and dry to touch. However, the cells reduce very little in length so wood reduces very little in length as it dries.

75

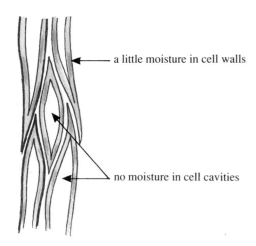

a little moisture in cell walls

no moisture in cell cavities

Below FSP

How to calculate the MC

The weight of moisture remaining in a piece of wood is expressed as a percentage of the dry weight of that piece. This is known as the MC of wood.

The traditional method for finding the moisture content of a piece of wood is known as the oven method.

Method

1. Take a piece of wood and weigh it. This is its original weight.

Weigh wood before and after drying

2. Place it in a low heat oven, usually 105°C, for 18–24 hours until its weight fails to drop after repeated weighing. This weight is its dry weight.

3. The difference between its original weight and its dry weight is known as its lost weight.

Wood in low heat oven

$$\% \text{ Moisture content} = \frac{\text{lost weight} \times 100}{\text{dry weight}}$$

e.g.

   1. Original weight = 177 grams.

   2. Dry weight = 150 grams.

   3. Lost weight = 177 −150 = 27 grams.

$$\% \text{ MC} = \frac{27 \times 100}{150 \text{ dry weight}}$$

$$= \frac{27 \times 10}{15}$$

$$\% \text{ MC} = \frac{27 \times 2}{3}$$

$$= \frac{54}{3}$$

$$= 18\% \text{ MC}$$

An MC of 18 per cent means that the weight of water in the wood is 18 per cent of the weight of dry matter in the wood.

Wood is not an inert material, however. It is said to be **hygroscopic**: it picks up and releases moisture. If you leave a wooden garden seat outside during the winter the wood will absorb moisture. During the summer this wood will shrink. The MC of wood will depend on where it is to be used. You will need a different MC for wood used in a garden shed and wood used in a radiator shelf.

What should the MC of both be?

Exterior and interior use

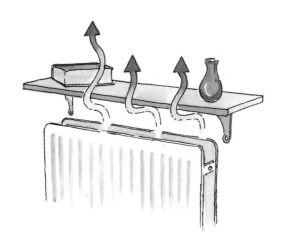

May require different moisture contents

Moisture meter

For measuring the MC of wood.

Moisture meters work on the principle that wood is a poor conductor of electricity whereas moisture is a good conductor.

In a moisture meter electric current passes between two electrodes. The meter measures the resistance of the moist wood and gives an instant reading of the moisture content as a percentage.

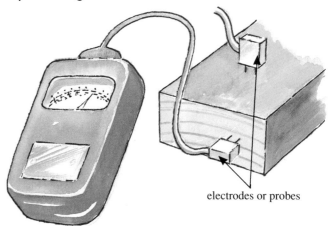

electrodes or probes

Moisture meter for measuring MC

How to use

Insert the electrodes into the wood at various points along the board or plank to check the average MC. The meter reads off instantly the percentage MC of the piece of wood.

Recommended % MC levels in wood

Fungus can only grow when wood has a percentage MC which exceeds 20 per cent and the area is not ventilated. Therefore all wood should be dried below an MC of 20 per cent.

Use	% MC
Structural: rafters, joists, etc.	18%
Garden furniture	16%
Occasionally heated rooms	12–14%
Normally heated rooms	11–13%
Continuously heated rooms	9–11%

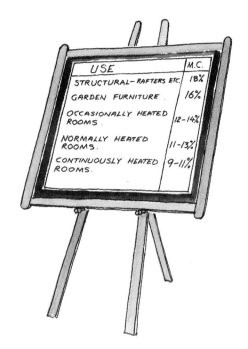

USE	M.C.
STRUCTURAL - RAFTERS ETC.	18%
GARDEN FURNITURE	16%
OCCASIONALLY HEATED ROOMS	12-14%
NORMALLY HEATED ROOMS	11-13%
CONTINUOUSLY HEATED ROOMS	9-11%

Use and moisture contents

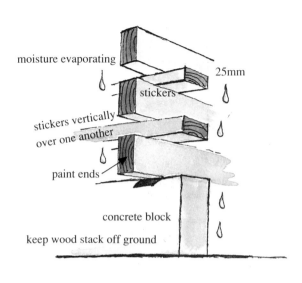

moisture evaporating

25mm

stickers

stickers vertically over one another

paint ends

concrete block

keep wood stack off ground

Air drying timber

Methods of seasoning timber

There are two main methods of seasoning timber:

a) natural or air drying;

b) artificial or kiln seasoning.

Natural or air drying

Air drying is the traditional method of reducing the MC of wood. The wood is first sawn into the sizes required, as it is almost impossible to season wood in the log.

It is then stacked in the open air where it is dried by the prevailing weather conditions.

Strips of wood called **stickers** are spaced 600–750mm apart to allow the air to circulate between the boards. The air circulation is controlled by the thickness of the strip. The wood should be stacked perfectly level and clear of the ground to allow air to circulate. The ends of the boards or planks will check and split as they dry out quickest unless they are painted. A covering should be placed over the stack to protect it from rain and direct sunlight.

Drying times

As a rough guide it takes one year for every 25mm thickness of hardwood and about half that time for softwoods. The MC of air-dried timber is usually 18–20 per cent which is not suitable for internal use, and such timber needs to be further dried.

One year per 25mm thickness

Kiln drying

Wood for interior use needs a MC of 8–10 per cent.

Wood is dried to this MC in a special chamber called a kiln.

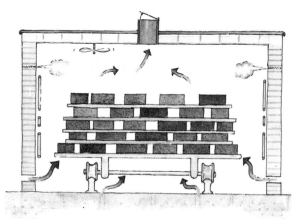

Kiln drying. Ends should be painted to prevent cracking

Stacking

The wood is stacked on trollies with stickers between them as for air drying and rolled into the kiln.

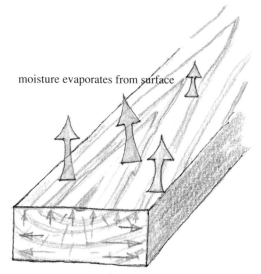

moisture evaporates from surface

moisture moves to replace lost moisture

Moisture loss

How does the wood dry?

Moisture evaporates from the surface. This causes the moisture from the inside to move towards the surface by capillary action. The aim of kiln drying wood is to control the rate of evaporation so that the drying process is gradual, with moisture moving at a constant rate outwards to replace the moisture that has evaporated. If this rate is too fast the wood will split or check at the surface or cause internal collapse called **honeycombing**.

Inside the kiln

Hot air is introduced to heat up the wood. However, since rapid evaporation of moisture would cause damage to the wood, moisture in the form of steam is introduced at the same time and is circulated by fans to slow down the evaporation of moisture from the wood. The humidity is gradually reduced inside the kiln, the temperature increases and the moisture in the wood gradually evaporates, until the MC falls to the required level, usually 8–10 per cent.

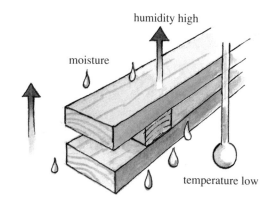

humidity high

moisture

temperature low

Inside the kiln

Equilibrium moisture content (EMC)

Wood will continue to shrink as it dries until its moisture content is in equilibrium or balance with the relative humidity of the surrounding air. Wood which has been over dried will swell until it reaches EMC. An external door in winter will often swell because in winter there is more moisture in the air, the humidity is higher.

Moisture content in equilibrium

Wood should be dry before painting or varnishing

Stacking of wood after drying

Kiln-seasoned timber should be stacked under cover to prevent it absorbing moisture. If it is stacked for a long period out of doors its MC will increase until EMC is reached. It is then little better than air dried timber. Sometimes kiln-dried wood is wrapped in polythene.

What are the advantages of seasoning timber?

- It is lighter, easier to handle and transport than green timber.

- Fungi will not grow below an MC of 20 per cent, therefore dried timber is more resistant to fungus attack.

- Because the cell walls have shrunk, the wood is stronger when dry.

- Seasoned timber is easier to saw, plane, sand and finish.

  Exception: some wood turners prefer to turn when the wood is green, allow it to dry and then finally turn and finish it.

- Seasoned timber will not further shrink, warp, check or distort.

- Dry surfaces take paints, varnishes, stains and adhesives better.

- It is easier to penetrate with preservatives as the cell walls and cavities do not contain water.

- Corrosion of ferrous metals is stopped or reduced because of the very low moisture levels present.

Advantages of kiln seasoning

- Timber can be dried to an exact MC and to an MC much lower than that of air-dried timber.

- The heating of the timber while drying kills all eggs, larvae and adult boring beetles.

- Carefully controlled conditions can minimise degrade, i.e. seasoning defects which occur during drying.

Shrinkage in wood

All woods shrink as they dry out. The shape of the board can change as it dries out.

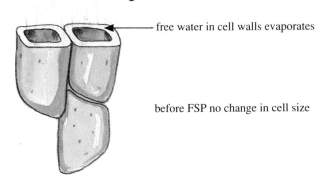

free water in cell walls evaporates

before FSP no change in cell size

Before shrinkage

It is almost impossible to dry timber in log form. Shrinkage does not begin until after fibre saturation point is reached.

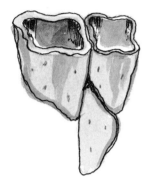

free water evaporated

water in cell walls reduced: shrinkage occurs

below FSP, cells are smaller, harder and stronger

After shrinkage (length changes little)

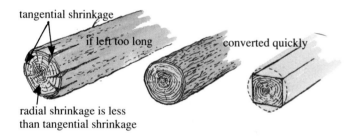

a log must be converted quickly after felling, otherwise it will split as shown

tangential shrinkage

if left too long

converted quickly

radial shrinkage is less than tangential shrinkage

Convert soon after felling

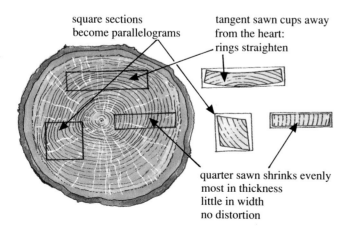

square sections become parallelograms

tangent sawn cups away from the heart: rings straighten

quarter sawn shrinks evenly most in thickness little in width no distortion

Results of different conversion methods

Activities

1. What is meant by the term 'seasoning'?
2. Why is it necessary to season timber?
3. What is 'green' timber?
4. How is moisture contained in freshly felled wood?
5. What is meant by the MC of wood?
6. What is meant by FSP? Illustrate with sketch.
7. At FSP what is the moisture content?
8. As wood begins to dry describe the process.
9. If wood were dried too rapidly describe what would happen.
10. Describe two methods of determining the MC of a piece of wood.
11. Wood used in different conditions has different MC.

    Show with the aid of sketches two different conditions and give suitable MC.
12. What is meant by the term 'hygroscopic'?
13. Describe with notes and sketches how wood should be stacked for air drying.
14. Give approximate times for air drying.
15. State what precautions are necessary:

    a) to protect the end of the wood;

    b) to prevent rising damp.
16. List the advantages and disadvantages of air drying.
17. State the steps necessary before air-dried wood could be used inside.
18. With the aid of sketches show what a kiln is.
19. How does a kiln work?
20. What is meant by relative humidity?
21. How does relative humidity affect the drying process?

22. List advantages and disadvantages of kiln-dried wood.

23. What is meant by EMC?

24. Show how the EMC of wood varies.

25. List the methods by which the EMC of wood may be regularised for areas of changing humidity, e.g. kitchen press doors?

26. Why does wood shrink?

27. With the aid of sketches show what happens when wood shrinks too rapidly.

28 How can tangential shrinkage be minimised?

29. Why are quarter-cut boards suitable for flooring?

30. Show what precautions may be taken to minimise distortion when making a table top.

Irregularities and defects in timber

Wood is a diverse and interesting material. No two boards from the same tree are identical. Wood can contain many different irregularities and defects. However, whether something is a defect or not depends on what the wood is being used for. If the wood is being used to support weight then a large knot would be a defect but to someone else a knot may be a thing of beauty, when not being used to support weight.

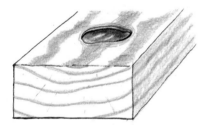

Dead knot

Defects may be caused in many ways:

a) natural defects: defects present in the growing tree;

b) artificial defects: caused by poor felling, seasoning, bad preservation, careless handling or stacking.

Natural defects

Heart rot: caused by a fungus which rots the pith of the heartwood.

Spike knot: can seriously reduce the strength of the wood.

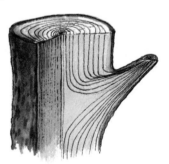

Spiral grain: the tree may twist when growing.

Felling defects

Defects through careless felling: the fibres separate when the tree falls on the ground; can also be caused by storm and lightning attack.

Stacking defects

Defects through poor stacking during seasoning.

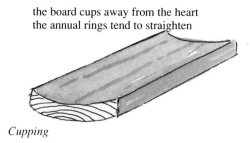

the board cups away from the heart
the annual rings tend to straighten

Cupping

Heart shake

the timber is said to be 'in wind' or in twist

Twisting

Star shake

bow: stickers not properly placed in wood pile

Bowing

Cup shake

Springing: curves on the width

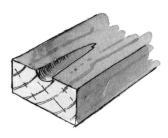

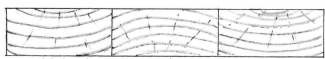

join boards to prevent cupping;
alternatively heart side up/heart side down

Grain arrangements to prevent cupping

Seasoning defects

Honeycombing: internal splits caused by too rapid kiln seasoning – greatly reduces strength.

Collapse: too rapid drying out. Moisture is being withdrawn too fast for it to be replaced by air.

Case hardening: incorrect drying schedule. Moisture withdrawn too quickly from outside layer. The outside case hardens but the core or centre remains wet.

End checks or splits: natural or artificial seasoning, too quick evaporation from end grain.

Conversion defect: Waney edge; bark left on.

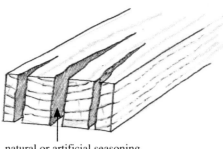

natural or artificial seasoning
too quick evaporation from end grain

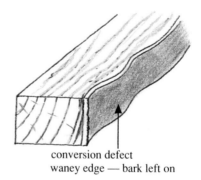

conversion defect
waney edge — bark left on

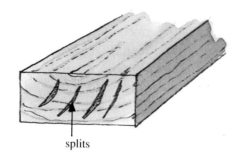

splits

Honeycombing

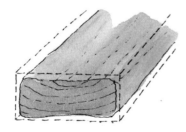

Collapse (dried too rapidly)

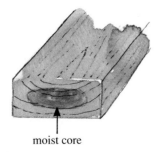

moist core

Case hardening

Activities

1. What is meant by a natural defect?

2. With the aid of sketches list four natural defects.

   Show how these defects affect the structural properties of wood.

3. List and describe some felling defects.

   Show how these may be minimised.

4. With the aid of notes and sketches show how bad stacking can lead to defects occurring in timber.

5. Show how some of these defects may be corrected.

6. What is meant by the term 'in wind'?

7. Poor seasoning leads to defects occurring in timber. Show with notes and sketches how these defects occur and why.

8. How can these defects be prevented?

Decay in wood

Some woods are naturally very resistant to decay. Elm was used for water pipes. The centre was hollowed out to form the bore. Beech, although a very hard wood, will decay very quickly if used externally. We use the term **durability** to describe the resistance of wood to decay.

So wood is said to be a) very durable, b) durable, or c) non-durable.

The main agents which attack timber are:

a) fungi, b) insects, c) marine borers.

Fungi

Fungi are very simple plant forms. Certain fungi attack wood, causing it to rot. Fungi require four conditions for their growth:

- food – the wood;

- moisture – properly dried wood cannot be attacked by fungi;

- air – fungi thrive in areas of still air;

- heat – warm conditions encourage the growth of fungi.

When these four conditions are present wood can easily be attacked by fungi.

Fungus attacks

1. **Sap stain**. Certain fungi feed on the sapwood of timber. This causes a bluish stain on the sapwood and it is sometimes known as blue sap stain. However, the fungus does not cause decomposition in the wood. It cannot attack properly seasoned timber.

Causes

It often occurs in freshly cut timber that is not properly stacked, e.g. wood stacked without stickers, or in dried wood that is stacked out of doors or in wood that is stacked in damp conditions.

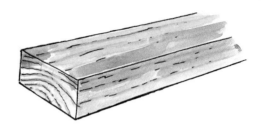

Sapwood discoloured by fungus

Treatment

Sap stain can be treated with preservatives that prevent attack and kill off existing fungus.

2. **Dry rot** is caused by the fungus *serpula lacrymans* which attacks damp timber. It is so called because the timber eventually becomes dry and crumbly. Dry rot is the most common form of decay in wood. Floor joists that are not properly vented, roof timbers subject to leaks, joists in contact with damp walls are all very prone to dry rot attack.

How dry rot develops

Spores (seeds) of dry rot are blown around in the air. When they land on damp wood they send out very fine hairlike roots into the wood. These spores can only be seen through a microscope.

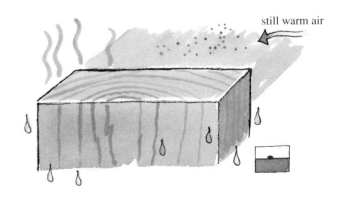

still warm air

Spores on damp wood

The very fine roots (*hyphae*) spread right through the wood, using up the moisture in the wood and causing the wood to dry and crumble, hence the name.

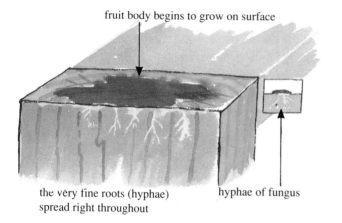

fruit body begins to grow on surface

the very fine roots (hyphae) spread right throughout

hyphae of fungus

Beginning to grow

A thick fleshy mat of tiny orange-brown fruit bodies forms on the surface of the wood. When these ripen they shoot out millions of spores, which again expands the dry rot. These rootlets can travel in the walls, behind plaster, and eventually whole areas of wood and wall become infested. The wood develops cracks, then crumbles even when pressed by hand and eventually collapses.

thick fleshy mat forms on wood

Feeds on wood causing decay

Prevention

Dry rot will not occur in wood with an MC below 20 per cent, therefore if the wood is properly dried and kept dry then dry rot will not occur. Wood should also be treated with preservative.

Wood infected by dry rot

Treatment

The presence of dry rot is very serious and the treatment is drastic.

Cut away infected wood and treat surrounding areas and new wood with fungicides. This is usually dealt with by specialists.

3. **Wet rot** is also caused by a fungus, *conophora puteana*, but can only survive in very wet wood, hence its name. In wood with a moisture content of less than 30 per cent the fungus soon dies. It is often caused in areas of localised wetting such as is caused by plumbing faults and leaks. The most common form of wet rot is known as cellar fungus.

Wet rot: result of not painting or protecting

How wet rot develops

It develops in the same way as dry rot. Spores land on the wood and send out rootlets or hyphae. The fungus is whitish in colour and often forms a white mat on the surface of the wood. If the moisture persists then eventually the wood will split as it decays and loses its strength.

Eradication

On most occasions if the source of dampness is fixed the rot ceases. However, if the wood is structurally weakened it has to be cut away and replaced with new wood treated with preservatives. Wall treatment is not usually necessary.

Preservation of wood

Wood is a biological material and decays with age. It can be attacked by fungi and insects. However, its life can be considerably lengthened by the proper treatment with preservatives.

When wood was cheap and plentiful many of the components used were oversized. However, nowadays things are different. Most of our native softwood comes from fast-growing pines and spruces and often contains a lot of sapwood. This sapwood is easily attacked by fungi and insects. There is a tendency, especially in Ireland, to use naturally weather-resistant tropical hardwoods for doors, windows and external cladding. This need not be so. Properly treated softwoods can give a life of equal length to some of those hardwoods. The tropical hardwoods are getting scarcer every year. We may well have to look to our own softwood supplies to meet our needs. Treatment of timbers before installation, known as **pretreatment**, is very important. It is only then that all surfaces can be properly treated. This also means that cheaper timbers can be used instead of the more expensive hardwoods.

How is timber treated?

There are three main types of wood preservatives:

1. tar oils;
2. water borne;
3. organic solvent.

1. Tar oils (creosote)

Wood can be dipped in creosote, creosote can be applied under pressure to wood or it can be painted on with a brush. It is really only suitable for external use as it has a very strong unpleasant smell. It is also very difficult to paint over creosote as it keeps 'bleeding' through the paint. It is very effective when used in telegraph poles, railway sleepers and external fencing.

Telegraph poles treated with creosote

Brush application of preservative

2. Water-borne preservatives

Water soluble chemicals such as boron and copper chrome arsenic are used as preservatives. The timber is saturated with water during this process and must be redried.

It is usually not used for joinery timber and finished sizes may vary after redrying. It is mainly used for treatment of poles, posts, carcassing timber, etc.

3. Organic solvent preservatives

These are solutions of fungicides and insecticides in an organic solvent similar to white spirits. Most of the preservatives you buy over the counter are of this type. Some of them are coloured, e.g. green or brown, to make it easier to see the treated areas. However, those dyes may show through light-coloured paintwork, and clear preservatives should be used if you want to paint or stain the wood.

How to apply preservatives

1. Brushing or spraying

Simplest to use. Organic solvent preservatives normally used.

However, penetration of preservatives is quite shallow and the treatment must be repeated at regular intervals. Usually used in repair work where any other treatment would be difficult to apply.

2. Immersion

The timber is immersed in a tank of preservatives for about three minutes.

Suitable for external joinery that is to be painted and for internal joinery.

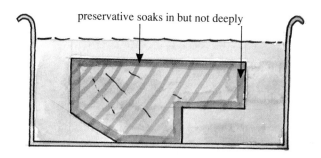

preservative soaks in but not deeply

Immersion treatment

3. Double vacuum

This has now become the most widely used treatment of timber in building and construction work. Organic solvent preservatives are mainly used.

All the necessary machining of the wood is done first – tenons, mortises, grooves etc. – so that all surfaces can be treated. If any surfaces are cut after treatment they should get two brush coats.

Initial vacuum: the timber is placed in a special chamber and a vacuum is created to remove the air from the wood.

Impregnation: the timber is then flooded with preservatives, the vacuum being maintained. Pressure is applied to force the preservatives into the wood. This can be either atmospheric pressure or positive pressure within the chamber.

Pressure chamber

Final vacuum: the chamber is emptied of preservatives and a second vacuum is drawn designed to withdraw excess preservative from the timber and to produce a dry surface.

Different cycles are applied for different timbers and the cycle depends on the the use to which the timber is being put – a longer cycle for very exposed timbers.

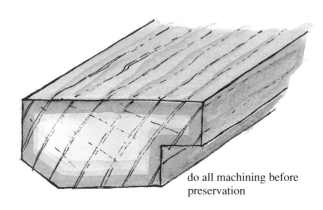

do all machining before preservation

Vacuum-applied preservative. Notice deep penetration

Permeability: what is it?

Unfortunately it is not possible to preserve all timbers equally well. Some timbers are more permeable than others, i.e. some timbers allow preservatives to flow through them under pressure more easily than others. Therefore some timbers are more suitable for outdoor use than others.

Health and Safety

particularly in the DIY area

- read instructions carefully;
- use protective clothing, gloves, etc.;
- allow plenty of ventilation;
- no children or pets allowed near while preservative is being applied.

Follow safety instructions

The grading of homegrown softwoods

Timber has many uses but principally

a) joinery: doors, windows;

b) structural: timber that carries a load, e.g. rafters, flooring joists, etc.;

c) cabinets, tables, chairs, presses.

Structural timber is graded by two methods:

a) Visual grading.

Specially trained graders check for structural defects visually. Such defects may be large knots, splits, checks, shakes.

Visual grading

Durability

Timber that has been vacuum treated with preservatives will be resistant to fungus and insect attack for a minimum of 30 years and for up to 60 years, depending on the cycle used. It more than justifies its initial cost.

There are two general grades:

- general structural (GS);
- special structural (SS).

b) Machine grading.

The wood is fed through a special grading machine. A series of rollers automatically loads the piece and measures its bow or deflection. The more it deflects the weaker the wood.

Preservatives prolong life of timber

91

The end of each plank is marked to show its stress grade.

Any machine-graded timber conforms to standard M75.

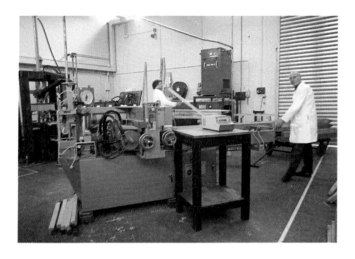

Machine grading

Wood boring insects

Wood boring insects cause great damage to wood. Many people bring in infested wood without realising the damage it can cause. One adult beetle can lay over 50 eggs, that means 50 insects attack the wood. They have a cycle of roughly three to five years in the wood and then transform into an adult beetle. If half are female and those 25 lay another 50 eggs each, after thee to five years you have 1250 beetles attacking the wood.

Five years later you have 1250 beetles or, say, 600 females laying eggs and that could mean 30,000 beetles boring the wood within a ten-year period. So it pays to be vigilant and to treat wood with insecticides where it may be in danger of an attack.

Lifecycle

The lifecycle of the insect falls into four stages similar to that of the butterfly:

Stage one: the egg

The female beetle lays its eggs in cracks and crevices in the wood. After a few weeks the eggs hatch into little worms or grubs.

Stage one: the egg

Stage two: the larva

The larva is the worm or grub. It eats its way into the wood causing great damage. In a severe attack the wood is completely destroyed and eventually crumbles. The grub can live in the wood from two to ten years according to the type of beetle.

dust on the surfaces as the larva is active
no holes at this stage
1–7 years: the grub is active

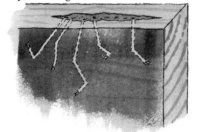

Stage two: the larva

92

Stage three: the pupa

The grub or larva changes into a pupa or chrysalis near the surface of the wood. This stage lasts about a month and during it the grub changes into a beetle. It develops wings that enable it to fly.

Stage three: the pupa

Stage four: the adult beetle

The adult beetle bores its way to the surface of the wood and emerges from small holes (1–3mm diameter). It flies off to mate and begins the cycle again by laying its eggs in cracks and crevices in other wood. It can lay up to 200 eggs and then dies. The new larvae continue the destruction.

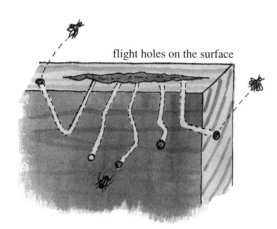

flight holes on the surface

Stage four: the adult beetle

Treatment

Timber that has been pretreated with a preservative that contains an insecticide is resistant to attack by wood-boring insects. If insect attack is noticed apply an insecticide liberally. Apply to adjoining wood in case it is infected.

Eggs of the furniture beetle

Small but hardworking larva

93

Some common wood-boring insects

The term woodworm is used to describe a variety of different beetles that attack wood. The woodworm holes that you see in wood are caused by the adult beetle as it bores its way out of the wood to mate, lay eggs and continue the cycle.

1. The common furniture beetle

This is by far the most widespread beetle to infest wood in Ireland. The adult lays its eggs in cracks and crevices in the wood. The larva bores through the wood for two to three years, after which the wood it forms a pupal chamber near the surface and changes into the adult beetle. It then bites its way to the surface, leaving a hole 1.5mm in diameter. In April to August about 80 per cent of insect damage in Ireland is caused by this beetle.

Common furniture beetle (actual size)

2. The wood-boring weevil

The next most damaging beetle after the common furniture beetle, which it resembles. However, it only attacks wood already infested by rot or cellar fungus. Both the adult beetle and the larva burrow into the wood. It is very prolific, having up to three lifecycles per year.

Wood boring weevil (actual size)

3. The death watch beetle

It is related to the common furniture beetle but is larger, leaving an exit hole 3mm in diameter. Its lifecycle on decaying wood can be as short as four years, and as long as ten years in hardwood. It has a well-known tapping sound caused by the head of the beetle and this is a mating call during the flight season in spring. It is often found in churches, hence its association with death reflected in its name. It attacks mainly hardwoods.

Death watch beetle (actual size)

4. The house longhorn beetle

It is easily identified by its oval flight hole about 10mm long and 6mm wide. It attacks only softwoods and causes immense damage, boring through them for some four to seven years.

The adult beetle lays up to 200 eggs.

House longhorn beetle (actual size)

Note. There is always the danger that other insects might be brought into this country in imported timber, especially in green and air-dried softwoods. Recently there has been concern about a pinewood rematode found in imported Canadian timber in Ireland.

Activities

1. List three agents which attack timber.

2. What is a fungus?

3. List the conditions necessary for the growth of fungus.

4. Name three types of fungus that attack timber.

5. List the characteristics of sap stain.

6. Why does sap stain occur?

7. Very often sap stain is followed by other fungus attacks. Why?

8. How does *serpula lacrymans* attack wood? Give its common name. Why is its occurrence so widespread?

9. With the aid of notes and sketches show how dry rot develops.

10. List the steps necessary to eradicate dry rot.

11. List the steps necessary for its prevention.

12. What are the conditions necessary for the growth of *conophora puteana*?

13. How do these conditions differ from those of dry rot?

14. How is wet rot eliminated?

15. Why is it necessary to protect wood in certain conditions?

16. What is meant by durability?

17. Why are some woods naturally more durable than others? Give examples.

18. List the three main types of wood preservatives.

19. Give an example of the use of tar oils.

20. List the advantages and disadvantages of creosote as a preservative.

21. What is meant by water-borne preservatives?

22. List two water-borne chemical preservatives.

23. Give examples of where they are used.

24. What is meant by organic solvent preservatives?

25. List the names of three organic solvent preservatives in common use.

26. *a)* List three methods of application of preservative.

    b) List the advantages and disadvantages of each method.

    c) Compare the longterm effects of each method.

27. Which method would you recommend for the following situations:

    a) fencing posts; *b)* garden seat;
    c) telegraph poles; *d)* garden shed.

28. Why is an attack of wood-boring insects potentially so harmful?

29. How may they unwittingly be introduced into a house?

30. Give the lifecycle of a wood-borer. Illustrate with sketches.

31. Describe the lifecycle of the common furniture beetle.

32. List three other beetles, and give a description of them.

    Illustrate your answer with sketches.

33. Show how wood can be treated

    a) to prevent infestation; *b)* to eradicate it.

Communication of design

Freehand drawing

Freehand means what is says: drawing without the help of equipment such as set squares, rulers, protractors, etc. Solutions to design problems can be solved using just pencil and paper. As we go through this chapter we will see that different ideas can be presented in different ways.

Primitive cave painting

The basic tools

Leonardo de Vinci (1452–1519)

During the Renaissance this Italian designer, painter and architect used drawings to express his ideas. Of course, as we know, he was ahead of his time, designing helicopters, tanks, parachutes, etc. Unfortunately the technology was not there to put his ideas into practice.

We have come a long way from a time when drawings were done with a piece of stick on sand, or painted on walls and ceilings of caves more than 30,000 years ago. These were done to help people identify different animals or even ward off unfriendly spirits. Later on designs were given to craftsmen to help them understand what was needed to be made.

Leonardo da Vinci

Nowadays we have much of the technology we need to put our drawings into practice. Modern aids make this task more enjoyable and the designer now has the help, not alone of pencil and paper to communicate her/his ideas, but also of computer graphics.

With practice you can make simple sketches very quickly

Starting out

Freehand sketching requires you to be observant. Like the fish in the bowl, look around you. Careful observation and a good sketch book will go a long way to help you.

Be observant

Everyone can draw

Remember how you practised when you learnt to ride your bike? It's the same with freehand drawing. Practice makes perfect. Of course, some will draw better than others, but everyone can learn to draw.

You can start drawing using a 2B pencil and up to 4B for shading a drawing. Clutch pencils may also be used and leads are available in a wide range of hardness and thickness.

Never sharpen your pencil too close to the drawing because the lead dust will smudge. If handing a pencil to your classmate, always keep the topped end pointed towards yourself.

Have you ever noticed that words cannot always describe the proportion, shape, form, colour, etc. of an object? A picture will show this very clearly. To demonstrate this have a student from your class choose an object from any page in this textbook without you looking at it. Let the student describe the object to you and then try and sketch the object described.

97

Loosening up

You notice before a game the way players loosen up. We must do the same in drawing. Begin by drawing a series of horizontal lines as shown. Then progress on to diagonal lines and finally vertical lines.

Horizontal lines

- Try keeping the pencil on the paper at all times.
- If you are right handed draw from left to right. If you are left handed draw from right to left.
- Do not grip the pencil too tightly and keep your wrist firm.

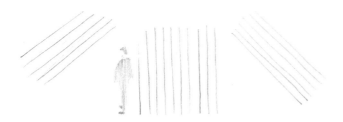

Vertical and inclined lines

- You can 'ghost' the line, i.e. move the pencil backwards and forwards in the direction of the line, just touching the paper. When you are satisfied with the direction draw the line boldly.

Now try placing some dots on your sheet and start to join them up. This will help you to learn to control your pencil. Next, draw lines at right angles to each other, and finally squares and rectangles.

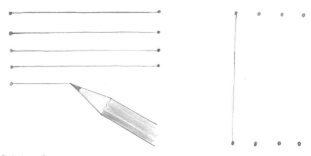

Joining dots

We have now formed **shape.** There are two kinds of shapes: **random** and **geometric**. Some are also **symmetrical**, i.e. if we divide them by a centre line each half is the same.

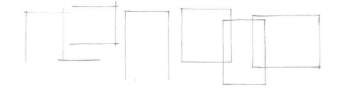

Familiar shapes

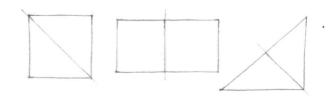

Geometric shapes

When drawing circles make several circular movements holding the pencil above the paper. When you feel you have the correct shape lower the pencil, drawing lightly on the sheet, then drawing more heavily. Make several attempts. Then try making a circle touch each side of a square.

Another way is to draw two axes, showing the points where the circle will cross them. On each quarter in turn join the points to form a circle.

Circles build-up

3D Representation

If we wish to have a drawing illustrated properly, we will need to use three dimensions; in other words, showing objects as solid rather than flat, two-dimensional shapes.

A two-dimensional shape has only two dimensions of measurement: height and length. A three-dimensional shape has three dimensions of measurement; height, length and width.

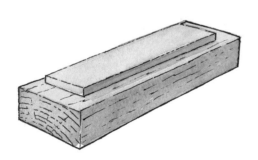

CHOOSE A FAMILIAR BOX-SHAPED OBJECT FROM YOUR WOODWORK ROOM AND SKETCH IT IN 3D

A very good way of drawing an object is to imagine a box or crate around the object. First look at the object and then imagine a crate around it. Draw the crate at the view that suits you best. Try not to draw anything else until the crating looks right.

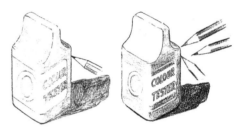

find the points where the colour tester touches the crating — place these on your drawing — join up the points making a drawing of the colour tester

Freehand build-up using crating

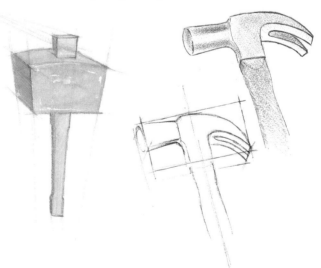

make a sketch of an object which contains circular or curved shapes — practise drawing some of the hand tools in your woodwork room by crating — crate the circle as shown — when viewed from the angle it appears elliptical

Identify the shapes

Isometric grid paper is available to assist in drawing in 3D. By sketching carefully along the lines it will give you help in visualising good proportion of an object.

You can also use the isometric grid as a backing sheet to be placed underneath your drawing paper. You may need to go over the grid lines with a thin black felt-tipped marker.

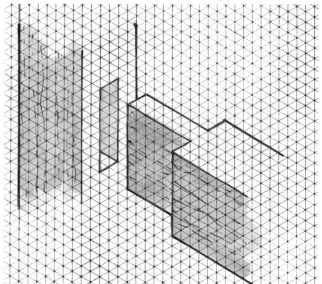

Using isometric grid. Do not become too dependent on the grid system. Freehand drawing should be what it says.

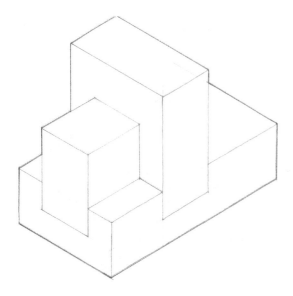

Plain paper over grid paper

If we wish to make our drawing more realistic we can use perspective projection. Perspective drawing is a depth indicator.

In this scene the point at which the tracks converge is called the **vanishing point** or **vp**.

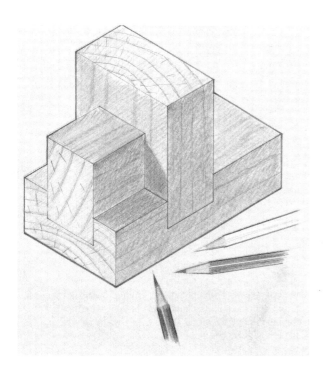

Adding colour

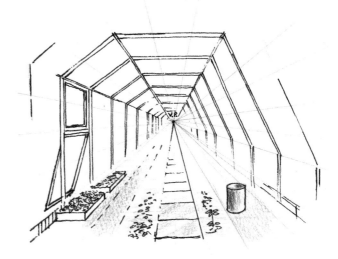

Perspective sketching. In this drawing the point at which the lines converge is called the vanishing point or VP

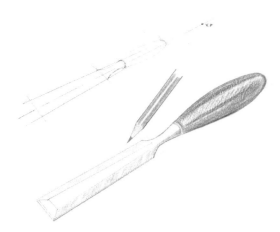

An example of two-point perspective

Colours and textures

Primary Colours

All colours are derived from three basic colours: red, yellow and blue. These are called primary colours.

Secondary Colours

When we mix two primary colours in equal proportions a secondary colour is produced.

blue + yellow = green

red + yellow = orange

red + blue = violet (purple)

The colour wheel

Tertiary Colours

If we mix a primary with a secondary colour in equal proportions a tertiary colour is produced, e.g. blue + orange.

You will have noticed that some colours look better together than others. Colours close together on the colour wheel create harmony. Colours opposite each other on the wheel are called complementary colours and so contrast with each other.

Example of warm colours

Warm colours are red, orange, yellow.

Cool colours are blue, green.

Example of cool colours

The effect of colour rendering on an object can be quite attractive and can give a feeling of solidity to an object. Observe the four objects below. By showing a little colour rendering it becomes apparent what each object is. Try to identify them yourself.

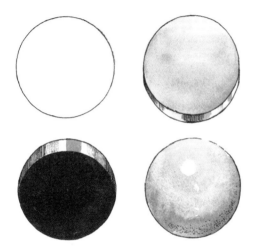

Effect of rendering

Shown below are five objects in plan. Now try to identify these objects. Draw an elevation of each. In fig. f devise your own form and show this in elevation. You can see from these drawings that colour identifies shape and form, and objects drawn without adding shade and/or colour can appear flat and sometimes cannot be identified. Pencil shading, of course, can also give us a good effect in our drawings.

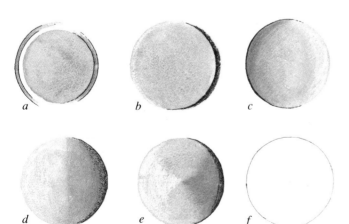

Effect of rendering

Give as many reasons as you can think of why colour should be used in drawings.

Black pencil drawing

What colouring material should I use?

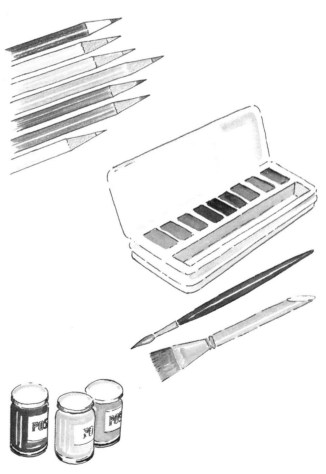

Finally: practise, practise, practise.

Measured drawings

'A sketch is worth a thousand words.'

Drawings are extremely important for many reasons. It is often much easier to explain an idea or project by using drawings or sketches than by writing long descriptions. Most people by nature understand drawings more easily than writing. Your younger sister or brother probably could understand quite complicated drawings even when very young. Drawing is a language and forms a very good means of communication; for example, a sketch of a chair will be understood all over the world, in Germany, France, Russia, etc. Unfortunately the same cannot be said about the written language.

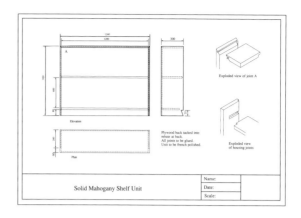

Working drawing

A working drawing requires the use of drawing instruments and we will now look at these in more detail.

Drawing instruments

Paper

The paper used should always be kept clean and tidy, and should be of good quality. Drawing paper usually comes in the following sheet sizes: A4, A3, A2, A1 and A0.

Freehand drawing

Drawings and sketches are also useful when trying to plan a new project. In fact, one of the best types of plan is a drawing. It can help us to imagine what the project will look like and if we do not like it we can easily change it, without wasting time. Usually a freehand drawing will suffice for this, but after this stage we need a drawing produced by using instruments: a **working drawing**.

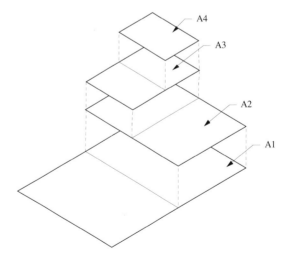

Relationship of sheet size

Drawing boards

These come in a variety of sizes to accommodate the various sheet sizes. They must have a smooth, flat surface and have straight edges. A desk can also be used.

Tee square

The tee square gets its name because it looks like the letter T. It has two parts, the stock and the blade, and these are fixed together to form a 90° angle.

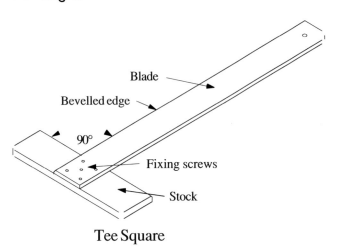

Tee Square

A 90° angle is often called a right angle or sometimes a square angle and this is where the tee square gets the second part of its name.

A very important part of your drawing equipment, the tee square is often abused. It should not be dropped or scratched as this can dent the blade. It is usually made from beech, mahogany or perspex.

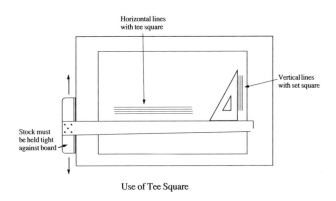

Use of Tee Square

The tee square is used with its stock tight against the edge of the drawing board or desk and is essential for drawing horizontal lines on the sheet. It is also used as a platform for set squares.

Set squares

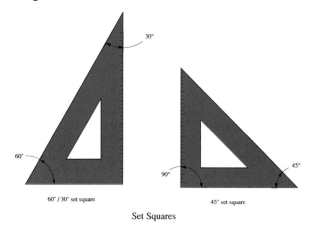

Set Squares

These are triangular shapes usually made from plastic and are used to draw vertical or inclined lines. The 45° set square has a 90° angle and two 45° angles, while the 60°/30° set square has a 90°/60° and 30° angle.

Clips

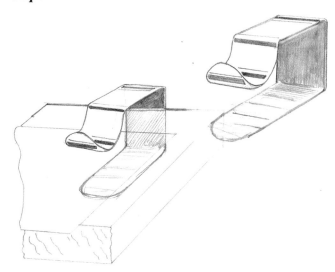

Drawing clip

These are used to hold the sheet of drawing paper steady on the board or desk. Alternatively you can use masking tape at each corner.

Compasses

There are many types of compasses available. It is worth buying a good-quality one as it can quite easily last a lifetime. The cheaper type of compass is designed to hold a pencil; the best of these are made from brass.

Brass compass   Springbow compass

The better types of compass are the springbow compass and the geared compass. The lead used in the nibs of these compasses should be sharpened to a chisel point rather than a conical point. This will wear more evenly and is easily sharpened using a piece of fine sandpaper.

Pencils

The first thing we must note is that not all pencils are the same. Some have soft leads which give dark lines and some have hard leads which give light lines. A 2H or H pencil is suitable for general drawing and a HB for printing and sketching.

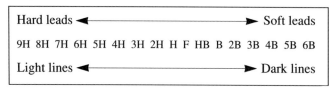

Lead gradings

As we have said earlier, drawings and sketches are very important means of communicating ideas; they can be used as a type of language.

When speaking about drawing there is a distinct difference made between freehand sketches and drawings produced by using drawing instruments. The main reason for this is because sketches are rarely produced using exact measurements, exact angles or carefully produced curves and circles, whereas drawings made using instruments usually are. Furthermore sketches are useful for quickly conveying ideas, while working drawings give much more information, such as exact sizes and shapes. When actually making something from a drawing it is essential that you have such information. For example, if you had a sketch or even a photograph of a toy truck that you wished to make, it would be still very difficult to make it: no measurements would be available, no exact details. On the other hand, if you had a 'working drawing' produced, using instruments, you would have far fewer problems.

Scaling and measurement

Before producing a drawing we must first understand the ideas of measurement and scale. All measurements are now made using the metric system of metres (m), decimetres (dm), centimetres (cm) and millimetres (mm).

10mm = 1cm

10cm = 1dm

Therefore there are 1,000mm in one metre.

10 millimetres = 1 centimetre

10 centimetres = 1 decimetre

10 decimetres = 1 metre

1,000 metres = 1 kilometre

milli = 1 thousandth

centi = 1 hundredth

deci = 1 tenth

kilo = 1 thousand

Whenever possible it is desirable to draw an object to its actual size, full size. For obvious reasons this is not always possible. To draw a map or a house full size you would need an enormous piece of paper. Similarly, there may be some objects which when drawn actual size are too small for any detail to be seen. In both these cases we need to draw to scale. Drawing to scale can either enlarge or shrink an object from its true size, depending on the scale used. A scale of 1:5 (one is to five) means that every millimetre on the drawing represents five millimetres on the object. The finished drawing will be five times smaller than the object being drawn. A scale of 1:10 (one is to ten) would result in the drawing ending up one tenth the size of the object being drawn. These are **reducing scales. Enlarging scales** will have the larger number first, e.g. 2:1, 5:1, 10:1 etc. A scale of 10:1 will magnify the drawing by ten times.

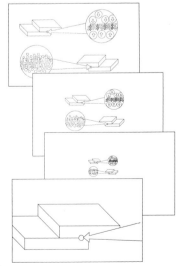

Not all scales are suitable

Choosing the correct scale is very important. When a drawing is finished the scale used should give us a clearly legible drawing which fills the sheet without giving the appearance of being cramped. Before starting any drawing, therefore, a little care should be taken to calculate the correct scale. The scale chosen should also be one that is commonly used and can be calculated easily. For example, a scale of 1:9 would be a ridiculous scale to use for two reasons.

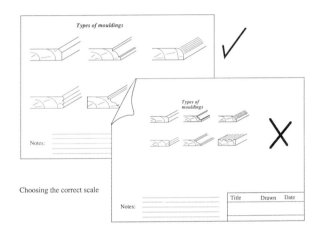

Choosing the correct scale

First of all it would be difficult to divide all fullscale measurements by nine. Secondly 1:9 will result in a drawing very similar in size to that produced by a scale of 1:10 which is a much easier scale to use. It is possible to buy a **scale rule.** This is a ruler with all the frequently used scales already calculated out on it.

1:5 One-fifth 1:2 one-half 1:1 full size 2:1 twice full size

Objects may be scaled *up* or *down*

Orthographic projection

Working drawings are usually presented using a system called orthographic projection. Using orthographic projection we view an object from different angles, getting a different drawing for each view. When these two, three or sometimes four drawings are looked at as a unit we can build up a comprehensive idea of what the object looks like and its size.

The word orthographic is made up from two words, 'ortho' and 'graphic'. Ortho comes from the Greek work *orthos* which literally translated means 'straight' or 'right'. 'Graphic' as you have probably guessed means 'picture'. Orthographic projection, therefore, means pictures projected at right angles.

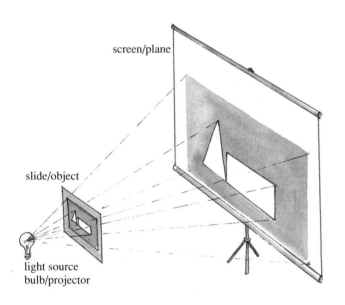

How an image is projected

The way images are projected in orthographic projection can be compared to the way slides are projected onto a screen. Here the film image is enlarged by means of a strong light. The further away the screen is moved the larger the image gets; the closer it is moved the smaller it gets until eventually when the screen and slide are together the image will not be enlarged but will rather be the exact same size as the slide. This happens because the rays of light from the bulb radiate outwards. When the screen is far away these rays have had space to spread, thus producing a large picture, when close to the slide the rays have not spread out as much, resulting in a smaller image.

We refer to the screens used in orthographic as **planes.** Two particular types of plane are used, vertical and horizontal.

But what is a plane?

> A plane is a flat, even surface. It has no actual boundaries, but rather can continue on indefinitely.

A wall could be considered to be a vertical plane whereas a floor or ceiling could be considered to be a horizontal plane.

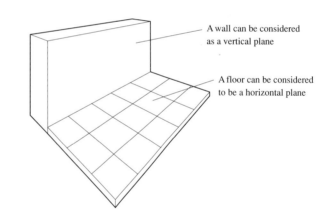

A wall can be considered as a vertical plane

A floor can be considered to be a horizontal plane

Horizontal and vertical planes

When the image of an object is projected onto a plane in orthographic the image produced will be the exact size of the object, no matter how close or how far away the plane is. This is because in orthographic, the light rays are said to be parallel. The image produced will always remain the same size.

107

We will now try to build up a simple orthographic drawing of a radio. The first view is got by looking straight in at the front of the object. A vertical plane is placed behind the radio onto which the image is projected. The drawing that results is called a **front elevation**.

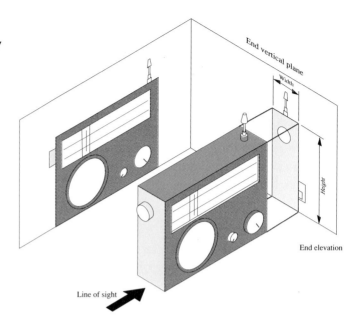

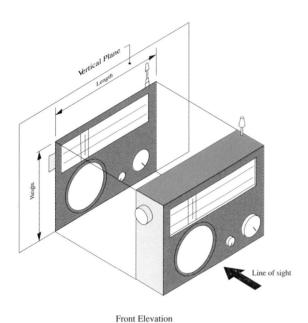

Front Elevation

This drawing by itself does not show all the details of the radio. It gives us the heights and lengths, but no widths can be seen.

To overcome this problem we must look in at the radio from either the left or the right. Again, the image is projected onto a vertical plane. This plane is perpendicular to that used for the front elevation. On this end plane we can see an image of the side of the radio, called the **end elevation**. The front elevation gives us information about the length and height of the radio, the end elevation gives us information about the width and height of the object.

A third plane, a horizontal plane, is now introduced underneath the object. To project an image onto this plane we must look straight down on the radio. This bird's eye view is called a **plan**, and gives us details of the radio's width and length.

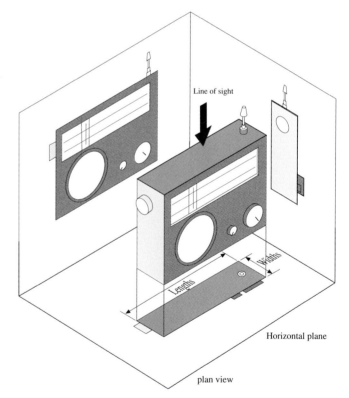

plan view

We can now remove the radio and we are left with an orthographic projection on the three planes: the front elevation, the end elevation and the plan. The shape and size of the radio are fully described in the drawing. It can be seen that to do this, at least two views were necessary. Sometimes three views or more are required.

It should be noted that all images in orthographic are inter-related. By changing part of the front elevation, for example, you will also change the other views.

If the aerial and tuning knob are removed from the front elevation, then they will also have to be removed from the plan and the end elevation.

It would be very difficult to produce orthographic drawings if we always had to fold our sheet to form our three planes (vertical plane, end vertical plane and horizontal plane), before we started drawing. The solution is simply to fold back the end vertical plane and fold down the horizontal to give us the three planes on one surface.

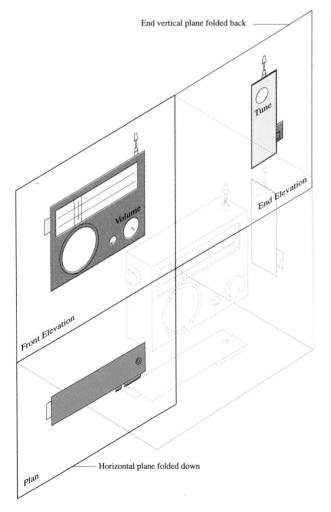

Planes folded out flat

We can see that:

The plan must always be directly below the front elevation, and the end elevation must be directly to the left or right of the front elevation.

Furthermore:

If you look in at an object from the left, the end elevation is to the right, and if you look in from the right, the end elevation is to the left.

When you get used to reading these drawings they will give you a three-dimensional image in your mind of the object being drawn.

Orthographic projection is the type of drawing which is ideal for giving sizes and measurements. It is not so good for giving an overall view of an object's shape or form. It is the most frequently used drawing system, being particularly suitable in manufacture.

Dimensioning

Drawings are usually made to convey information or ideas, particularly orthographic drawings. An essential part of those drawings must be the measurements. When measurements are put in on a drawing they are called dimensions. In order that everybody can understand our dimensioning it is important that there is a set of rules to follow.

The main points to note are:

1. all dimensions should be shown in millimetres;

2. all measurements are read from the bottom or right-hand side of the paper;

3. arrowheads should be sharp, small and neat;

4. dimensions should be spaced well away from the drawing;

5. dimension lines and extension lines should be lighter than the drawing outline;

6. drawings should not be confused or overcrowded with dimensions;

7. the limit lines or extension lines should not touch the drawing outline and should extend just beyond the dimension line;

8. smaller measurements should be placed closest to the drawing;

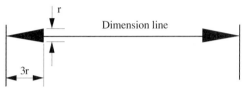

Arrowheads should be dark and in the proportions shown.

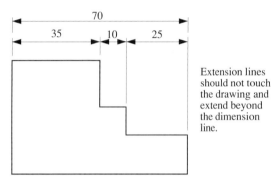

Extension lines should not touch the drawing and extend beyond the dimension line.

Small measurements should be placed closest to the drawing.

9. where possible dimension lines should not be drawn within the drawing itself but should be outside the perimeter of what is

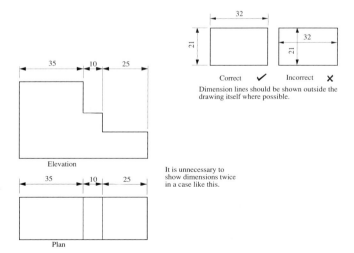

Elevation

Plan

Correct ✓ Incorrect ✗
Dimension lines should be shown outside the drawing itself where possible.

It is unnecessary to show dimensions twice in a case like this.

being drawn.

We spoke earlier of drawing objects to scale. When dimensioning these drawings it is the **actual size** of the object whose measurements we write down, not the sizes on the drawing. In other words, although the actual dimensions are smaller or bigger on the drawing because of the scale, it is the real measurements of the project which are written down.

Pictorial drawing

The human eye is accustomed to seeing in three dimensions. It is for this reason that we have some difficulty interpreting two-dimensional drawings like orthographic projection. Remember in our drawing of a radio the front elevation only had length and height, two dimensions; the plan had length and width, also only two dimensions. It is for this reason that pictorial drawings are so useful. These are drawings which attempt to show an object in

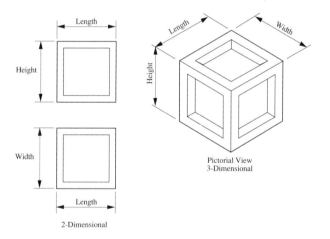

Pictorial View 3-Dimensional

2-Dimensional

three dimensions, height, length and width.

There are several traditional methods of drawing pictorial drawings. We will briefly look at three of these:

1. Oblique projection;

2. Isometric projection;

3. Perspective.

110

Oblique projection

The word oblique means slanted or at an angle. It is one of the simplest ways of drawing with instruments in three dimensions. Although oblique projection can be used in isolation it is generally used in conjunction with orthographic projection to give a better understanding of it.

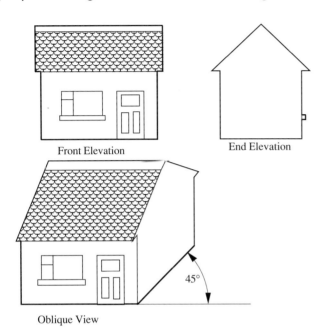

Front Elevation

End Elevation

Oblique View

To draw in oblique the first surface is first drawn in its true shape. The other two visible surfaces, top and side, are drawn back at an angle of 45°. Sometimes the lines which go back at 45° are reduced in length by half in order to give the more realistic appearance to the object. If there is a circle on any of the surfaces that are projected back at 45° it will be distorted into an oval shape (an ellipse). An ellipse unfortunately cannot be drawn with a compass.

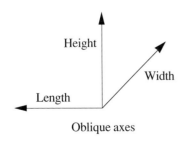

Oblique axes

Isometric projection

Isometric projection gives a much more realistic pictorial view than oblique projection. The object is seen as if it is standing on one corner. Lines are drawn vertically and at 30° to the left and right forming the axes by which all measurements are made. True measurements can only be done in these three directions. The sides will all be distorted, none showing their true shape. Lines which are parallel, however, will remain so in the drawing. Again, circles will be distorted on these surfaces into elliptical shapes.

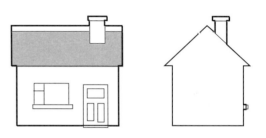

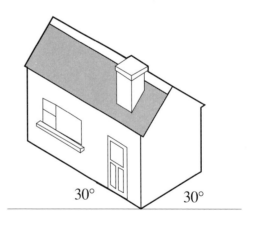

Isometric Projection

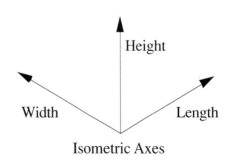

Isometric Axes

Perspective

The most realistic pictorial drawing which can be produced using instruments is perspective. Perspective takes into account the fact that parallel lines appear to converge to meet in the distance. Everybody is familiar with this in everyday life. Railway tracks or a long straight road appear to vanish at a point on the horizon; the rails or the side of the road appear to get closer together in the distance. A row of houses appears to get smaller in the distance. Perspective drawing tries to copy this phenomenon.

Curves and circles in pictorials

Circles and curves can generally be drawn with a compass in orthographic projection. In the pictorial drawings mentioned, however, this cannot be done because the surfaces are distorted in the projections.

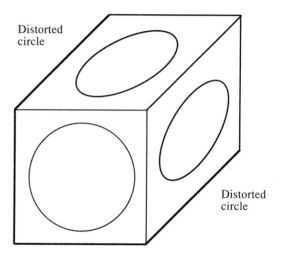

Distorted circle

Distorted circle

The Circle on the front surface of an oblique is drawn with a compass

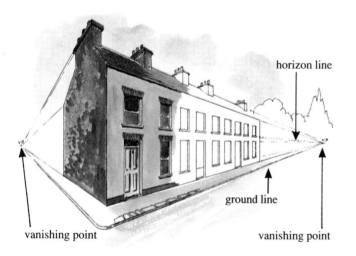

horizon line

ground line

vanishing point

vanishing point

Perspective

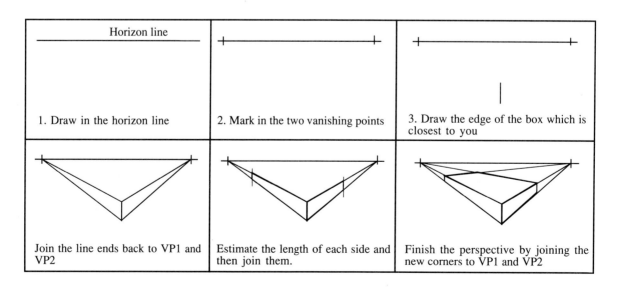

Horizon line		
1. Draw in the horizon line	2. Mark in the two vanishing points	3. Draw the edge of the box which is closest to you
Join the line ends back to VP1 and VP2	Estimate the length of each side and then join them.	Finish the perspective by joining the new corners to VP1 and VP2

Simple method of drawing a perspective

112

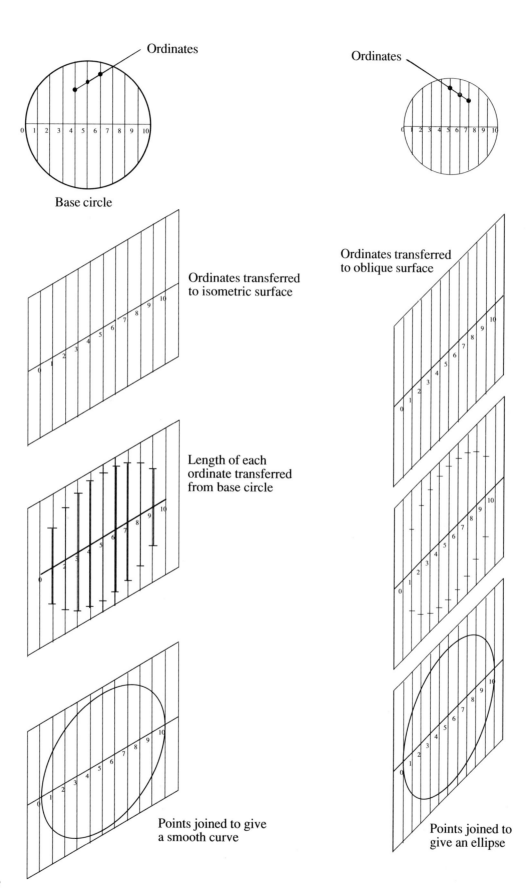

Ordinates

Base circle

Ordinates

Ordinates transferred
to isometric surface

Ordinates transferred
to oblique surface

Length of each
ordinate transferred
from base circle

Points joined to give
a smooth curve

Points joined to
give an ellipse

Curves in pictorials

Note: If there is a circle in the front surface of an object drawn in oblique, it can be drawn with a compass. This surface is a true shape, it is not distorted and as such any circles on it will not be distorted. If you need to draw an object in oblique, therefore, try to arrange the object so that any circular features are to the front of the drawing.

When it is necessary to draw a circle or curve on a distorted surface of an object either in oblique or isometric we can use a system called the **ordinate method**. A circle of the required radius is drawn to the side and divided, using vertical/horizontal lines, into a number of ordinates. Using a similar set of measurements those ordinates are then drawn on the required surface in the pictorial. When drawing these ordinates you must remember to draw them to the correct angles. Once the length of each ordinate is transferred onto the pictorial the ends can be joined with a freehand curve. The resulting curve is called an **ellipse.** No set number of ordinates are specified. The only requirement is that the spacing and number of them are the same as on the base circle.

Note: Drawing circles in perspective is slightly more complex and will not be dealt with here.

Working drawings

Once you have designed an object it is important to produce working drawings so that what has been designed can be made. Working drawings need to convey details such as dimensions, materials to be used, construction details and assembly instructions. They can be done in any form as long as all this information is present. Generally orthographic is used, with pictorials to aid understanding.

Small complex areas can be circled, brought out to the side and enlarged. Notes and hints on the method of construction and assembly should be detailed on the drawing where it is deemed necessary. Finally, exploded views may be used to help illustrate how a mechanism or series of joints are assembled.

Occasionally if the object to be produced is very complex it may be necessary to use **schematic drawings** in conjunction with working drawings. These are a series of drawings containing minimal detail which show the steps or procedures to be followed. The first drawing gives the first step and each successive drawing after this shows the next step to be followed. It is important to note that only essential pieces of information are shown on each drawing. Photographs could easily be used for this.

Interpretation of independently prepared graphical data

Everything that we make does not have to be designed beforehand by us. It is often much easier to use somebody else's design, somebody else's drawings or plans. Fortunately if this information is given in the form of drawings or sketches it will present no problem, as the rules laid down for drawing are international ones and as such are easily understood.

If you are struggling for a solution to a design problem why not look to see how other people have solved a similar problem? You do not have to rely solely on your own ideas. With a little research we can easily build up a useful body of knowledge.

Where should we look?

Reference books are an obvious place to start. Your school library or a public library will have many books which may be relevant. Many great ideas can be found in Do It Yourself books, craft books and woodwork books. A good library should also have a supply of magazines. They are a great information source but are often forgotten or ignored.

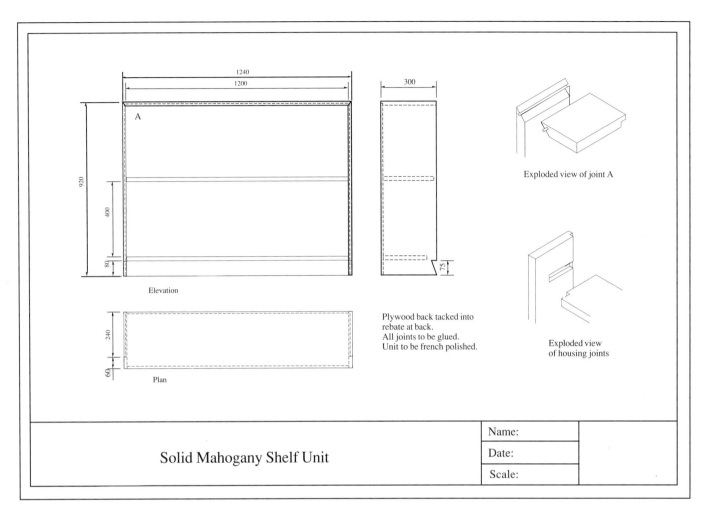

1240
1200
920
400
80
A
Elevation

300
75
Plywood back tacked into rebate at back.
All joints to be glued.
Unit to be french polished.

Exploded view of joint A

Exploded view of housing joints

240
60
Plan

Solid Mahogany Shelf Unit	Name:	
	Date:	
	Scale:	

Basic working drawing

The library is an excellent source of information

Apart from books we have television as a source of ideas. Nowadays there are many specialist programmes for people doing woodwork, metalwork or crafts. These programmes can often give useful hints.

The most important source of inspiration is, of course, people. If you are designing a bread board for the kitchen who better to ask than your mother? A tool rack for the garage, your father will know best. Your brothers or sisters and friends can also help. Do not be afraid to ask for help. Advice is cheap. People love to give a helping hand.

Report writing and presentation

Graphical data

Graphical data is an important element of any report, and presenting it in the right form can make all the difference between a good and bad one. Your report should reflect your **stages of work**. It would be foolish to have your working drawing at the beginning and your design sketches near the end. The drawings should follow a logical sequence from your preliminary design sketches up to your final working drawings, fully dimensioned and with all working notes.

A report should not contain pages and pages of solid writing. Where possible, each page should have at least one **diagram** which is relevant to the text. This will help to brighten up the page, to make it more interesting to the reader.

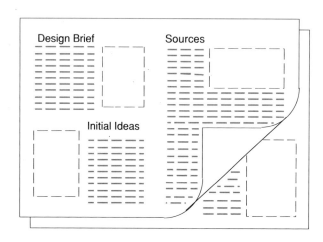

Design reports should be neat and to the point

All diagrams should be neat and where necessary have a short accompanying note explaining what is happening.

Colour can be used on sketches and diagrams but should not be used on working drawings.

If you wish to use a drawing produced on the computer, make sure that the text and dimensions are large enough to be seen when printed.

The **layout** of your drawings and text should be thought out carefully. A staggered layout is preferred rather than having all your drawings on the top, bottom or to one side of the page. When mounting groups of drawings you must consider layout very carefully or the finished page may look untidy. The final display should be interesting but balanced.

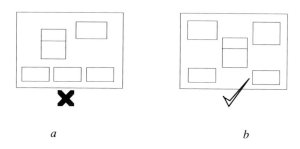

a   *b*

Poorly balanced layout (a)
Well balanced layout (b)

Written information on your drawings can be **presented** in several ways. It can be handwritten; printed; done by using stencils; or by using dry transfer lettering. Of these four methods the transfer lettering gives the most professional appearance. The transfers come in many different letter styles. Their main disadvantage is that they are very expensive.

When writing a report you should follow the same rules that are followed when writing an essay for English. In other words, each section should have an organised **structure**: an introduction, main body of information/ideas and a conclusion. Paragraphs, of course, are essential, as is good sentence structure.

Important information can be underlined or highlighted using colour.

Methods of representing the time taken for the various activities

Bread board project	
Tasks	**Time (hrs.)**
Initial ideas/sketches	1
Investigation	2
Sketches/working drawings	1.5
Making	4.5
Finishing	1.5
Report/evaluation	1.5
Total	**12 hours**

Activities represented by piechart

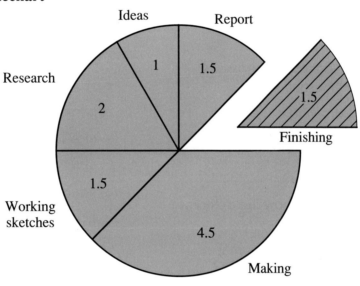

Activities represented by barchart

Bread board project

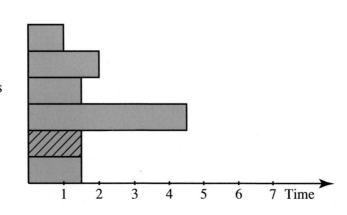

Finally, when writing a report remember that a **concise, to-the-point approach** makes for much more pleasant reading.

Bar and pie charts

A report may often involve a small section of statistics, i.e. information given in the form of numbers or percentages. For example, you may want to say how much time you spent researching, designing, making and finishing a model. This sort of information is best presented in the form of bar or pie charts. These charts portray the information both quickly and neatly. Remember, however, that a chart which is not clearly labelled is of no use at all.

Activities

1. Explain what is meant by the phrase 'A sketch is worth a thousand words'.

2. How can we call drawing a universal language?

3. What are the differences between freehand drawing and drawing with instruments?

4. Explain using a diagram how the different sheet sizes relate to each other.

5. How did the tee square get its name?

6. Sketch a tee square, name its parts and describe its important features.

7. Draw the two types of set squares and mark in the angles on each.

8. How should the point of a compass pencil be sharpened? Why?

9. Describe how the numbers and letters on a pencil tell us about its lead.

10. Write down four units of measurement and explain how each one is related to the other.

11. Why are scales so important in drawing? Give an example of a reducing scale and an enlarging scale and describe how each effects the drawing of an object.

12. What does the word 'orthographic' mean?

13. Explain what a plane is and give two examples of a horizontal plane and two examples of a vertical plane.

14. Using a sketch describe how the front elevation of a television would be achieved.

15. When drawing why is it so important to choose the correct scale?

16. Draw an enlarged dimension arrowhead and show how it should be proportioned.

17. Draw a dice in the three following types of projection:

    a) oblique;

    b) isometric;

    c) perspective.

    Which looks the most realistic?

18. Explain the words

    a) vanishing point;

    b) horizon;

    c) ground line.

9

Design and Making

Project example 1: Key rack

Brief: With the theme 'The Sea', design and make a key rack using the following materials:

One piece of softwood 120 x 75 x 12mm. (Scots pine).

One metal hook (L-shaped).

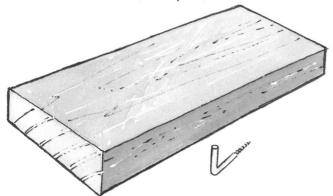

Materials supplied

Ideas

Use the outline of a fish as the shape for the key rack.

Materials (properties)

Scots pine (red deal) is classified as a softwood.

Origin: Europe.

Colour: reddish/yellow.

Features: distinctive grain.

Texture: fine.

Hook: mild steel.

Key rack

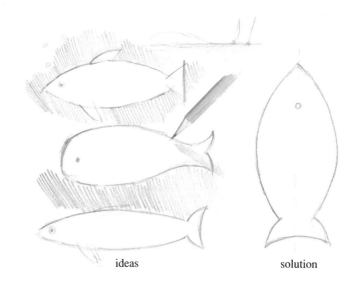

ideas   solution

Design ideas

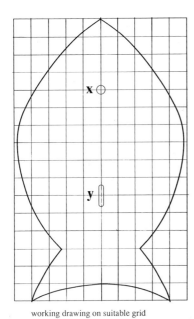

working drawing on suitable grid

3. Cut close to outside of line with coping or scroll saw.

4. When cutting is completed clean off saw marks with a fine rasp or surform. Sand across the edge with 100 grit sandpaper and finish with finer grades, moving with the grain.

5. Use bradawl at point *y* to provide pilot hole for hook.

6. Clean off and sand face and back of project.

7. Apply finish.

Planning

1. Transfer shape to timber.

2. Drill hole (it is easier to hold a rectangular shape when drilling).

3. Cut out shape.

4. Clean off and sand edges.

5. Use bradawl.

6. Clean off and sand face and back.

7. Apply polish.

Realisation (making)

1. Draw a 15mm grid 120 x 75 on an A4 drawing sheet. Transfer points *a*, *b*, *c*, etc. to this grid, draw the outline. Fold sheet along one edge of the grid and fix this edge to one side of the timber with tape.

   Place a sheet of carbon paper under the pattern and trace the outline onto the timber. Mark positions *x* and *y*.

2. Drill 6mm hole at point *x*. (Clamp timber firmly.)

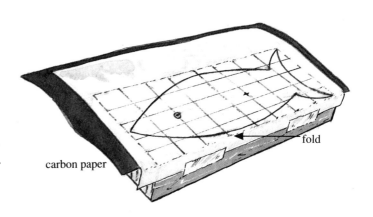

Transferring the shape to the wood

Dust off project. Apply one coat of transparent French polish, with French chalk added (one tablespoon to 500ml of polish), allow to dry overnight. Cut down (sand lightly), polish and apply a second coat. When applying polish do so sparingly and apply it with a polishing mop.

Leave a few minutes to dry and insert hook.

8. Compile a report on your project. Include your drawing and notes on the materials and techniques used. Examine and comment on your project.

Tools and equipment

Coping saw with fine-toothed blade, or scroll saw. Fine rasp, surform or spokeshave.

Sandpaper 100 to 280 grit and sanding pads.

6mm drill bit and hand or power drill.

Bradawl.

Polishing mop.

French polish. Made from shellac and methylated spirits (industrial alcohol). Shellac is derived from the secretion of the lac insect.

Health and safety

- Use safety glasses when using the drill.
- Wear a dust mask in dusty conditions.
- Never use finishing materials near a naked flame. Use only in well-ventilated areas.

Finishing the edge

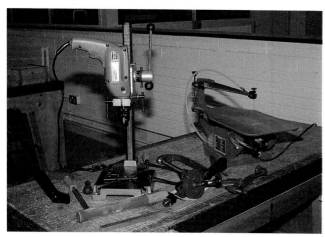

Tools required

Processing

121

Project example 2. Marquetry pattern

Brief: Design and make a marquetry pattern in the shape of fruit, overall size not greater than 150 x 150mm, using the following materials:

Selection of veneers.

MDF board 150 x 150 x 6mm.

Contact adhesives (brush on).

Tape (a masking tape).

Picture hook. Adhesive cleaner.

Materials

Marquetry pattern

Materials

Veneer is a thin sheet of wood usually 0.6 to 0.8mm thick. Exceptions are sawn veneer which is thicker and 'micro wood' veneer which is paper thin with a paper backing to give it strength. Veneer is available in a wide range of natural woods and some dyed woods.

MDF (medium-density fibreboard) is a manufactured board made of compressed wood fibres. It has no grain pattern. Its smooth surface provides a good base for veneers.

Contact (impact) adhesive is a synthetic rubber/resin adhesive, which bonds on contact. It gives off an inflammable vapour.

Wax: most waxes are made from beeswax or a combination of waxes in solvent, e.g. turpentine.

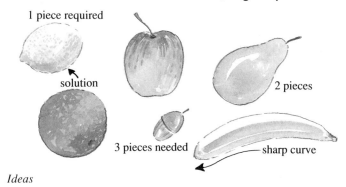

1 piece required

solution

2 pieces

3 pieces needed

sharp curve

Ideas

Planning

1. Working drawing; select veneers.
2. Prepare equipment, cutting board, knives, etc.
3. Tape veneers to cutting board (mat).
4. Trace outline onto veneer.
5. Cut out and tape pattern.
6. Fix pattern and backing to ground work.
7. Trim veneer, sand edge, face and back.
8. Apply finish.
9. Compile report.

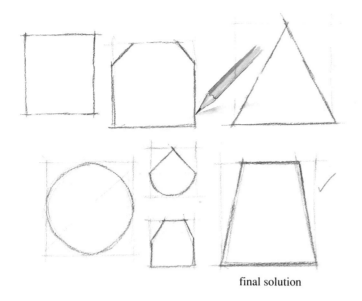

final solution

Background shape: ideas and solutions

Realisation (making)

1. Tape working drawing (pattern) onto cutting board.

2. Tape leaf of veneer along one edge onto the cutting board. The pattern will determine its exact position.

3. Tape second leaf onto the cutting board, overlapping first leaf. Place tape along a different edge.

4. Place carbon paper between drawing sheet and veneer and using a pointed dowel trace outline onto one leaf of veneer. Flip back drawing sheet (do not remove) and remove carbon paper.

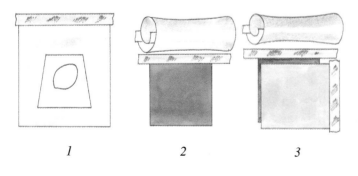

1   *2*   *3*

5. Using a scalpel with a number 10A or 11 blade cut along the outline. Move the knife carefully using your free hand behind the knife to hold the work steady. Rotate the cutting board so that your knife hand is in a comfortable position. Repeat this process until you have cut through both veneers. Keep the knife perpendicular to the work during cutting.

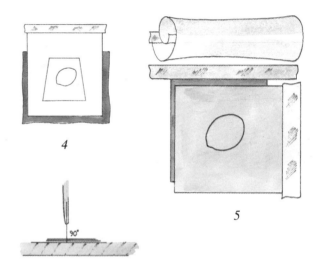

4

5

Tools and equipment

Cutting mat (rubber), cutting board. Straight edge (timber) 250 x 40 x 6 or 400 x 40 x 8.

    Knives: modelling knife with replaceable blades.

Veneer press

Scalpel with number 10A or 11 blades (no. 11 for small radius curves).

Veneer hammer.

Press.

Tools and equipment

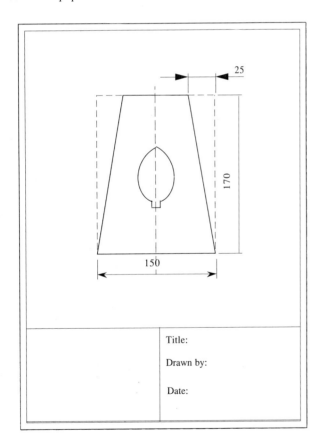

Working drawing

6. When the veneers are cut through, the inner pieces can be picked up with the point of the knife and placed to one side. Flip back the top leaf and fit the cherry insert into the walnut background. Fix in position by taping the joint.

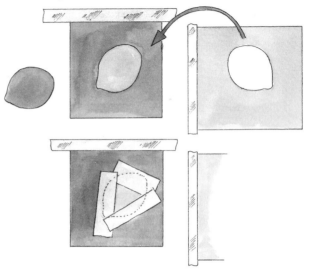

7. Before bonding the pattern to the groundwork, check that all the joint lines are sealed with tape to prevent the adhesive coming through to the finished surface.

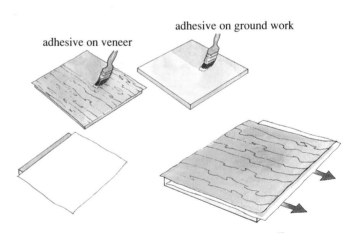

adhesive on veneer

adhesive on ground work

To apply the 'brush on' contact adhesive, place the backing veneer on the groundwork. Brush on an even film of adhesive to the veneer and leave to one side. Now apply a coat to the groundwork. When the adhesive is touch dry (five to ten minutes), use a slip sheet to position the veneer on the groundwork. When the veneer is correctly positioned, remove the slip sheet and apply pressure. Hand pressure is normally sufficient, but a press may be used with advantage. Trim any surplus veneer.

Repeat the process to bond the marquetry pattern to the other face of the groundwork.

8. Trim and clean up edges. Sand to a smooth finish. Remove tape and prepare for polishing.

Trim edges vertically

Description of materials

Contact (impact) adhesive is a synthetic rubber/resin adhesive, which bonds on contact. It gives off an inflammable vapour.

Adhesive cleaner is a solvent and must be compatible with the adhesive.

Health and safety

- Use knives with care and when cutting straight lines use a straight edge with the edge of at least 5mm thick.

- Contact adhesives should only be used in a well-ventilated area.

- Do not use near a naked flame.

- As with any material containing solvent, avoid contact with the skin.

9. Dust off. Apply a coat of finishing wax (e.g. beeswax and turpentine) by taking a small amount on a soft cloth and rubbing into the wood using a circular motion. When the wax begins to build up on the surface finish off by removing any surplus. Leave for a few minutes and burnish with a clean dry cloth. This process should be repeated two or three times at intervals of 24 hours.

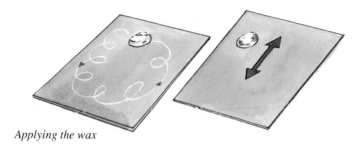

Applying the wax

Fix picture hook to back of pattern shown with short pins or screws.

10. Evaluate your work and compile a report.

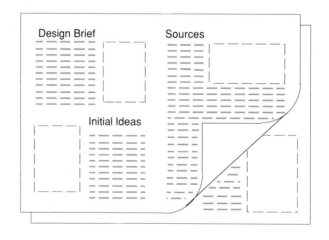

Logging your work

125

Project example 3: Chopping board

Brief: Design and make a kitchen chopping board, with an incised design on one side, using:

One piece of beech 250 x 180 x 18mm.

The finished product

Ideas

Materials (properties)

Beech is classified as a hardwood.

Origin: Europe, Japan.

Colour: white to brown.

Features: prominent rays.

Texture: fine.

Good bonding properties.

Vegetable oil: non-toxic (cooking oil).

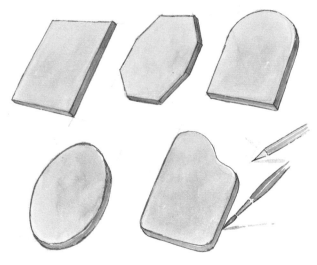

Shape of board

Planning

1. Working drawing on grid.
2. Transfer design and shape to timber.
3. Work design.
4. Cut board to shape.
5. Sandpaper project and apply finish. (Non-toxic finish to be used).
6. Report.

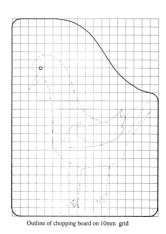

Outline of chopping board on 10mm grid

Working drawing

126

Tools and equipment

Vee chisel or parting chisel.

Coping saw or scroll saw.

Bench holdfast or G cramp.

Cloth to apply finish.

Tools and equipment

Realisation (making)

1. Draw a 20mm grid on an A4 sheet. Draw the design on this grid, using the method described in project 1.

2. Transfer design and outline of the board to timber (as described in project 1).

3. Hold timber in vice or cramp it to bench with a holdfast or G cramp. Use a vee tool to cut out design on timber. Using the vee tool, follow the lines on the wood, working with the grain where possible.

Vee tool

Push vee tool with one hand and guide and control it with the other, always keeping both hands behind cutting edge, and working away from your body.

4. Cut out shape of board.

5. Clean up and sandpaper chopping board to a smooth finish. Dust off, and apply vegetable oil with a cloth, working in a circular motion. When the wood cannot absorb any more oil, rub with a dry cloth. Leave for 24 hours and repeat process.

6. Compile a report on your project. Include sketches, drawings and notes on the materials and techniques used. Evaluate and comment on your project.

Health and safety

- When using a chisel keep your hands and body behind the cutting edge.

- Use safety glasses when using a scroll saw.

- Never place your hand or fingers directly in front of the blade of a scroll or fretsaw.

- Use only non-toxic finishes e.g. vegetable oil (cooking oil) when finishing projects which may come in contact with food.

Activities

Design and make any of the following:

1. A bread board; make a working drawing and include some form of decoration.

2. A simple frame for a photograph. Consider the size of photograph and the materials available.

3. A simple trophy or plaque.

4. A pencil holder from a single block of wood to hold six pencils.

5. A clock, overall size not greater than 200 x 200 x 50mm. (Time piece will be required.)

Options *a)* to be made from one piece of wood;

     b) to be made from one piece of plastic;

     c) use any material;

     d) use a combination of materials.

6. A puzzle: fretwork.

7. A small moveable toy, to be small in scale.

8. A letter rack. It should have some form of embellishment. Consider the size required.

9. A notepad block.

10. A paper-towel holder, to be made from the minimum amount of material. Consider the size and weight of the paper-towel roll.

11. A nameplate for a house. Try to associate your design with the name, e.g. 'Woodlawn' would include the shape of a tree or trees as part of the design. Remember to use a durable wood, as the nameplate may be exposed to the weather. Make out a working drawing and a plan of procedure.

12. A letter opener. The material is to be wood or plastic, or a combination of both.

13. A kitchen platter. Make a working drawing and also plan a work schedule. Consider the size, type of wood and non-toxic finish.

14. A paperweight which is to be carved.

15. A bookshelf, overall size not greater than 600 x 200 x 200mm deep. Include some form of embellishment.

16. A container to hold 12 sewing reels. Consider the size of the reels.

17. A matchbox holder, use any material.

18. A mobile box to hold 18 wooden blocks, size 40mm cubes.

19. A toothbrush holder to hold a number of brushes. Use any available material.

20. A cassette pack to hold ten cassettes. Check the size of a cassette.

21. A pipe holder from a material of your choice. Consider the various types and sizes of pipes.

22. A jewellery box, to be veneered. Consider the size and type of carcass.

23. A jewellery box; to be made from the solid.

24. A napkin holder to hold six napkins. Use a material of your choice.

25. An abstract piece of sculpture, overall size not greater than 200mm cube. Use any material.

26. A motorised truck. Consider the size, type and size of motor, wheels, battery, etc.

27. A kitchen knife holder to hold three knives. Consider the size of knives, holder to be free standing or wall mounted.

28. A fruit dish, turned or carved.

29. A plant hanger to hang four pots.

30. A hand mirror from the materials of your choice.

31. A bird box. Consider the environment into which it is to be placed, access for cleaning, durability.

32. A home for a pet animal: dog, cat, rabbit, etc. Take account of the size of the animal, type of access required, open plan or compartment, etc.

33. A plant holder to hold three flower pots 100mm diameter x 120mm high. Consider the arrangement of pots, for internal or external use.

34. A trinket box, to be turned.

35. A support for a book which is to sit on a desk, to make reading more comfortable. Consider the size, space on desk, materials.

36. Three bottles of milk are left on the doorstep each morning. Design a holder which is convenient to carry, allows bottles to be removed easily, protects the caps from birds.

37. A toast rack, to be made from wood, and the process of lamination is to be used in its manufacture.

38. Rings, bracelets and earrings are to be stood in a jewellery box. Design a box with separate compartments for each; a musical jingle may be included in the design which should operate when the box is opened.

39. A container to hold all of your pencils, pens, drawing instruments etc. neatly and as compact as possible. Work on the basis of the materials which are available to you.

40. A picnic table and seats which should fit in with the environment into which they are to be placed.

10

Joining wood

When deciding which is the best method to join two or more pieces of wood together, it is necessary to ask yourself a number of questions. For example:

- What types of wood are being joined (e.g. hardwood, softwood or manufactured boards)?

- Will the joint have to resist heavy or light loads?

- Will the joint need to be permanent (as in a glued joint) or semi-permanent (as in a screwed joint)?

- Will the joint need to allow for movement between the various elements of the joint? (Remember, timber can expand or contract, depending on the amount of moisture present in the atmosphere.)

- How important will the appearance of the joint be in relation to the appearance of the finished item?

- Can you suggest some other questions which you might need to ask before deciding which method of jointing is most suited to the job in hand?

Forces

To be effective, a joint must be capable of resisting a force (or a combination of forces) which may act on the joint during the course of its everyday use.

Exerted forces

For example, to prevent this chair from collapsing, the forces acting externally on the joints in the chair must be balanced by the internal forces. These internal forces depend to a large extent on the methods used to join together the various parts of the chair.

In order to design a joint to serve a particular purpose, you must determine what type of force the joint is likely to be subjected to.

The four basic types of force or stress to which woodworking joints are exposed to are:

a) compression;

b) tension;

c) shear;

d) torsion.

a) When an object is stressed in a manner which would tend to make the object shorter the object is said to be subject to a **compressive force** or to be **in compression**.

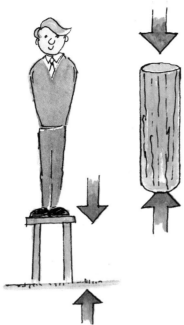

the legs of this stool are said to be in compression
— compressive forces tend to shorten the object they act upon

Compressive forces

b) An object is said to be **in tension** when the forces applied to it try to make the object longer. This situation can also be described by saying that the object is being acted upon by a **tensile force**.

this piece of string is said to be in tension
— a tensile force or a tensile stress tends to make an object longer

Tensile force

c) **Shear forces** try to push parts of the same object in opposite directions. Some cutting instruments such as scissors, operate on the principle of shear.

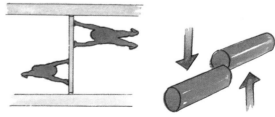

this wooden fence is said to be in shear
— a shear force tends to push parts of the same object in different directions

Shear force

d) **Torsional forces** are forces which tend to twist an object or part of an object. **Torsion** is the type of force used when you unscrew a bottle top.

a torsional force is needed to loosen this nut
— torsion tends to twist an object

Torsion force

Activities

1. Describe at least three situations where each of the following forces may be found (use sketches to illustrate your answers where necessary):

   a) compression;

   b) tension;

   c) shear;

   d) torsion.

2. Examine a piece of timber. Can you suggest how the structure of the wood enables it to resist the forces listed in question 1?

3. Can you suggest which forces the following materials are most able to resist?

   a) steel wire;

   b) copper pipe;

   c) sheet plastic;

   d) aluminium bar.

4. Investigate how the shape of a thin material such as paper, cardboard or light plastic, changes its ability to support a weight.

   For example, how will the strength properties of the folded paper shown below compare to the strength of unfolded paper?

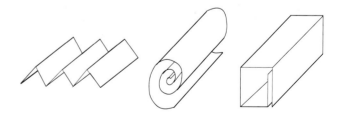

Joint design

There are only a few basic joints used by the woodworker and these have been developed and perfected over many years. However, there are countless variations of these basic joints which are used to overcome problems posed by different situations.

To illustrate, look at these variations of the **mortise and tenon joint.**

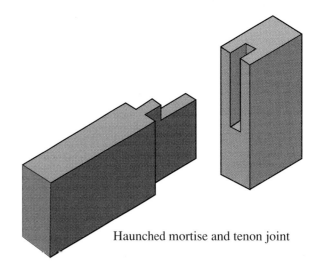

Haunched mortise and tenon joint

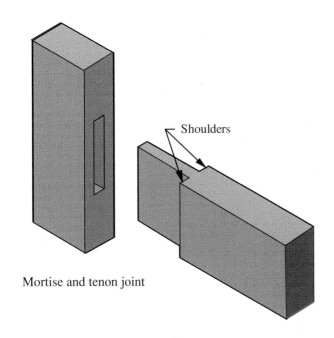

Shoulders

Mortise and tenon joint

One variation of the basic mortise and tenon joint is known as the **haunched mortise and tenon joint**. This is commonly used to join two pieces of timber to form an external right angle, such as at the corner of a door or window.

A third variation of the mortise and tenon joint is a **rebated mortise and tenon joint** in which the shoulders of the tenon are not of equal length. This version is used when the pieces being joined include a rebate.

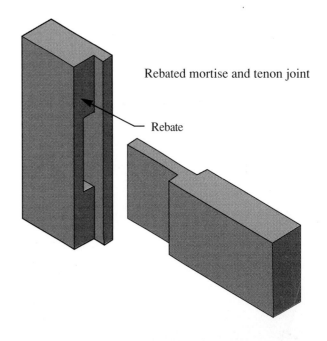

Rebated mortise and tenon joint

Rebate

The mortise and tenon joint is one of the most frequently used joints in woodwork. It is a particularly strong joint and it is used in the manufacture of doors and window frames. The strength of the joint relies to a large extent on having accurately fitted shoulders.

Even though there are a great many joints which may be used in woodwork, there are only a few basic or core joints. In general, most joints can be said to belong to one of the following groups:

Housed joints

Mortised joints

Bridled joints

Dovetailed joints

Edge/Butt joints

Each group consists of a number of variations, some examples of which are illustrated on the opposite page.

These diagrams (below) indicate the different ways in which a woodwork joint might be stressed. The chart on page 135 shows a number of basic joints and illustrates their ability to resist these forces. Note that the joints are assumed not to be glued or fastened.

A = Torsional shear

B = Tension

C
D } = Horizontal shear

E
F } = Vertical shear

G = Compression

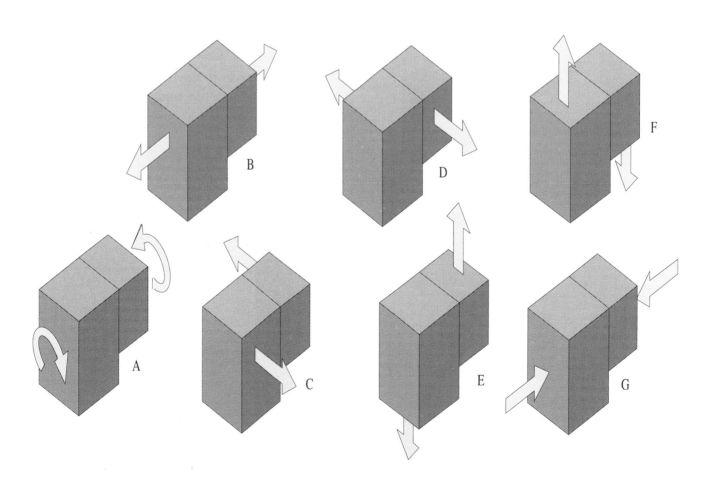

	A	B	C	D	E	F	G	Housed joints: variations
	X	X	√	X	√	√	√	

	A	B	C	D	E	F	G	Mortised joints: variations
	√	X	√	√	√	√	√	

	A	B	C	D	E	F	G	Bridled joints: variations
	√	X	√	√	√	√	√	

	A	B	C	D	E	F	G	Dovetailed joints: variations
	X	√	√	X	√	√	√	

	A	B	C	D	E	F	G	Edge/Butt joints: variations
	√	X	√	√	√	√	√	

Glued joint

135

Activities

1. What are the basic considerations to be taken into account before deciding upon the best method of joining pieces of timber?

2. What are the basic groups of woodworking joints and which joints are contained within each group?

3. What forces are present in each of the following situations?

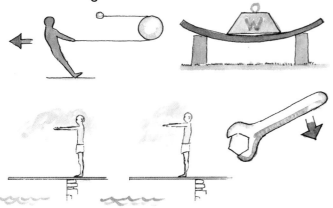

4. Are all materials able to resist all forces equally? Give examples to illustrate your answer.

5. Examine the materials which have been used to construct your classroom. Determine if each material is capable of resisting compression, tension and torsion and fill in the chart below.

Material	Tension	Compression	Torsion

6. Sketch woodwork joints which are capable of resisting the following stresses:

   a) tension; b) torsion; c) shear.

7. Examine a small block of timber. Suggest how the structure of the wood affects its ability to support a heavy load.

   In which direction do you think the block of wood can support the greater weight? Why?

8. Examine the following artifacts in your home and produce sketches to describe the types of joint used to make them:

   a) timber external door

   b) timber window and frame

   c) timber cabinet door

   d) timber shelved unit

9. Make a number of dovetail halving joints, changing the angle of the slope for each one.

   What effect does changing the slope have on the strength of the joint?

   What do you notice about the likelihood of the timber chipping at point 'x'?

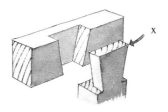

10. Design woodwork joints which would be suitable for use in each of the following situations. (Use sketches to illustrate your suggestions.)

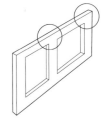

Adhesives

A glued joint is said to be more **mechanically efficient** than a joint which relies solely upon nails, screws, rivets or bolts. This is because the adhesive binds the pieces of material together over the whole area of the joint. Screws and nails only act on a portion of the joint area and may actually weaken the timber if too many fasteners are used.

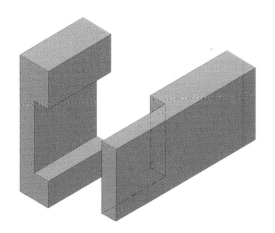

Contact area for glueing

The diagram above shows a disassembled tee halving joint. It shows the areas where the two timbers will be bound by the adhesive.

A joint which relies on screws or nails may fail as shown here if it is not carefully designed.

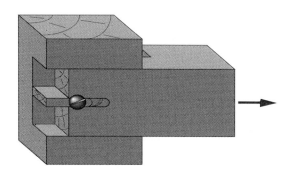

With wood to wood bonds a gap of 0.076mm to 0.15mm gives the greatest strength. Therefore, it is essential that all joints which are to be glued must be worked accurately. Refer to the sections of this book dealing with the designing and processing of joints.

When choosing an adhesive for a particular job a number of points will influence the final choice. These are:

1. the type of materials which are to be bonded;

2. the conditions under which the finished product will eventually be used;

3. the scale of production, i.e. a once-off job or a mass-produced item;

4. the type of joint being glued and the accuracy to which it is worked;

5. whether or not the wood has been treated with any chemicals.

How adhesives work

An adhesive binds two pieces of material together in two different ways:

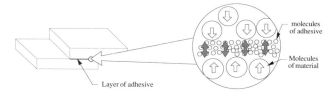

a) Specific adhesion: where the molecules of the adhesive are attracted to the molecules of the materials being joined;

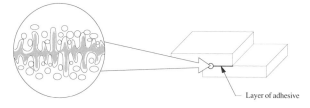

b) Mechanical adhesion: where the adhesive enters into pores or cracks in the materials surfaces and then sets.

In practice a joint usually relies upon a combination of both specific and mechanical adhesion. However, a joint may exhibit more of one type of adhesion than another. For example, joining a smooth material such as glass would depend almost exclusively on specific adhesion.

Almost all of the adhesives used to join wood are stronger than the timber itself. Therefore the durability of the adhesive and convenience in use will usually influence choice of adhesive.

> But, regardless of which type of glue is most suitable, do not use any adhesive unless you have permission from your teacher to do so.

There are a great number of adhesives readily available and their durability varies widely. The ability of an adhesive to remain effective in a particular environment is examined in BS 1204 (standards for close-contact and gap-filling adhesives) and a number of classifications for glues are recommended.

Abbreviation	Classification	Durability
INT	Interior	Suitable only for use in dry conditions. Will survive damp conditions for a short time only. They may also be prone to attack by insects and micro-organisms.
MR	Moisture-resistant	Will not survive prolonged exposure to hot water. They can withstand prolonged exposure to cold water and are resistant to attack by micro-organisms.
BR	Boil-resistant	Will withstand prolonged exposure to cold water and offer good resistance to micro- organism attack. Offer good resistance to exposure to boiling water.
WBP	Weather-Boil-proof	Suitable for use in areas exposed to severe weather conditions. They remain effective when subjected to cold or boiling water, micro-organism attack, steam or conditions of dry heat.

Some terms associated with adhesives

1. Shelf life

This is the length of time that an adhesive can be stored before its performance in use would be reduced. Storage of the glue in accordance with the manufacturer's recommendations is essential if premature deterioration of the adhesive is to be avoided.

2. Pot life

This is the time available for using the adhesive after it has been prepared. Pot life is timed from the moment the water is added to a glue in powder form or, in the case of a two-part adhesive, from when the hardener is added.

In the case of PVA adhesives which do not require the addition of water or hardeners, pot life refers to the time taken for the adhesive to become excessively stiff or when a hard film begins to form on the surface of the glue. Pot life is also known as **open assembly time**.

3. Closed assembly time

This is the period during which the parts being bonded can be moved and positioned before a final bond begins to form. The closed assembly time of an adhesive is an important consideration when choosing an adhesive. Some adhesives such as contact adhesives and cyanoacrylate adhesives (superglue) have a closed assembly of only a very few seconds.

Can you suggest how temperature, moisture and the types of materials being bonded might affect a) shelf life b) pot life and c) closed assembly time?

Adhesives types

When classifying adhesives it is usual to group them under one of three broad headings:

- **Properties of the adhesive:** e.g. if the glues are for internal or external use.

- **Materials to be joined:** e.g. wood to wood, fabric to wood, plastic to plastic, etc.

- **Composition of the adhesive:** i.e. what the adhesive itself is made from.

We will examine glues under the heading of composition of adhesive and our examination will be divided into three sections:

1. adhesives made from natural products;
2. adhesives made from synthetic products;
3. rubber-based adhesives.

1. Adhesives made from natural products

Animal glues are sensitive to moisture and are prone to attack by micro-organisms. They are therefore rarely used but they do provide an excellent bond under dry conditions. The adhesive is made of bones and hides from animals and from fish offal. Animal glues are provided in solid form such as in pearls and slabs and they must be heated to melting point before being applied with a stiff glue brush.

Casein glues are made from the curds of milk, dried and ground to a fine powder. This powder is then mixed with hydrated lime and certain other chemicals. Casein adhesives have good resistance to reasonably high temperatures provided that conditions are generally dry. However, they deteriorate if exposed to wet or damp conditions and are also prone to attack by micro-organisms (moulds and bacteria). Adhesives based on casein are suitable for bonding timber to plasterboard, linoleum and plastic. They may also be used for general bonding of wood to wood for internal use.

2. Adhesives made from synthetic products

Synthetic resins

    Polyvinyl acetate (PVA)

    Urea formaldehyde

    Urea-melamine formaldehyde

    Phenol formaldehyde

Resorcinol formaldehyde

Epoxide resins

Cyanoacrylates

Polyvinyl acetate (PVA)

Very popular as a wood adhesive; it is used cold, requires no preparation and when dry it sets to a hard but flexible transparent film. In addition, it sets at room temperature and will not blunt cutting tools. It can be applied by brush, roller or glue stick and is suitable for bonding joinery, cloth and leather for use in dry conditions.

PVA adhesives soften at around 70°C and their resistance to water is greater than that of animal glues.

Urea formaldehyde

Widely used in conditions which are not exposed to weather. They are also used in the manufacture of plywoods. Will break down if continuously exposed to extreme weather conditions, but they are immune to attack by micro-organisms.

Urea-melamine formaldehyde

The durability of these resins can be improved by the addition of melamine. Immune to micro-organism attack and have an improved resistance to boiling water. Comparatively expensive and, like UF adhesives, they tend to blunt cutting tools when set.

Phenol formaldehyde

Immune to attack by micro-organisms and possess high strength properties even under conditions of severe exposure. More expensive than UF glues but they are resistant to many acids, solvents and wood preservatives.

Resorcinol formaldehyde

Very expensive but very durable and effective. Classified as WBP, immune to micro-organism attack and perform effectively in severe weather conditions. Have a long shelf life and a pot life of one to five hours depending upon temperature.

Epoxide resins

Cost prevents them from being widely used but they are capable of bonding many different materials very effectively. They do not shrink on setting and are ideal for bonding non-porous materials such as glass and metals. Usually supplied as two-part adhesives.

Cyanoacrylates

These one-part adhesives produce a strong bond very quickly and are sometimes referred to as 'superglues'. Caution is needed when using the adhesive as there is a risk that skin may become adhered.

3. Rubber-based adhesives

Adhesives made from natural or synthetic rubbers are usually designed as **contact adhesives**. This means that a thin coat of adhesive is applied to the surfaces to be bonded and allowed to dry for ten to thirty minutes. When the surfaces are then brought together, the bond is formed immediately. Therefore, care must be taken to position the parts accurately.

A wide range of contact adhesives is available and they are used to bond wood, metal, polyurethane, rubber, rigid PVC, leather and laminated plastics. They are generally used to bond thin flat sections of material together and are not suitable for the bonding of woodwork joints.

Tapping a rubber tree

Health and safety

- When using adhesives ensure that the area in which you are working is well ventilated as the vapours from some types of glue can cause drowsiness if inhaled.

- Also, if any adhesive comes in contact with your skin, remove the glue immediately by washing with water in some situations. It is advisable to wear gloves or to apply a barrier cream to your hands. A barrier cream will prevent any direct contact between your skin and the adhesive.

Application

Depending on the nature of the job and the type of adhesive being used, glues may be applied in a number of ways.

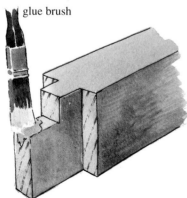

glue brush

Adhesive can be applied to joints and other small areas using a stiff **glue brush**. PVA and casein glues can readily be applied in this way.

glue stick

Slightly larger areas, such as this edge joint, can be glued up using a shaped piece of thin wood usually referred to as a **glue stick**.

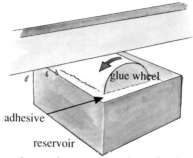

glue wheel

adhesive

reservoir

Where there are a lot of edge joints to be formed, it may be beneficial to use a **glue wheel**. This consists of a reservoir of glue and a wheel which remains partly submerged in the adhesive. Timbers which are passed over the top of the glue wheel are given a uniform coat of adhesive.

An electric glue gun

The **glue gun** uses adhesive which is supplied in the form of sticks of solidified glue. An electric element liquefies the glue by heating it. The glue re-solidifies after application as the adhesive cools and this forms the bond. Some brands of adhesive are colour coded according to their specialist function, e.g. yellow for wood, cardboard and paper.

Large flat areas can be covered quickly and uniformly with the aid of a hand-held **roller** which has its own reservoir of adhesive. A roller of this type is often used with PVA adhesives.

Where contact adhesives are to be applied a **serrated spreader** is convenient. The serrations ensure that the adhesive is applied to the surface in ribbons of equal thickness.

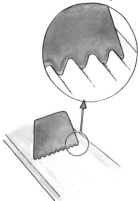

In some situations, adhesives may be applied to large areas using a **spray gun**.

A **mechanical glue spreader** can be used to apply adhesive to one or two sides of the timber. The spreader consists of two rollers, each of which has a reservoir to hold adhesive. This type of device is useful for quickly applying adhesive to timber laminates.

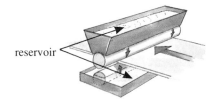

reservoir

Application of pressure to joints

Framing or Sash cramp
Used where a large number of items (e.g. when jointing a number of boards to provide a wide table or worktop) need to be secured temporarily while the glue forms a permanent bond. Extension bars are available for very wide frames or areas.

Sash cramp

Small items or narrow sections of wood can conveniently be held with the aid of one or a number of 'G' cramps.

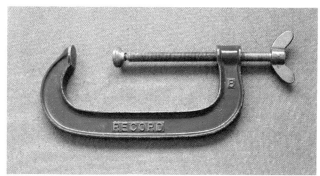

G cramp

Long sections of timber can be bonded to sheet materials with the aid of a screwing or nailing strip. This strip facilitates the easy removal of screws and/or nails after the glue has set.

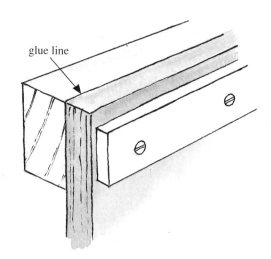

glue line

Nailing or screwing strip

How adhesives set

Depending upon the chemical composition of the adhesive, glues set to a final hardened condition in a number of ways.

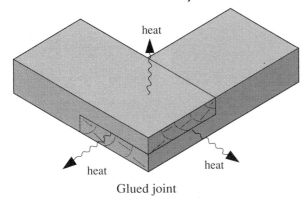

Glued joint

Animal glues return to a hardened state as they cool. They can be returned to a liquid state by exposing the joint to heat.

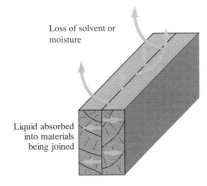

Polyvinyl acetate and some rubber-based contact adhesives set by way of a loss of moisture or solvent. The adhesive loses moisture or solvent by evaporation into the atmosphere. Depending upon the nature of the items being joined, some of the liquid may be absorbed into the material.

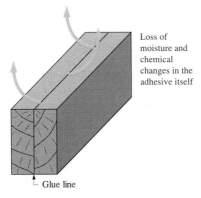

Casein glues and synthetic resins such as urea-, phenol, and resorcinol formaldehyde adhesives set due to a loss of moisture coupled with some chemical change in the glue itself.

Epoxide resins undergo a chemical reaction which is initiated by the addition of a hardener or catalyst which is mixed with the adhesive during preparation. The chemical reaction changes the glue from a liquid state to a solid state.

In the case of many adhesives, the time necessary for the final bond to occur can be reduced by exposing the joint to increased temperatures.

The load or stress that a glued joint can safely withstand will depend to a large extent upon the type of stress that the joint is subjected to.

When an adhesive is being tested, the glued joint is subjected to four different forces:

Shear

A shear force tends to move the parts of an adhesive bond in opposite directions. A correctly designed and fabricated glued joint will normally be highly resistant to shear forces, due to the fact that a shear force will be spread over the total bond area.

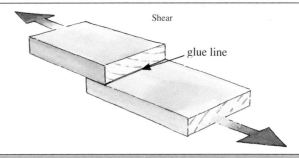

Tension

Tensile forces try to lengthen the bond stressed. Most adhesives are highly resistant to tensile stresses as the forces are distributed over the full bond area. However, if elements of the joint tend to twist or bend then 'peel' stresses may develop and the joint may fail.

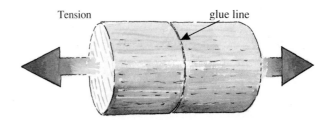

143

Torsion

Joints should not be subjected to torsional forces if possible as they tend to set up high stresses at one side of the joint. Therefore, the stresses are not spread over the whole bond area and failure of the joint may occur.

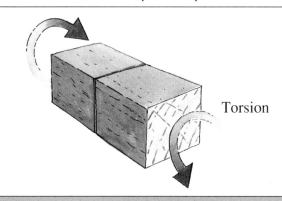

Torsion

Peel/Cleavage

A glued joint is usually at its weakest when it is subjected to a peel or cleavage stress. As with a bond subjected to a torsional stress, a peel or cleavage force concentrates loads on only one part of the adhesive bond and the joint is therefore prone to failure.

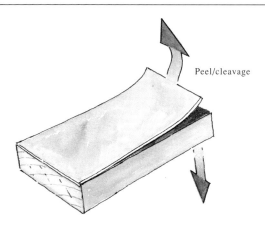

Peel/cleavage

Factors affecting strength of glued joints

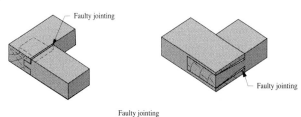

Faulty jointing

Faulty jointing

Faulty jointing

Badly designed or poorly made joints prevent the whole of the joint area being effectively bonded. Joints of reduced strength will result.

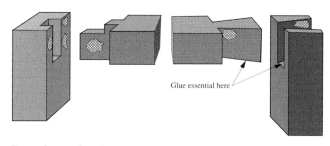

Glue essential here

Poor glue application

Strength of joint is reduced by the unequal application of adhesive to the joint area.

Strength will also be reduced if insufficient adhesive is applied to key areas of the joint.

Pot life of adhesive

Glues which are not prepared in accordance with the manufacturer's recommendations, or adhesives which are used after their recommended pot life has passed, may result in glued joints of reduced strength.

Selecting the correct adhesive

It is very important to select an adhesive which is designed to bond the materials you wish to join. The chart on page 145 is a quick guide to glues suited to bonding particular materials. Note that the chart is only intended as a starting point and you need to investigate the situation in which the adhesive is to be used before making a final choice.

MATERIAL						
	Wood	Metal	Acrylic	Melamine	Rubber	Expanded Polystryrene
Wood	Polyvinyl acetate	Epoxy resin	Epoxy resin	Contact adhesive	Contact adhesive	P.V.A
Metal	Epoxy resin	Epoxy resin	Epoxy resin	Contact adhesive	Contact adhesive	P.V.A
Acrylic	Epoxy resin	Epoxy resin	Epoxy resin (e.g. Tensol)	Contact adhesive	Contact adhesive	P.V.A
Melamine	Contact adhesive	Contact adhesive	Contact adhesive	Contact adhesive	Contact adhesive	P.V.A
Rubber	Contact adhesive	Contact adhesive	Contact adhesive	Contact adhesive	Contact adhesive	P.V.A
Expanded Polystyrene	P.V.A	P.V.A	P.V.A	P.V.A	P.V.A	P.V.A

(leftmost vertical label: MATERIAL)

Using the chart

The chart suggests that a contact adhesive may be used to bond acrylic to melamine. You must now determine which grade of contact adhesive is suitable for the job.

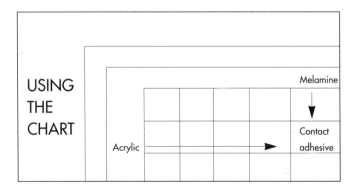

Activities

1. Explain why a glued timber joint is usually stronger than a joint which relies solely on nails or screws.

2. Explain the difference between 'specific adhesion' and 'mechanical adhesion'.

3. What do the following abbreviations stand for?

    WBP, INT, MR, BR.

4. What are the primary safety precautions to be observed when using adhesives?

5. Name two types of adhesive which could be classified as:

    a) interior grade

    b) boil-resistant grade

    c) weather-boilproof

    d) moisture-resistant

6. In what situations is it sometimes convenient to use a 'contact adhesive'?

7. Describe four factors which could reduce the strength of a joint which has been glued.

8. Name five different ways to apply adhesives and describe the different situations in which each method is used.

9. Briefly explain how each of the following types of adhesive sets:

    a) animal glues

    b) epoxide resins

    c) casein glues

    d) polyvinyl acetates

10. Explain the following terms associated with adhesives:

    a) pot life

    b) shelf life

    c) closed assembly time

11. Describe four methods used to secure the components of a joint while the glue is setting.

12. Reproduce the chart below and fill in the
    remaining sections:

Use	Adhesive	Reasons for choosing
Mass-produced timber furniture		
Bonding fabric sheets to plywood		
External timber doors		
Bonding sheets of laminated plastic to MDF sheets		
Bonding acrylic to acrylic		
Timber framing to be used in exposed conditions		
Bonding wood veneers to plywood to be used internally		

13. Apply excess PVA glue to the surface of a
    piece of timber. Allow the adhesive to dry.
    Apply a range of different finishes to the
    wood (such as varnish, French polish, wood
    stains, etc.) and assess how the quality of
    each finish is affected by the excess glue.

14. Design a poster (A3 size) which could be
    displayed in the workshop to promote the
    safe use of adhesives.

15. Write an essay describing how the type of
    buildings, furniture, etc. would be different
    if designers and builders did not have the
    use of modern adhesives.

11

Hand tools

Important eras in human history are sometimes identified by referring to the material used to make tools, e.g. the Stone Age, the Bronze Age and the Iron Age. The ability to make and use tools is regarded as one of the most important skills possessed by humans.

Classification of hand tools

Hand tools may be conveniently classified according to the type of operation they perform.

Tools to hold and support work

Woodwork and metalwork benches are normally fitted with a vice to hold the material while it is worked. Other holding tools are the bench holdfast and the G cramp.

Marking-out tools

This group is sometimes referred to as geometrical tools and includes tools used to measure distances and angles, test the straightness of edges, and to mark circles and curves.

Percussion or impelling tools

Hammers, mallets and screwdrivers are used to assemble joints or to drive nails or screws into the material. Some percussion tools also include a cutting or chopping action such as the axe or the adze.

Saws

Saws may be used to reduce the size of large sections of material or to work very fine joints. There are many saw types and choice will depend upon the material being cut and the profile of the cut, i.e. whether the cut is straight or curved.

Paring or shaving tools

Planes and spokeshaves are used to accurately reduce timber to a finished size and to produce a smooth finished surface by removing thin shavings of material. The wood chisel can be used to pare and carve timber to the desired shape.

Abrasive and scraping tools

Tools do not always use a sharpened edge to remove material. Tools such as the surform and rasp remove small particles of material using small teeth on the blade of the instrument.

Selection of hand tools

Boring tools

Some tools use a rotary action to cut material. The most frequently used boring tool is the drill and there are many attachments available to bore holes in a range of materials.

Setting-out tools

The try square

Has two parts: the stock and the blade. The stock is made from rosewood or mahogany, the blade from steel and is joined to the stock with rivets. The stock is protected from excessive wear with a brass strip. The most important thing about a try square is that it makes an angle of 90°, so care should be taken not to drop it. The size of a try square is determined by the length of the blade and is usually 150mm long. When using a try square it is important to keep the stock tight up against the wood and against either the face side or the face edge.

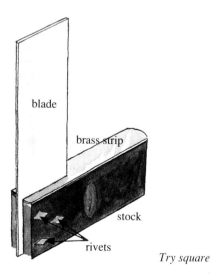

Try square

Sliding bevel

Like the try square, has got a stock and blade but in this case the angle between the two can be set to any angle. Instead of rivets we have a half wing nut to secure the blade. The slotted blade can slide into the stock when the tool is not in use.

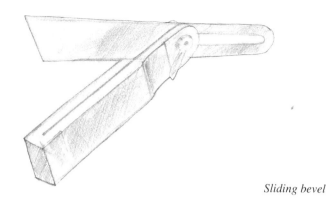

Sliding bevel

The rule

A very accurate tool for measuring. The graduations are in millimetres and centimetres. The usual length is 300mm but metre rules are available.

The tape measure

An extendible, flexible steel strip, coiled in a container. The tape measure is spring loaded and retracts into the case when released unless it is locked into position. A hook rivetted to the end ensures accurate measurement.

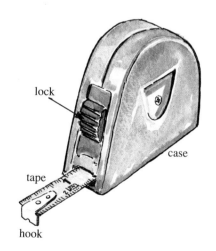

Tape measure

The marking knife

A simple tool, it is used to score lines which are to be sawn. Its function is to sever the outer fibres of wood, thus giving a cleaner, neater cut.

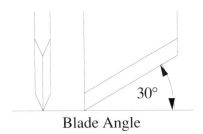

Blade Angle

30°

Marking knife blade

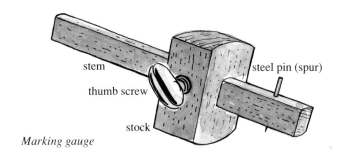

stem

steel pin (spur)

thumb screw

stock

Marking gauge

> Only lines which are to be sawn should be marked with the marking knife.

The blade is ground on both sides and is drawn towards you when being used.

The bench hook

Is made from beech and is used as an aid to bench cutting. Two end blocks are jointed at right angles across the base board, one on the top surface and one on the bottom. The bottom one is hooked over the edge of the bench or held in the vice while the work is held firmly against the other. The bench hook also saves the bench from getting damaged when sawing.

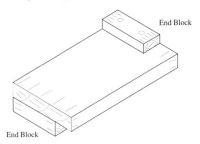

End Block

End Block

Bench hook

The gauge

Used to mark lines on wood parallel to one of its edges. The two most commonly used are *a*) the marking gauge and *b*) the mortice gauge.

The **marking gauge** has four parts: the stem, the stock, the spur and the thumb screw. The stock slides up and down the stem and is fixed by tightening the thumb screw. To use this gauge the stock is run tightly down the edge of the wood while the spur marks the required line. The gauge is made from beech.

The **mortise gauge**, as the name suggests, is used predominantly to mark out mortise and tenon joints. It is like the marking gauge except that it has two pins. One pin is fixed and the other may be adjusted by a thumb screw mounted at the end of the stock.

This gauge is used in the same way as the marking gauge. The distance between the spurs should be set to the width of the chisel to be used to chop the mortise. The mortise gauge is made from rosewood or mahogany.

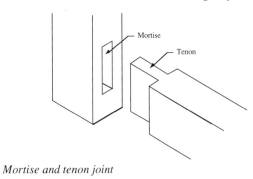

Mortise

Tenon

Mortise and tenon joint

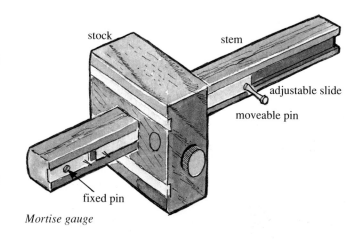

stock

stem

adjustable slide

moveable pin

fixed pin

Mortise gauge

Activities

1. What is the most important thing about a try square?

2. Sketch a try square and name its parts.

3. What is the main difference between a sliding bevel and a try square?

4. What is the function of the brass strip along the stock of the try square? Name two other tools that have similar brass strips.

5. Make a sketch of a marking knife.

6. What is the function of a marking knife?

7. Why is it important to only mark lines that are to be sawn with the marking knife?

8. Explain how a bench hook is used.

9. Make a neat sketch of a marking gauge.

10. Describe the differences between a mortise gauge and a marking gauge.

11. How did the mortise gauge get its name?

12. Do a little research to find two other types of gauge. Make drawings of each.

13. What used people to use before tape measures came on the market?

Percussion tools

Screwdrivers

There are three basic types of screw head which lead to three main types of screwdriver:

a) the slotted head giving the parallel tip screwdriver;

b) the philips head giving the philips screwdriver;

c) the pozidrive head giving the pozidrive screwdriver;

Parallel tip   Philips   Pozidrive

The size of a screwdriver is known by its blade length, which varies from 50mm to 300mm. The blade is made from hardened steel. Care must be taken in choosing the correct size of screwdriver to suit the particular screw to be driven. A badly fitting screwdriver will damage the screw head.

What length blade to choose?

Use the longest screwdriver convenient for the work. More power can be applied to a long screwdriver than a short one, usually because the longer screwdriver has a larger handle.

The tip must fit the screws both in width and thickness.

If the tip is too wide it will scar the wood around the head.

If the blade is too narrow and thin you will destroy the slot and the screwdriver tip.

Handles are of either plastic or wood. They should not be hammered as this can damage them or, as is the case with wooden handles, split or crack them.

Plastic moulded handle

Cabinet screwdriver with traditional wooden handle

Health and safety

- Never use a screwdriver near a live wire even if it has a plastic handle.

- Treat a screwdriver with respect. It can be a dangerous tool.

- Driving a screw is a two-handed operation. **Never** hold the work in one hand while driving a screw with the other.

Cabinet screwdriver

The traditional type of screwdriver. It has a wooden handle and a circular sectioned blade. The blade can be ground to a different width and thickness if necessary.

Philips and pozidrive screwdrivers

Both these have a crossed head tip formed by grinding flutes in the end of a pointed blade. The only difference between them is that the pozidrive is designed to fit into an additional square hole in the centre of the crossed slots of the screw.

Crossed head and tip of Philips screwdriver

Spiral or pump screwdriver

This tool drives screws by pressure, i.e. pushing down on the handle twists the bit. It can be twisted clockwise or anti-clockwise by using the ratchet. The bits are interchangeable if required. This screwdriver will drive screws much faster than the traditional screwdriver will.

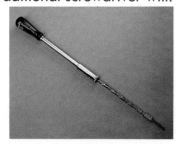

Pump-action screwdriver

Activities

1. Draw a cabinet screwdriver.

2. List and draw the three main screw tips.

3. Why is a pozidrive screwdriver better than a philips?

4. How is the size of a screwdriver given?

5. Draw three types of handle. What is the advantage/disadvantage of each?

6. Why is a screwdriver a dangerous tool?

7. Give six things which should not be done with a screwdriver.

8. Why is the size of a screwdriver head important? Explain.

Bradawl

Used to make small holes in wood, usually to mark the centre of a hole or as a pilot hole for small screws. The handle is usually beech but can be made from plastic or boxwood and has a brass ferrule. The blade is tempered steel and finishes in a wedge shape. To use the bradawl it is important to start by placing the blade across the grain. This will cut the wood fibres rather than split them. A downward pressure with short clockwise and anti-clockwise twists will bore the hole.

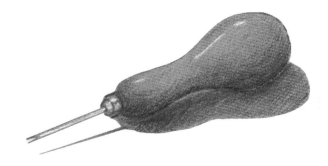

Bradawl

A bradawl should never be used as a small screwdriver as this will damage the blade tip and loosen the blade in the handle.

151

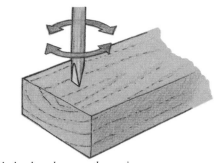

Blade placed across the grain

Nail punch

Nails should be preferably be punched below the surface of the wood, particularly in flooring and before timber is cleaned up and sanded. These punch holes can then be sealed and filled giving a much neater finish. The nail punch is made from steel, has a knurled handle and a hollow ground tip for gripping the nail head. Various sized punches are available, having different tip sizes. Obviously the small sizes should be used on smaller nails and the larger sizes on larger ones.

Nail punch

Activities

1. Why is the bradawl not used along the wood grain?

2. Sketch a bradawl and name its parts.

3. Suggest with the aid of diagrams how the blade could be joined to the handle.

4. How would you design a bradawl to prevent the blade becoming loose after a lot of use?

5. Why is the tip of a nail punch hollow?

6. Why are nails in floors punched below the surface?

7. Sketch a nail punch.

8. Why is it important to choose the correct punch size when punching nails?

Hammers

There are two types of hammers commonly used in woodwork nowadays:

a) the Warrington hammer

b) the claw hammer.

The Warrington hammer

The handle is made from ash or hickory and the head from forged steel. Generally used for light work, this hammer can vary in weight from 170g up to 450g. The head of all good hammers is wedged on, which fixes it very firmly to the handle.

Cross pein Warrington hammer

Health and safety

- Never use a hammer with a loose head. It is very dangerous.

The claw hammer

A heavier hammer than the Warrington hammer. The claw is used to pull nails. To withstand the force of pulling nails the head is usually fixed to the handle, using two or more steel wedges in conjunction with a wooden wedge. Claw hammers vary in weight from 450g up to 680g.

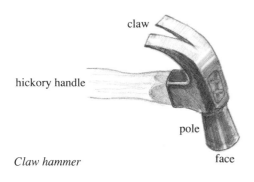

Claw hammer

claw

hickory handle

pole

face

Use of hammers

1. Hold the hammer at the end of the handle; this delivers more powerful blows and the hammer head will hit the nail more squarely.

2. Never use the side of the hammer.

3. Never use a hammer with a loose head.

4. Use the correct-sized hammer for the job in hand, i.e. a light small hammer for small nails and tacks and a heavy hammer for large nails.

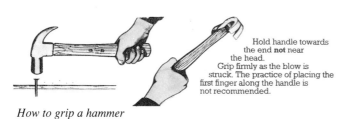

Hold handle towards the end **not** near the head.
Grip firmly as the blow is struck. The practice of placing the first finger along the handle is not recommended.

How to grip a hammer

5. Keep the head of the hammer clean or it will slip while driving nails.

6. Do not try to pull very large nails with a claw hammer. You may break the handle.

7. Never use a hammer on a chisel handle.

A dirty hammer face will tend to slip and cause damage.

KEEP CLEAN AS BELOW
PRESSURE

Emery cloth or fine glass paper

Always keep hammer face clean

The mallet

Used to strike the handle of the chisel when making a mortice, and for assembling and disassembling joints. Usually the mallet head and handle are made from beech. This is a good wood to use because it is hard and dense enough to withstand the stresses involved and yet it is soft enough not to damage the chisel handle. The handle is tapered and therefore the head tightens when the mallet is used. The two striking faces are not parallel but are tapered towards the handle.

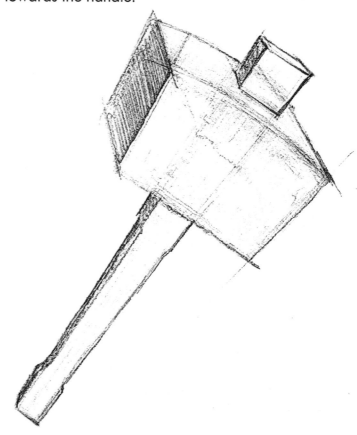

The mallet

The carver's mallet

The head is made from beech and the handle from ash. The head of this mallet is round to enable the carver to work from a variety of angles without changing grip. The carver's mallet fits snugly in the hand and is easily wielded.

Carver's mallet

> The carver's mallet should only be used for carving work.

Pincers

The carpenter's pincers is used to remove nails from timber and for cutting the heads off small nails and tacks. Pincers come in various lengths varying from 150mm to 200mm. When using the pincers grip the nail as near to the wood as possible. A piece of waste wood should always be placed below the jaws to protect the wood surface.

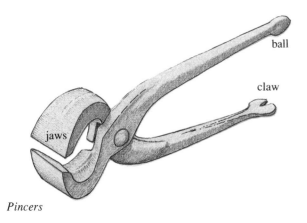

Pincers

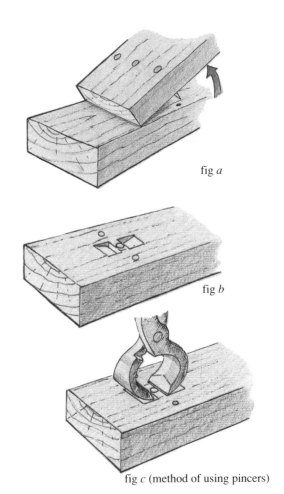

fig *a*

fig *b*

fig *c* (method of using pincers)

When the nail head is flush with the surface. If the two pieces of wood can be prized apart then knock the nail through wood to expose head (fig a). Otherwise cut two recesses using an old wood chisel or a cold chisel (fig b). This allows a pair of pincers to be used to grip the nail and remove it (fig c).

Activities

1. Make a diagram of a claw hammer.
2. Compare the use of a claw hammer to that of a Warrington hammer.
3. Why should a hammer be held at the end of its handle?
4. Give four reasons for a nail bending when being driven.
5. Why is beech such a good wood for mallets?
6. Sketch a carver's mallet.
7. Compare the way a hammer's head and a mallet's head are secured to their handles.

8. Explain why the faces of the mallet are not parallel.

9. Sketch a pincers.

10. Describe the use of a pincers.

11. Why are waste pieces used underneath pincers and claw hammer jaws when pulling nails?

Saws

Saws for cutting wood can be divided into two main groups: *a)* saws for straight cutting; *b)* saws for curved cutting. For cutting metals and plastics we use a hacksaw.

Variety of saws

Straight cutting	Curved cutting
Tenon Saw	Bow Saw
Cross-cut Saw	Coping Saw
Panel Saw	Compass Saw
Dovetail Saw	Pad Saw
Rip Saw	Hacksaw

Saw teeth

The design of the saw tooth depends on the type of timber to be cut. For cutting across the grain use a saw with cross-cut type teeth and for sawing with the grain use one with a rip-saw tooth pattern. Tooth size is also important. Large teeth with deep spaces or gullets are best suited for softwoods, while hardwoods require smaller teeth. Furthermore rough sawing can be done with a large-toothed saw whereas fine work such as joint cutting should be done with a smaller toothed saw.

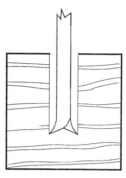
Cross-cut saw teeth

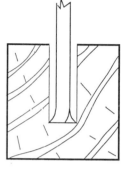
Rip saw teeth

Cross-cut saw teeth are sharpened to points and cut the fibres while rip-saw teeth work in the same way as a chisel.

A very important feature of all saws is the set. The saw cut must be thicker than the blade otherwise the saw will become stuck. To achieve this alternate teeth are bent slightly to the left and right. The kerf which is produced allows the saw to pass freely through the wood.

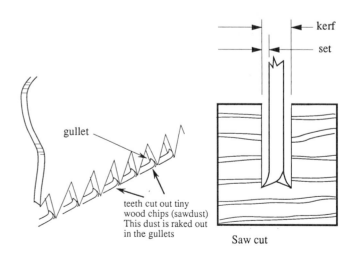

gullet

teeth cut out tiny wood chips (sawdust) This dust is raked out in the gullets

kerf

set

Saw cut

Saw set (with saw)

Cross cut saw

The tenon saw

This saw is used for light bench work and for cutting joints, particularly tenons, hence its name. The parts of the tenon saw are the handle, blade, teeth and rib. The handle is fixed onto the blade using screws. The blade is made from high-quality steel and varies in length from 200mm to 300mm. The teeth are of the cross-cut type and there are 10–15 points per 25mm.

The panel saw

Used for light work such as sawing plywood or hardboard; work which is too heavy for a tenon saw and too light for a cross-cut saw. It is similar in appearance to the cross-cut saw but slightly shorter, having a blade length of about 500mm. It has 10–12 teeth per 25mm and these are of the cross-cut type.

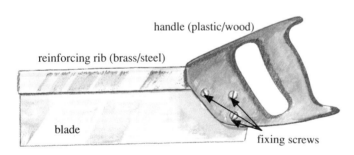

reinforcing rib (brass/steel)

handle (plastic/wood)

blade

fixing screws

Tenon saw

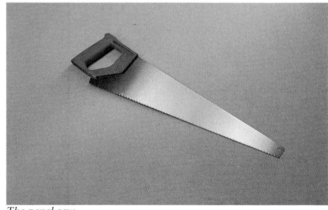

The panel saw

The cross-cut saw

This saw is used, as the name suggests, for cutting across the grain of the wood; for cutting boards to length. It is not suitable for cutting small pieces of wood. The handle can be wooden (beech) or plastic. The blade made from cold rolled high carbon steel is about 600mm long. This saw has 6–8 teeth per 25mm. The backs of these larger hand saws can be straight or skew backed.

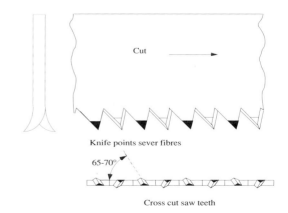

Cut

Knife points sever fibres

65-70°

Cross cut saw teeth

The dovetail saw

This saw is like a tenon saw in every way except that it is smaller. Usually the handles are open. It is used for very fine light work such as cutting dovetails. The blade length is between 150mm and 200mm and has 18–20 teeth per 25mm. The teeth are sharpened to the rip saw pattern because most of the sawing done with this saw is along the grain.

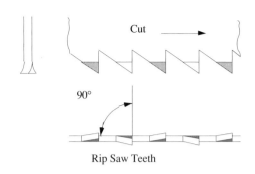

Rip Saw Teeth

Dovetail saw

The rip saw

Used to saw timber with the grain and has a similar appearance to the cross-cut saw. The blade length varies from 600mm to 650mm. Teeth are large, there only being 4–8 per 25mm. The design of the teeth on the rip saw is quite different to cross-cut teeth. They cut with a chisel action and are sharpened across at 90°.

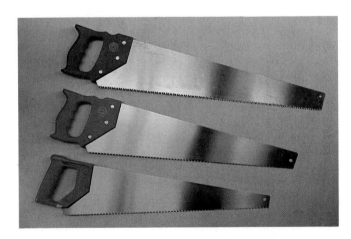

Rip saw

Saws for curved work

None of the saws mentioned so far are suitable for curved work because the blades are wide and they could not turn around a curve. All saws suitable for curved work, therefore, have narrow blades.

The coping saw

Has a narrow blade with fine teeth, 14–16 per 25mm. The blade is under tension by the springing of the frame and tightening of the handle. Although the blade is easily broken it is inexpensive to replace. Ensure that the sight pins remain in line. Unlike most other saws you use two hands on the handle of the coping saw. The work must therefore be held firmly in the vice. It must be noted here that the coping saw is only suitable for light thin material. The blade teeth should point towards the handle.

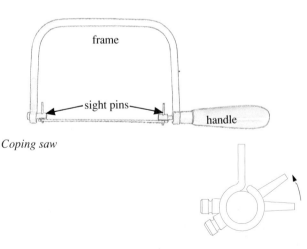

Coping saw

The cross pins must remain in line at all times

The compass saw or lock saw

The blade is narrow and tapers along its length to a point. The handle is of the open type.

The pad saw

Often used to cut keyholes, it consists of a blade slotted into a handle and secured in place using a locking nut. The blade is usually 200mm long with 10 teeth per 25mm. Since the blade is only supported at one end, at the handle, it can be easily bent, even though it is thicker than most saw blades. The minimum length of blade should be allowed to protrude.

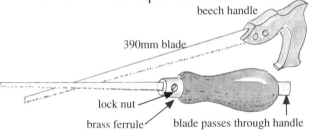

Compass saw (top) and pad saw

The hacksaw

Used to cut both metals and plastics. The saw frame is adjustable to take different blade lengths. Teeth are small and are usually set in a wavy pattern. Two hands are used on this saw, one on the frame and one on the handle.

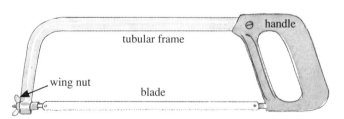

Hacksaw with tubular frame

Use and care of saws

Saws for straight cutting are all held in the same way. The index finger is placed along the handle to help steady and support the saw. One hand only is used in these saws, the other is often used to support the wood.

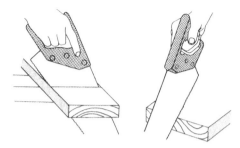

Whatever pattern of hand or back saw you use, note the position of the first finger. This helps balance and gives better control

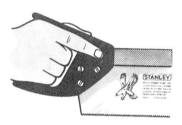

How to hold the saw

Whatever pattern of hand or back saw you use, note the position of the first finger. This helps balance and gives better control.

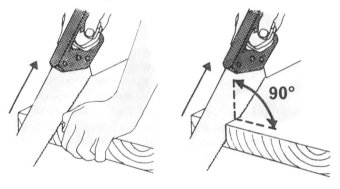

Start the cut by drawing the saw backwards a few times. Use your thumb as a steadying gauge for this initial cut. Ensure the saw is square to the wood.

Health and safety

*   Always be aware that a saw can give a very nasty cut, so keep your hand away from the cutting line in case it hops out of the saw cut, except of course when you are starting the cut.

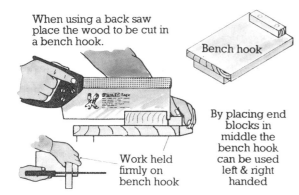

When using a back saw place the wood to be cut in a bench hook.

Bench hook

By placing end blocks in middle the bench hook can be used left & right handed

Work held firmly on bench hook

Using a tenon saw

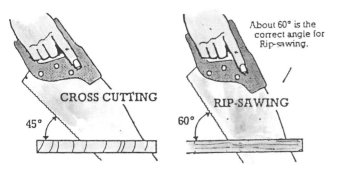

CROSS CUTTING

45°

RIP-SAWING

60°

About 60° is the correct angle for Rip-sawing.

Correct cutting angle

- When starting a saw cut draw the saw backwards for three or four strokes. Your thumb can be used as a steadying gauge and a guide for these starting cuts. When sawing proper begins your thumb should be tucked in out of danger.

The different teeth on various saws determine how they are used. Saws with cross-cut teeth are best used at 45° to the wood while those with rip-saw pattern teeth work best when used at 60° to the wood. The tenon or back saw is best used horizontally with the aid of a bench hook.

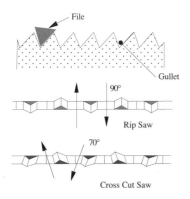

File

Gullet

90°

Rip Saw

70°

Cross Cut Saw

Sharpening

Done with a saw file which is a file having an equilateral triangular section (the angle between each tooth of any saw is 60°). Cross-cut saws are filed at an approximate angle of 70° to the blade and rip saws at 90° to the blade.

Activities

1. List four saws for straight cutting and four for curved cutting. In your own words describe the main difference between each group.

2. Explain with the aid of diagrams the following terms:
   a) kerf;
   b) set;
   c) gullet;
   d) teeth per 25mm.

3. List the saws that have cross-cut style teeth.

4. Using diagrams explain the difference between cross-cut saw teeth and rip-saw teeth.

5. How does the size of a saw's teeth effect its use?

6. If the saw sticks in the wood can you suggest possible causes of and possible solutions to this problem.

7. Sketch a tenon saw and name its parts.

8. Why does the tenon saw have a reinforcing grip? Why do all saws not have this?

9. Explain the following terms:
   a) straight back;
   b) skew back;
   c) taper grinding.

10. Which would you prefer, plastic-handled saws or wooden-handled saws? Give reasons for your answer.

11. What are the differences between a dovetail saw and a tenon saw?

12. Why is a coping saw called a tension saw? Name another tension saw.

13. Sketch a pad saw. Why is its saw blade so thick?

14. What is the important thing to remember when using a coping saw?

15. Why is a hacksaw suitable for cutting metal and plastic when the other saws are not?

16. Why is the index finger placed along the handle when sawing?

17. Explain how to sharpen a rib saw, and a cross-cut saw.

18. What safety precautions would you give to somebody using a saw for the first time?

Paring tools

Bench planes and block plane

Planing is a way of removing waste wood or smoothing a surface before a finish is applied. The two types of plane most commonly used are:

a) the jack plane;

b) the smoothing plane.

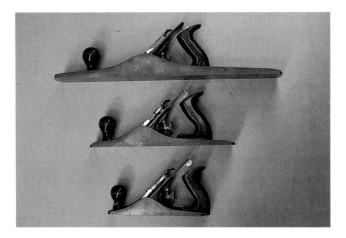

Planes: Try plane (top); Jack plane (centre); Smoothing plane (bottom)

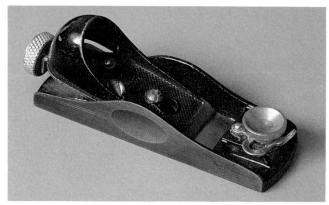

Block plane

Jack plane

Smoothing plane

The smoothing plane, jack plane and try plane have what is known as a **double blade**. The cutting iron is the part of the plane which actually cuts the wood. The cap iron helps the wood shavings to curl away smoothly from the cutting edge of the blade and prevents tearing of the wood surface.

TYPE	USES	LENGTH	BLADE WIDTHS
Block Plane	A small plane which has its blade set at a lower angle than the jack or smoothing planes. This reduces the risk of chipping the blade. The block plane is used with one hand only and is useful for planing plastic laminates	140–180mm	35mm 40mm
Smoothing Plane	Used primarily to smooth and clean timber before it is glass papered. The smoothing plane is lighter than the jack plane and easier to control.	213–245mm	45mm 50mm 60mm
Jack Plane	Designed to plane uneven surfaces straight and true. It is ideal when cutting away a lot of waste wood down to a finishing line	355–380mm	50mm 60mm
Try Plane	A large plane which requires considerable skill to use accurately. The long sole of the plane allows long pieces of timber to be planed straight and true.	460–560mm	60mm

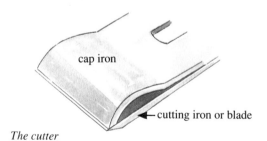

The cutter

Cap iron

Using a plane

- If the person using the plane is right handed then they will stand with their right side nearest the work bench.

- Make sure that the timber to be planed is secured in the vice or by a bench stop.

- Stand behind the workpiece with your feet apart. This will give you better control (see drawing).

Correct stance

Parts:

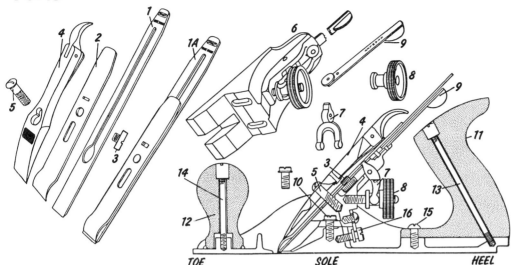

1A Double Plane Iron
1 Single " "
2 Cap Iron
3 Cap Iron Screw
4 Lever Cap
5 Lever Cap Screw
6 Frog Complete
7 "Y" Adjusting Lever
8 Adjusting Nut
9 Lateral Adjusting Lever
10 Frog Screw
11 Handle
12 Knob
13 Handle Bolt & Nut
14 Knob Bolt & Nut
15 Handle Screw
16 Frog Adjusting Screw

TOE SOLE HEEL

Parts of the plane

- In order to keep the sole of the plane flat on the surface of the wood, the point at which most of the the downward pressure is applied must change between the start of the cut and the end of the cut. Note also that you must use the plane in the direction naturally followed by the wood, i.e. 'with the grain'.

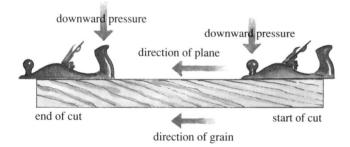

if you try to plane from one end to the other, pieces will split off and spoil the work piece

one way to overcome this is to plane from each end to the centre

Health and safety

- Always keep the cutting iron sharp: it is safer and will give better results.

- Do not run your fingers along the sole of a plane.

- Place the plane on its side in the well of the bench between planing operations.

- When the plane is not in use the cutter should be retracted.

Planing end grain

Grinding and sharpening

To ensure that planes and chisels perform to their best, it is important to regularly sharpen their cutting edges.

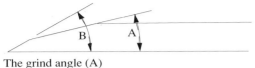

The grind angle (A)
The sharpening angle (B)

The cutting edges of chisels and planes have two important and distinct angles:

- the grinding angle;
- the sharpening angle.

It is not necessary to grind a cutting edge every time it is to be sharpened but you will need to re-grind when:

a) the bevel has become round due to careless sharpening;

b) the bevel has become worn due to sharpening;

c) the cutting edge has become chipped from use.

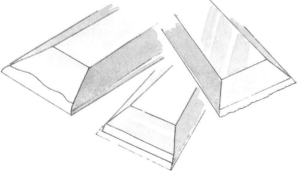

If a chisel or plane cutting iron needs to be re-ground the best method is to use a large diameter, slow-running grindstone. Many modern grindstones are made from artificial stone and are oil lubricated.

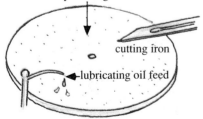

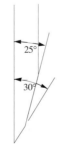

Grinding and sharpening angles for chisels and planes

Grinding Angle 25°
Sharpening Angle 30°

Sharpening a plane cutting iron

1. Remove plane irons from plane.

2. Lay the blades flat on the workbench and use a screwdriver to remove the cap iron.

3. Sharpen the cutting iron on the oilstone. Use the fine side of a combination oilstone and use a light machine oil to keep the stone lubricated. Remember the sharpening angle for cutting irons is 30°.

Position of hands when using oilstone

4. Remove birr on the oilstone, making sure to keep the blade flat on the oilstone.

5. Wipe the blade with a cloth and replace in plane.

Note. The cutting edge of a chisel is sharpened in a similar manner and to the same angle as the cutting iron in a plane.

Chisels

The chisel is one of the most important tools used when working with wood. Chisels are available in sizes ranging from 3mm to 38mm, which refers to the width of the blade. In the workshop the most common sizes are 6mm, 12mm, 18mm and 25mm.

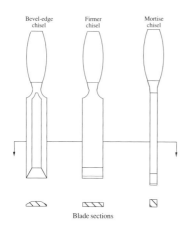

Blade sections

The blade of the chisel is cast steel, hardened and tempered. The handles of most modern chisels are made of plastic, but some chisels have timber handles. Beech, ash and boxwood are the most popular timbers used.

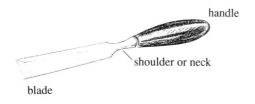

Bevel edged chisel

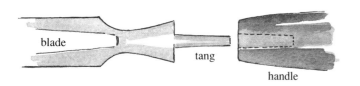

Stanley bolster construction

Health and safety

• When using any chisel ensure all parts of the body are kept behind the cutting edge of the chisel.

There are three different types of chisels commonly used:

1. the bevel-edged chisel;
2. the firmer or square-edged chisel;
3. the mortise chisel.

The bevel-edged chisel is used for general purpose woodworking and is particularly useful when paring trenches with sides at an angle of less than 90°. It is also used for the cutting of dovetails. Here it is being used horizontally.

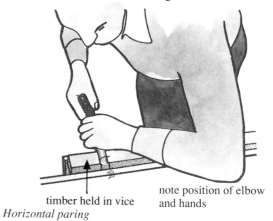

Horizontal paring

The square-edged firmer chisel is used for general purpose woodworking and for light chopping and mortising. Here it is being used to pare vertically.

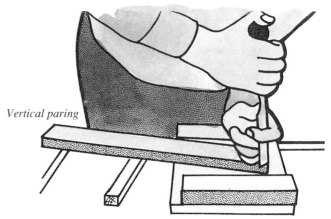

Vertical paring

timber supported; note position of hands

The mortise chisel is used with a mallet to cut mortises. The blade and handle are reinforced to withstand the blows from the mallet.

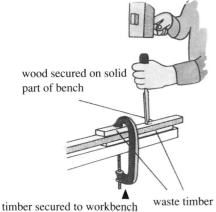

wood secured on solid part of bench

timber secured to workbench with 'G' cramp

waste timber

Chopping and mortising

Gouges

A gouge may be described as being similar to a chisel but having a curved blade.

The two types of gouge most frequently used are:

a) the firmer gouge;

b) the paring gouge.

The firmer gouge is ground on the outside which makes it very suited to the paring of curved recesses.

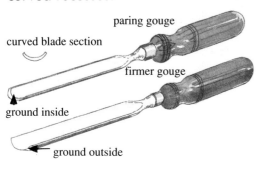

paring gouge

curved blade section

firmer gouge

ground inside

ground outside

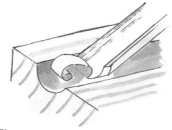

Firmer gouge

The paring gouge is ground on the inside and is therefore suited to working concave curves. It is also useful for paring a curved surface on the edge of a workpiece.

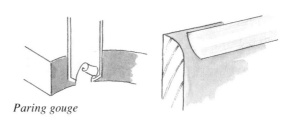

Paring gouge

Sharpening gouges

The firmer gouge is bevelled on the outside and can therefore be sharpened on the oilstone.

As the paring gouge is bevelled on the inside it is rather difficult to sharpen. It is sharpened with a curved oilstone known as a slipstone.

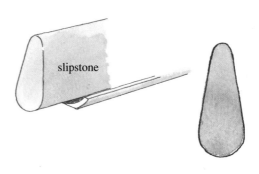

slipstone

Sharpening paring gouge

Slipstone section

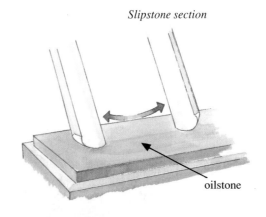

oilstone

Sharpening a gouge

Other useful planes

The rebate plane

When part of a piece of wood is is cut away to form a step, the space that is then formed is known as a rebate. A continuous rebate is commonly used where glass is to be inserted into a frame. The plane used for this type of work is shown below and is known as a rebate plane.

Rebate plane

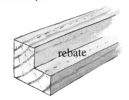

Timber framing

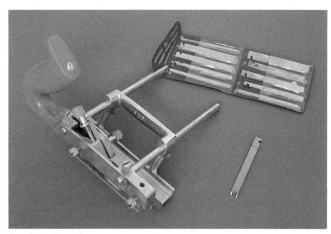

Combination plane

The plough plane

When it is necessary to cut a groove along the grain of a workpiece, a plough plane may be used. A range of different sized cutters is available. The most frequently used are between 3mm and 19mm in width.

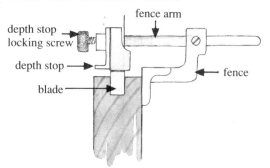

Front view of plough plane

The router

Very useful for levelling the bottom of a groove or trench. As it is fitted with a depth gauge the depth of a trench can be finished to the desired measurement. It is particularly useful when finishing a stopped housing joint.

The router

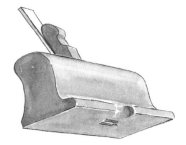

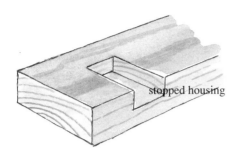

stopped housing

The spokeshave

A small, lightweight tool used to work curved surfaces on timber. There are two different types of spokeshave:

    1. spokeshaves which have a curved face and are used to work concave curves;

    2. spokeshaves which have a flat face are used to work convex curves.

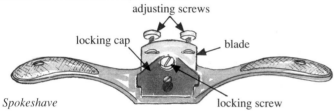

adjusting screws

locking cap

blade

locking screw

Spokeshave

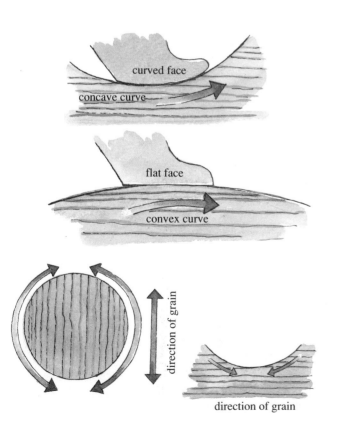

curved face

concave curve

flat face

convex curve

direction of grain

direction of grain

Abrasive tools

Surform

A cross between a plane and a file. They come in various shapes and sizes and are used to shape and sculpt timber, fibreglass, plastics and some light metals. Surforms are different from a conventional file or rasp in that they allow the waste material to pass through the blade. Surforms do not produce as smooth a finish as the conventional planes.

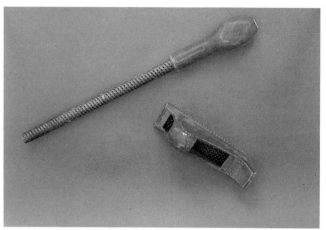

Surform tools

flat blade

Rasp

Used for similar purposes to the surform. It looks very much like a file but has much rougher teeth for cutting wood.

Rasp

167

Files

A useful tool for the shaping of metals and plastics. They come in a range of shapes and sizes and can be obtained with rough or smooth teeth. It is important to choose the correct file for the job you have to do.

Parts of a file

- If you are filing a long flat edge, then choose a large flat file.

- If you are removing a square or rectangular section from the inside of the workpiece choose a square file.

- If you need to file an internal angle which is less than 90°, use a three-square file.

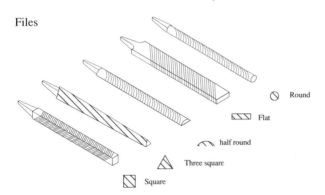

Files

Round
Flat
half round
Three square
Square

Cross filing

Cross filing is used to remove waste material and to file down to a line.

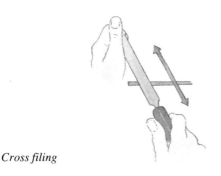

Cross filing

Draw filing

Draw filing is done with a smooth file to produce a smooth shiny finish to the edge of the material.

Draw filing

Boring tools

The rachet brace

A bit and brace are used to bore holes in wood. The smallest twist bit normally available is 6mm. Braces are of two main types, **plain** and **rachet**, and these are used to hold and turn the bit while boring.

The rachet brace is useful when working in a confined area which will not allow a full turn of the brace.

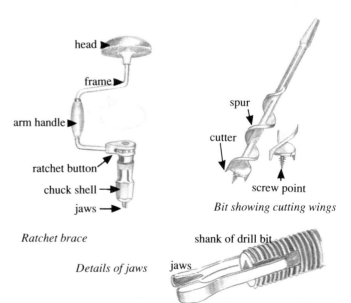

head
frame
arm handle
ratchet button
chuck shell
jaws
spur
cutter
screw point

Bit showing cutting wings

Ratchet brace

shank of drill bit
jaws

Details of jaws

A countersink bit is used to bore a small recess at the mouth of a bored screwhole. This recess allows the head of a countersunk screw to finish just below the level of the woodsurface.

If holes need to be bored to a certain depth you may:

(i) use a custom-made adjustable depth stop, or

(ii) make your own depth stop from a piece of waste timber.

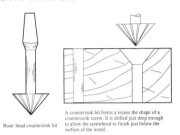

Rose head countersink bit

A countersink bit forms a recess the shape of a countersunk screw. It is drilled just deep enough to allow the screwhead to finish just below the surface of the wood.

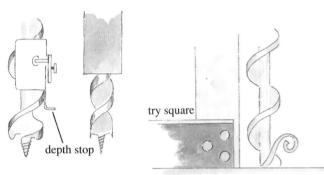

depth stop

try square

Usually holes have to be bored perpendicular to the surface of the timber. The accuracy of the boring can be checked by placing a try square on the workpiece.

Small holes to take screws, nails or rivets can generally be drilled with the hand drill. This tool is sometimes known as a **wheelbrace**. The hand drill usually takes drills up to 8mm.

> The centre of the hole to be drilled should be marked with a bradawl or centre punch. This will help to centre the drill and accurately bore the hole.

Larger hand drills are available which will take drills up to 15mm in diameter. They are designed to be pushed from the chest and are therefore known as **breast drills**.

Health and safety

- Care must be taken not to push the hand drill sideways while drilling. Twist drills are rather brittle and may snap in the hole.

The hand drill		
Type of drill	*Uses*	*Common sizes*
Twist drill	Used to drill holes in plastic, wood and light materials	3 to 12mm
Countersink drill	Used to taper the end of a hole, allowing screwheads to go below the surface, in wood, plastic and metal.	12mm
Hole saw	Used to bore very large holes in wood and some plastics. Can also be used to make discs	14 to 63mm

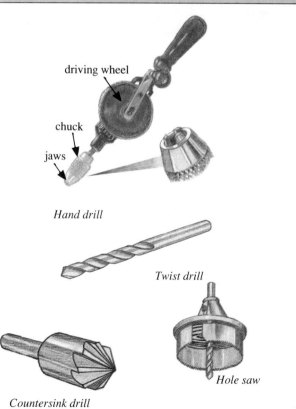

driving wheel

chuck

jaws

Hand drill

Twist drill

Countersink drill

Hole saw

169

12

Power tools

Woodworking machinery has been essential for the economic production of virtually all timber artifacts for many years. But in more recent times the use of portable power tools and light machinery has become popular in school workshops. Power tools greatly reduce the amount of time and labour need to perform many woodworking operations.

Powered circular saw and hand saw

Portable power tools fitted with electric motors are very popular but in some situations tools which are powered by compressed air are used.

Health and safety

- If used incorrectly, power tools and machinery may be dangerous. Therefore do not use any tool unless you have permission to do so and a supervising adult is present.

Recent advances in technology have facilitated the introduction of machinery controlled by computer.

CNC router

Computer numerically controlled (CNC) machinery allows the operator to programme the computer to instruct the machine to produce the required item. Therefore a large number of identical items can be produced.

The following section deals with the light machinery and portable power tools which may be used by pupils in the manufacturing of a project.

170

Check list

Before using a powered tool, ask yourself the following questions.

- Is the tool you wish to use suitable for the job you are doing?

- Is the area you wish to work in suitable?

- Is the mains electricity supply suited to the tool you wish to use?

- Have you been instructed in how to use the power tool?

- Do you have the permission of a teacher or an adult in charge to use the power tool?

- Is it necessary to use goggles or other protective clothing while using the power tool?

- Is the tool clean and in good working order?

- Is the plug on the appliance or the mains power socket damaged?

- Is the tool correctly wired and earthed?

- Is the appliance switched off before you plug it into the mains?

- Is the tool about to be started up while it is under load?

Health and safety

Always get permission from your teacher before attempting to use any portable power tool. Then, before using the tool, ensure that you make the following safety checks.

- Check that the machine is suited to the main power supply.

- Check that the lead and the plug are not damaged.

- Check that the power tool is switched off.

- Check that the socket is switched off.

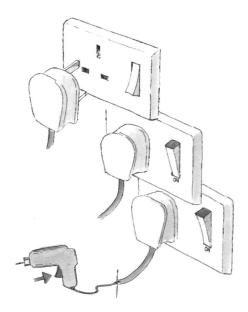

If the above safety procedures have been correctly followed you may now:

1. plug in the appliance;
2. switch on at the socket;
3. switch on at the appliance.

The mortising machine

The mortise and tenon joint is one of the most frequently used joints in woodwork, but it is also one of the most laborious to produce by hand. However, mortises can be quickly and accurately worked using the mortising machine.

Mortising machine

It consists of a motor, which is mounted on vertical slides, and an adjustable worktable. The worktable is fitted with a clamp to secure the material being mortised.

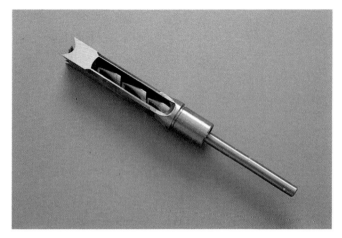

Hollow square chisel

The hollow mortise chisel cuts in two stages:

1. The auger removes the central section by boring.

2. The cutting edges of the chisel remove the remaining corners of the mortise in a cutting action.

Hatched area of mortise removed by auger

Hatched area of mortise removed by chisel

The lower end of the motor is connected to a collar to which different sizes of hollow square chisels can be fitted. A hollow chisel consists of two parts: the square chisel itself and an auger which runs within the hollow portion of the chisel.

It is important that there is a gap of 2–3mm between the cutting edges of the hollow chisel and the auger to avoid friction between the two parts.

The narrow bandsaw

Can be used to cut curved or intricately shaped items from timber and manufactured boards as well as from light metals and plastics. It is important to ensure that the correct type and size of blade is fitted to suit the operation in hand.

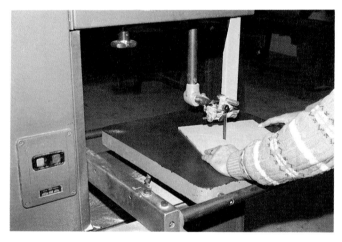

Bandsaw in use

A number of standard jigs are available and many more can be readily constructed to facilitate the manufacturing of large numbers of curved items.

The narrow bandsaw

Health and safety

- It is important to apply the brake after the machine has been turned off as the blade will continue to run for some time.

The sawblade itself consists of a continuous band which passes over two large wheels, one of which is driven by a motor. Narrow blades of about 3mm width are available and they are used when cutting small radius curves in light material. Generally speaking, the size of blade used will depend upon the thickness of the material and the radii of the curves being cut.

Bandsaw blade arrangement

To prevent the blade from being forced off the wheels while cutting, the back edge of the blade is supported by a hardened steel disc which is mounted on ball-bearings. As the back of the moving blade contacts the disc, the disc rotates and friction is reduced.

The jig-saw

Chiefly used for the cutting of intricate shapes in wood, metal and plastics. It is also useful for the cutting of internal pockets in timber, such as those cut into worktops to receive sinks. A range of blades for cutting different materials is available, and hardwood up to 60mm can be cut.

Jig saw

Using the jig saw

173

Can you give examples of situations where internal pockets need to be cut from materials using a jig-saw?

Health and safety

- Ensure that the work is firmly clamped down before beginning to cut. Also make sure that the blade is stationary before it is placed into or removed from a cut.

Router in operation

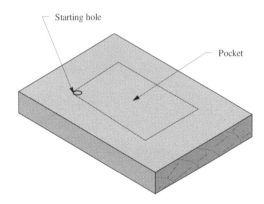

Cutting out a pocket

When cutting internal pockets the most convenient way of starting the saw is to bore a hole through the timber to receive the sawblade.

The router

An extremely useful and versatile portable power tool. It is capable of a wide range of operations, including moulding, ploughing, grooving, drilling, plunge cutting and trimming the edges of veneers and plastic laminates.

The router can be used with custom-made jigs or templates which allow intricate items to be accurately reproduced. An adjustable fence is also available which allows the operator to plough or mould parallel to a finished edge of the timber.

A range of cutters is available to suit most operations. Some examples are shown here.

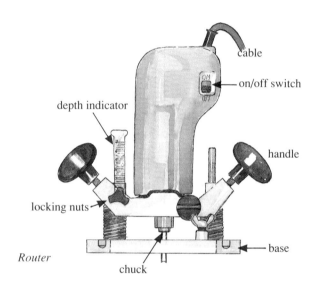

Router

There is a wide range of cutter profiles available

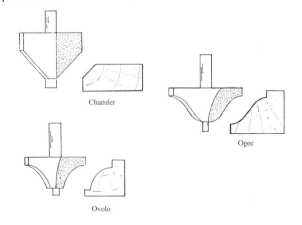

Chamfer

Ogee

Ovolo

Examples of cutter profile

Health and safety

- When viewed from above the cutter rotates in a clockwise direction. It is very important that the router is fed in the opposite direction to the rotation of the cutter.

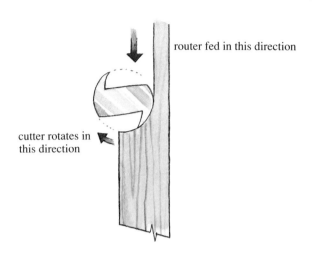

router fed in this direction

cutter rotates in this direction

The electric drill

The portable power drill is one of the most widely used portable tools. Two types are commonly used in woodworking: the heavy-duty drill and the general-purpose drill.

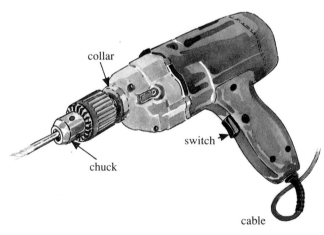

collar

chuck

switch

cable

Electric drill

Heavy-duty drill: bores steel up to 23mm thick and is useful for boring concrete and masonry to receive fastenings. The heavy-duty drill is usually fitted with a hammer action.

General-purpose drills are smaller and are capable of drilling steel up to 12mm thickness.

Both types of drill can be mounted on stands and used as a light bench machine.

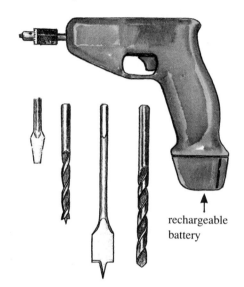

rechargeable battery

Cordless rechargeable drill with bits

A recent development is that of the **cordless drill** which is powered by a rechargeable battery and is very useful as a powered screwdriver. The cordless drill, as well as the heavy-duty and general-purpose drills, is capable of being fitted with a wide variety of attachments, examples of which are shown above.

Health and safety

- It is essential that the material being drilled is securely held in the clamp or vice.

By examining a number of attachments can you decide which are designed for boring a) metal, b) wood, c) masonry? Can you suggest reasons why these attachments have different designs?

The belt sander

Uses a continuous belt of abrasive material which passes over rollers at the front and back of the machine. Various grades of belt are available and the belt sander is suitable for sanding large flat surfaces.

The belt sander

Belt sander in use

Health and safety

- Ensure that the abrasive belt has stopped revolving before it is placed on the bench and released.

The disc sander

Ideal for producing a high-quality finish on the end-grain of timber. Sizes range from 12.5mm to 22.5mm and the rotating head has a flexible rubber backing to which the sanding material is fixed. Attachments which can be used with the disc sander include a variety of polishing pads and wire brushes.

Abrasive theory

Sanding discs and abrasive paper are made up of abrasive particles which are bonded to a backing fabric or paper. The individual abrasive particles have sharp edges, and it is the edges which remove layers of the material during the sanding operation.

The orbital sander

So called because of the rapidly rotating action of its sanding surface, it is an excellent tool for producing high-quality finishes on flat or curved surfaces. Due to its relatively light weight the sander can be used vertically as well as on horizontal surfaces. The abrasive sheet is secured on the flexible rubber base of the sander by two spring-loaded clamps. A cordless version of the orbital sander is also available.

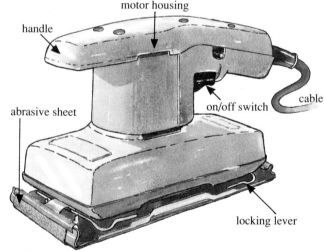

The orbital sander

The spray gun

Used in conjunction with an electrically powered compressor which first filters the air, pressurises it and then transfers the air to the gun by way of a flexible hose. The pressurised air is mixed with a liquid finish in the spray gun and the finish is deposited on the surface of the work in the form of very fine droplets.

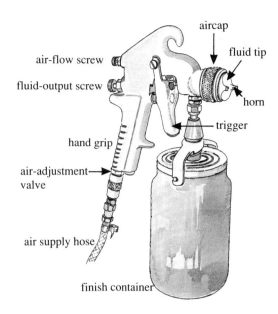

The spray gun

Labels: aircap, air-flow screw, fluid tip, fluid-output screw, horn, hand grip, trigger, air-adjustment valve, air supply hose, finish container

> When you are spraying indoors, it is important that you work in a specially constructed **spraying booth**. A spraying booth isolates the spraying area from the rest of the workshop. The booth must also be fitted with a special extractor fan to remove the flammable fumes from the spraying area.

Health and safety

- Follow the instructions and safety procedures included with each particular liquid finish.

- Wear goggles and a respirator at all times while in the spraying booth.

- Do not allow any naked flames into the spraying area.

- Do not clean the spray gun without first releasing the air pressure.

- If the gun becomes blocked disconnect it from the compressor before attempting to unblock.

Cleaning the spray gun

Unscrew the finish container and empty it. Pour some clean solvent into the container and reconnect it to the spray gun. In a safe area, operate the gun until a clear spray emerges.

Release the air pressure, disconnect the gun from the compressor and dismantle the spray gun. Then, clean each component with a clean cloth dampened with thinner. Reassemble the spray gun and store safely.

Activities

1. Outline four safety precautions regarding the use of portable power tools in the workshop.

2. What type of tool would be suitable for cutting a large hole or pocket in the centre of a wide piece of timber? Describe how you would use the chosen tool to remove the pocket of timber.

3. Describe, using sketches, how the mortising machine uses the hollow square chisel to work a mortise.

4. Name three different types of portable sander and describe the different uses of each type.

5. Neatly sketch a belt sander and name all parts of the appliance. Explain how a sander removes material from the surface of the wood.

6. Produce a detailed sketch of a portable power drill and name all parts. Sketch four different attachments which may be used with the drill.

7. Sketch and name the main parts of a cordless drill. What are the advantages and disadvantages of a cordless drill in comparison to a drill powered from mains electricity?

8. What are the advantages and disadvantages of power tools in relation to traditional hand tools?

9. Describe how the blade is fitted and guarded on the narrow band saw.

10. In which direction should the router be moved in relation to the direction in which the cutter rotates? Use a sketch to explain your answer.

11. Sketch and name the parts of a portable router. Sketch five different cutters which could be used with the router.

12. Describe four situations where it would be necessary to wear goggles when using a power tool.

13. Design and draw a poster (A3 size) which will promote the safe use of portable power tools in the workshop.

14. Examine a 3-pin plug as used on some power tools. Draw, to a large scale, an inside view of the plug explaining the correct way to wire the plug.

15. Examine four items in your own home, e.g. a timber door, cabinet or chair, and suggest which power tools might have been used during its manufacture. Use sketches to illustrate your answer.

16. Examine the appliances listed below and describe the built-in safety features which are used on each device, e.g. guards, fuses, special switches, etc. Suggest ways in which these features might be improved or any other changes which could make the tool safer to use:

   a) router;

   b) belt sander;

   c) power drill;

   d) mortising machine.

13

Fasteners

Nails

Nails are used as a quick and easy method of joining wood. Unfortunately nails alone rarely make a strong joint and they often look unsightly. Several things can be done to strengthen the joint. For example, glue can be used in conjunction with nails to give extra rigidity. The nails will hold the wood together while the glue sets. Alternatively nails can be clinched or we can use a method called **dovetail nailing** or **skew nailing**; more about this later.

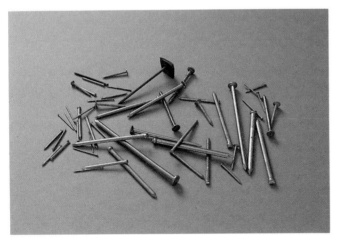

Examples of nails

Nails have been in use for thousands of years. Up until about a hundred years ago all nails were hand cut. Nowadays practically all nails are machine cut although some hand-cut nails are still used for particular types of work.

Nails have three parts: the point, the shank and the head. They are generally made from mild steel although copper, brass and hardened-steel nails are also available. Copper and brass nails will resist corrosion and are often decorative. Hardened-steel nails (masonry nails) are used for hammering into brick, or block walls.

Round wire nails

Both the head and the shank are circular. They give a strong fixing but the finished appearance is poor. They are used for rough carpentry, for construction mock-ups and for general-purpose work.

> Finish: bright mild steel
>
> Size: 18–150mm.

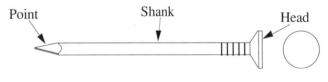

Point   Shank   Head

Round wire nail

Oval wire nails

The head and shank are oval in section. Again they give a strong fixing but the appearance is much better as the small head can be punched below the surface of the wood. These nails are designed to reduce the risk of splitting the wood and so the wide part of the section should be driven parallel to the wood grain.

Finish: bright mild steel

Size: 18–100mm.

Oval wire nail

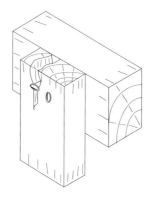

Oval nails should be driven with the wide part of the shank parallel to the grain. This reduces the chance of splitting.

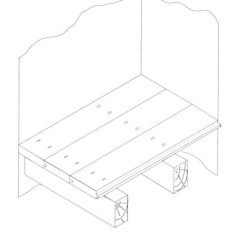

Lost head nails are often used for fixing floor boards

Flooring brad

Panel pins

These are a smaller version of the lost-head nail, having narrow shanks and small heads. They are used for securing thin plywood or hardboard and for fixing small joints. The thickness of the shank (gauge) is denoted by numbers.

Finish: bright mild steel, sometimes copper coated

Size: 12–50mm.

Panel pin

Lost-head nails

This nail is very like those mentioned above except that it has a very small head. They can be of round or oval section. More of a finishing nail, the head can be easily punched below the surface. These nails are often used for fixing floor boards.

Finish: bright mild steel

Size: 40–100mm.

Lost head nail

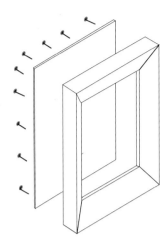

Panel pins are used to fix light panels

Clout nails

Clout nails are small sturdy nails with very wide flat heads. They are very useful for fixing metal sheeting or felt to wood. Usually used outside, these nails are galvanised to prevent corrosion.

Finish: galvanised

Size 15–62mm.

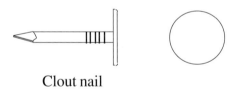

Clout nail

Cut tacks

This nail is designed for attaching fabric to wooden frames, and is used frequently in upholstery. Its sharp point is pushed into the wood ready for driving. The wide head grips the fabric.

Finish: blued steel

Size: 12–25mm.

Cut tack

Upholstery nails

As the name suggests, these nails are used for upholstery or for fixing leather to wood. These are thin nails with dome-shaped heads.

Finish: brass, chrome, bronze, nickel plated or black japanned

Size: 12–20mm.

Upholstery nail

The upholstery nail is often used on furniture

Wiggle nails or corrugated fasteners

Although not nails in the accepted sense, these fasteners are very useful when making mitres and butt joints in rough framing. Placed across the joint line the fastener is driven flush with the surface of the wood.

Finish: bright steel

Size: 6–25mm deep with 2–7 corrugation.

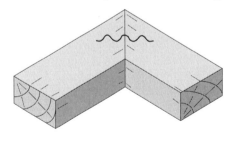

Used in framing

Wiggle nail

Staples

Staples are used for fixing wires or cables to wood. They have two shanks and points.

Finish: bright steel, galvanised steel

Size: 12–50mm.

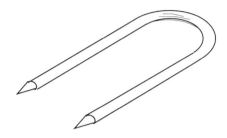

Staple

Use of nails

Where possible nails should always be punched below the surface of the wood using a nail punch. This allows the wood to be cleaned off afterwards with a plane without damaging the blade. If required the little nail hole can then be filled.

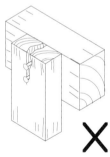

Putting nails in line along the grain can cause splitting.

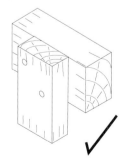

Staggering the nails is much less likely to crack the wood.

If you have a number of nails to put into a piece of wood never place the nails in a straight line along the grain as this can often cause the wood to split. The nails should in fact be staggered. If the wood still tends to split try blunting the point of the nail slightly; this often helps.

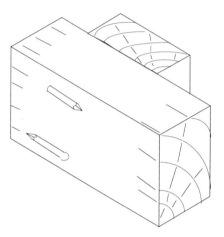

A clinched nail can often give added strength but can be difficult to remove and can look unsightly

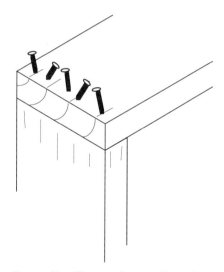

Dovetail nailing or skew nailing gives a much stronger joint.

Hardwoods in particular tend to split when being nailed. In this case a hole slightly smaller than the diameter of the shank of the nail may be drilled into the wood.

A better nailed joint is achieved if the nails are inclined to give a dovetailing effect. A clinched nail gives a very strong if perhaps unsightly joint. This is where the nail is driven through two pieces of wood and projects out at the back. The part that is projecting out is bent over parallel to the grain.

If the nails tend to bend when being driven try smearing a little oil on them before you start. Make sure that you strike the nail straight and also clean the face of the hammer with a small piece of emery paper.

Screws

Screws have not been in use for as long as nails have. Screws are primarily used for joining wood to wood, the clamping force they provide creating an extremely strong joint that is easily dismantled. They are also used for attaching fittings such as hinges and locks.

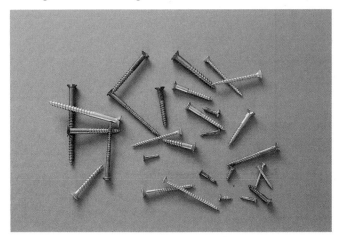

Examples of screws

The size, shape and material used in a screw depend to a large extent on the job to which it is to be put. There are three principal types of screw:

a) the countersunk head screw;

b) the round head screw;

c) the raised head screw.

Screw heads are slotted to take screwdriver blades. The most common type have a single slot to take a cabinet-type screwdriver. Others have cross-shaped slots to take philips and pozidrive screwdrivers.

Screws are usually made from mild steel, stainless steel or brass. Mild steel screws are often coated with nickel, chromium or are blued or black japanned. These coats can be strictly for decorative purposes or to prevent corrosion. Brass screws will not corrode and for this reason are more useful for outdoor use on timbers like oak which has a high acidic content.

The main parts of a screw are the head, the shank, the thread and the point. When buying screws you must specify the length, the type of head required, the material and the thickness. The thickness or gauge of a screw is determined by a scale of numbers between 0 and 24. The bigger the number the thicker the screw, e.g. a no. 5 screw is about 3mm in diameter and a no. 14 screw is about 6mm in diameter.

Length	Gauge Number															
6 mm	0	1	2													
9 mm		1	2	3			6		8							
12 mm			2	3	4	5	6	7	8							
16 mm				3	4	5	6	7	8		10					
18 mm				3	4	5	6	7	8	9	10	12				
22 mm					4		6	7	8							
25 mm				3	4	5	6	7	8	9	10	12	14			
32 mm					4	5	6	7	8	9	10	12	14	16		
38 mm					4		6	7	8	9	10	12	14	16		
44 mm							6	7	8	9	10	12	14	16		
50 mm							6	7	8	9	10	12	14	16	18	20
54 mm							6		8		10	12	14			
60 mm							6		8	9	10	12	14	16		
70 mm									8		10	12	14			
75 mm							6		8		10	12	14	16	18	20
89 mm									8		10	12	14	16		
100 mm									8		10	12	14	16	18	20

So to order screws you must specify four things, e.g. 50mm x 8 gauge brass raised head, or, 12mm x 2 gauge steel countersunk.

Countersunk head screws

These are flat-topped screws which when inserted fully lie flush or level with the top of the wood. They are used for general-purpose work; hinges, locks, framing, etc. They are made of a wide range of materials, mild steel being the most common. If they are to be exposed to dampness or acid wood (e.g. oak), brass or galvanised screws are more advisable. It must be remembered, however, that brass screws are more easily broken. The wood must be countersunk to the correct depth to receive the head of the screw. Lengths vary from 6mm up to 150mm.

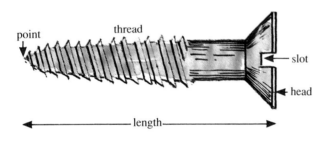

Countersunk head screw

Round head screws

Made from the same materials as countersunk screws, these are mainly used for securing metal fittings to wood, e.g. handles, name plates, finger plates. They are particularly useful when fitting sheet material which is too thin to countersink. The round head screw has a domed top and is quite decorative. The length of the screw is measured as shown on the diagram. Available in lengths from 12mm to 50mm.

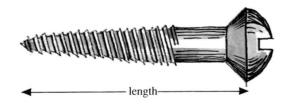

Round head screw

Raised head screws

This screw has a head which is a combination of the countersunk head and the round head. The countersunk part of the head must be sunk into the material. The domed top then lies proud of the surface. Generally used for fixing metal plates to wood where added strength is needed. The length varies between 10mm and 35mm and is measured as shown.

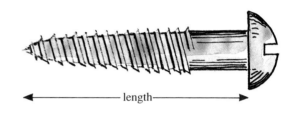

Raised head screw

Special screws

Twin threaded screws

A new generation of wood screws is made with coarse twin threads which provides a strong fixing even in chipboard. Compared to a conventional screw, more of the overall length is threaded and the shank is much narrower so there is less risk of splitting the wood. The steep pitch of the threads enable the screw to be driven quickly.

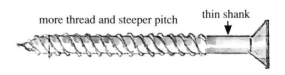

Twin thread screw

Clutch head screw

This is a thief-proof screw used for fixing locks or securing valuable objects. It is inserted with an ordinary straight-topped screwdriver. When an attempt is made to remove the screw, however, the tip of the screwdriver will get no grip and will ride out of the slot.

Clutch head screw

Although screws are extremely useful many woodworkers regard exposed screw heads as unsightly. There are several types of fitting that conceal screw heads or enhance their appearance.

Fittings for screws

Recessed screw cup

This is a durable brass collar that fits directly below the head of a countersunk screw. It lies flush with the surface.

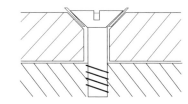

Recessed screw cup

Surface-mounted screw cup

Made from pressed brass, this fitting provides a raised collar for countersunk or raised-head screws. This is ideal for softwood since it increases the bearing area beneath the screw head. It also means that no countersinking has to be done.

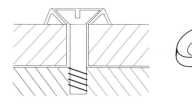

Surface mounted screw cup

Domed cover

This fitting comes in two parts. A plastic dome snaps over the rim of a matching screw cap to hide the head of the woodscrew.

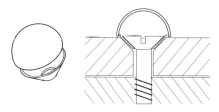

Domed cover and cup

Cross head cover

This is a moulded plastic cover with a spigot on the underside that provides a tight-friction fit in the screw slots. This type of fitting is used quite frequently on kitchen cabinets.

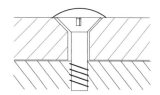

Cross head cover

Mirror screw cover

This fitting has a chrome or brass dome with a threaded spigot that screws into the top of special countersunk screws. Designed particularly to hold mirror glass, these may also be used for attaching plaques and nameplates to walls, etc.

Mirror screw and cover

Use of screws

The gripping power of a screw depends on the head being larger than the hole made in the top piece of timber or metal. It also depends on the thread getting a grip in the second piece of wood.

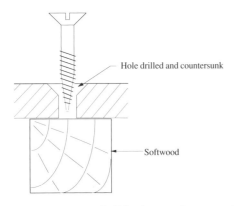

Hole drilled and countersunk

Softwood

It is necessary to drill holes in the wood to receive all but the smallest of screws. Boring can be done by a bradawl or a hand drill. The hole for the shank of the screw should be a clearance hole; being slightly larger than the shank diameter. In softwoods it is sufficient to bore the top piece of wood for the shank and countersink for the head if necessary. Hardwoods, however, because of their hardness and tendency to split, need a pilot hole for the thread in the second piece of wood. This hole should be about half the size used for the shank. It is very important that these holes are drilled to the proper sizes. If a hole for the shank in the top piece of wood is too small then you will have difficulty pulling the two pieces together. Alternatively if the pilot hole in the lower piece of wood is too large then the thread will have a poor grip, resulting in a weak joint.

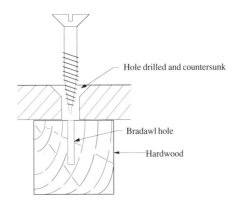

Hole drilled and countersunk

Bradawl hole

Hardwood

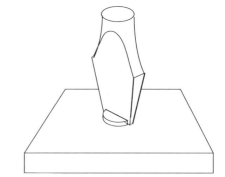

A screwdriver whose blade is too broad will damage the wood

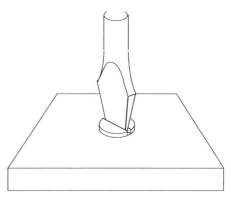

When the blade is too narrow it will damage the screw slot

When encountering problems driving a screw try greasing the shank and thread with soap, grease, wax or oil. Never use a hammer as this reduces its gripping power. Excessive force on a screw will cause it to snap; brass screws are particularly vulnerable to this. A solution to this would be to drive a steel screw into the hole first to cut a path and then replace it with a brass one.

When selecting a screwdriver always choose one whose tip fits the screw head exactly. It will drive the screw with the minimum of effort without damaging either the screw head or the work.

Activities

1. What is the main difference between nails and screws?

186

2. What advantage has an oval nail got over a round wire nail? Make a neat diagram of each nail.

3. Suggest four places where the lost head nail would be used.

4. Draw a diagram of a wiggle nail. Where would this be used?

5. Explain with the aid of a diagram the meaning of dovetail nailing. Why is this stronger than ordinary nailing?

6. Describe some of the problems which can be encountered when using nails. Suggest methods of solving these problems.

7. Describe what the term clinching means. What are the advantages and disadvantages?

8. Draw a diagram of any screw and describe its parts.

9. Compare steel screws with brass screws, giving details of when you would use each.

10. Draw diagrams of three different screw heads and name each.

11. Some screws have threads up along their whole length. What is the advantage of this?

12. Describe with the help of diagrams how you would bore holes for screws in

    a) softwoods;

    b) hardwoods.

13. What information do you have to give when buying screws?

14. How is a screw thickness specified?

15. Describe two types of screw cap and how and where they are used.

16. Give three handy hints on driving screws.

Knockdown fittings

When making large-scale constructions, especially those that have to be assembled on site, you will usually find it expedient to joint your work with mechanical fittings rather than with traditional joints and adhesives. The knockdown fittings are also convenient when you wish to build a workpiece which may be dismantled at some future date for transportation. In general knockdown fittings are designed for use with square cut butt joints and require precisely bored holes for accurate positioning. As a result they are most popular with woodworkers who are equipped with power tools and machinery.

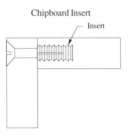

Chipboard Insert
— Insert

Chipboard insert

It is nearly impossible to make a really strong fixing in the edge of chipboard even using special wood screws. These threaded nylon inserts pushed into pre-drilled holes expand when woodscrews are driven into them thus making a secure joint.

Screw sockets

These work in a similar way to the chipboard inserts. In this case the sockets are metal and are screwed into a drilled hole using a screwdriver. A machine screw will then fit the threaded hole in the centre of the socket. These are used for bolting boards or solid wood together.

Screw sockets

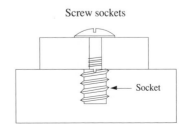

— Socket

Panel connectors

Used to bolt worktops edge to edge or for joining handrails, they can be very useful. To fit a connector, a stopped hole is drilled in each panel and a narrow slot is cut to link the two and to accommodate the connecting bolt. The connector is then inserted and by tightening the hexagonal bolt with a spanner the panels are pulled together.

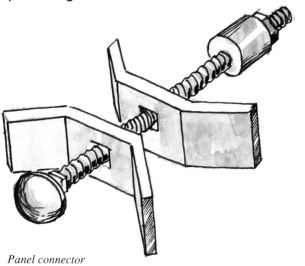

Panel connector

Block joint

Probably the most commonly used knockdown fitting, and is used to join panels at right angles. It consists of two interlocking plastic blocks. One block is screwed to each panel. A clamping bolt pulls the two blocks together.

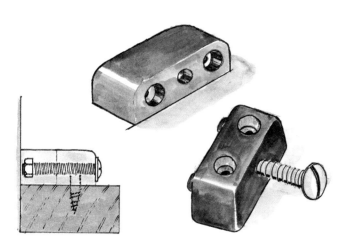

Block joint

Cabinet connector

A neat fitting for joining two cupboards, kitchen cabinets, etc. together side by side. The end with the ribbed 'nut' remains stationary while the threaded bolt is turned with a screwdriver.

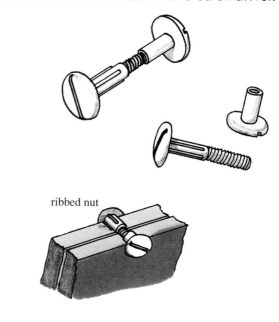

ribbed nut

Cabinet connector

Tee nut and bolt

A simple fixing for joining wooden framing. Identical holes are drilled in each component. The bolt and nut are inserted. As the bolt is tightened it pulls the nut neatly into the back of the wood. The teeth on the underside of the nut prevent it from twisting.

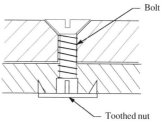

Bolt

Toothed nut

Tee nut and bolt

Bolt and barrel nut

An extremely strong and effective fastener, so effective in fact that it is often used on table and chair frames, two objects of furniture which get a

188

lot of abuse. Generally used in conjunction with wooden locating dowels, this fixing consists of a barrel nut and a bolt with an allen key head.

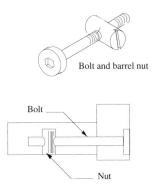

Bolt and barrel nut

Bolt

Nut

Taper connector

A concealed fixing for hanging wall cupboards. Both parts of the connector are dovetail shaped and tapered. Sliding one into the other locks them securely together.

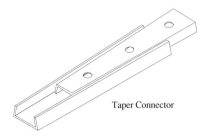

Taper Connector

Shrinkage plates

Designed especially for fixing solid wood table tops to an underframe. The plate is screwed to the inside of the rail so that it is flush with the top edge. A round head screw is then driven from underneath into the table top through whichever of the two slots runs perpendicular to the grain. In this way the slot will allow the top to move slightly whether due to shrinkage or expansion.

Corner plates

Used in table construction to hold the rails and leg together. Flanges on each end of the plate fit into slots cut in the rails. The plate is also screwed to

the rails. A hanger bolt is then screwed into the chamfer in corner of the leg, through a hole in the plate and tightened, using a wing nut. This pulls the leg tight against the rails.

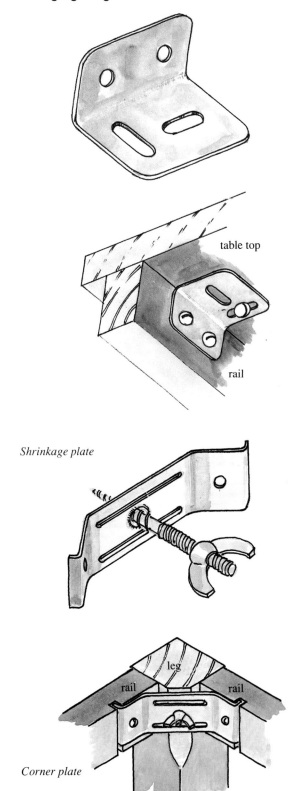

table top

Shrinkage plate

rail

Shrinkage plate

leg

rail   rail

Corner plate

Activities

1. Describe the meaning of the term 'knockdown' fittings.

2. Why are knockdown fittings becoming more and more popular in modern furniture making?

3. Draw a diagram of a panel connector and show how it is used.

4. Describe why shrinkage plates are designed specially for solid table tops.

5. Give two types of fitting which could be used for fitting kitchen units together. Which would you prefer to use? Give reasons for your answer.

6. Explain the design principles involved in the taper connector.

7. Why are block joints such popular knockdown fittings?

8. Sketch a cabinet connector and give two examples of where it could be used.

9. Chipboard inserts are such a simple fitting; how do they improve on a normal screwed joint?

10. What would be the steps to be taken when fixing a corner plate?

11. Describe the difference between a chipboard insert and a screw socket. How do each get their strength?

14

Hinges and fittings

Hinges

There are many types of hinge available. Some are for general use, others are designed for specific uses. For example, the hinge for fixing the lid of a jewellery box would be totally unsuitable for hanging a heavy wooden gate.

Hinges generally consist of two leaves and a knuckle. The knuckle is formed by interlocking parts of each leaf, usually an odd number. Through the centre of the knuckle runs a steel pin. The pin acts as an axis or axle about which the leaves can rotate.

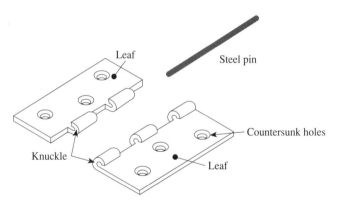

Parts of a hinge

Hinges are made out of brass or steel, brass being more decorative and corrosion resistant, steel being stronger. Like steel nails and steel screws, steel hinges can be coated both to resist corrosion and as a decoration. Common coatings are nickel plate, chrome plate, copper plate and black japan.

Hinges are usually fitted using countersunk head screws. These screws should have the same coating as the hinge.

Butt hinge

The most versatile and commonly used hinge, the butt hinge is also the most simple. Most doors, windows, box lids, etc. are all hinged using butt hinges. The solid brass butt hinge is the traditional cabinet maker's hinge although it is comparatively expensive.

There are many types of butt hinges which can be classified as separate hinges in their own right.

Butt hinge

Piano hinge

A piano hinge is a very long butt hinge. Generally made in 2m lengths, it is used where an especially strong fitting is required. This hinge can easily be cut to the length required. It is are extremely easy to fit and for this reason is quite popular.

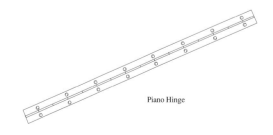

Piano Hinge

191

Lift-off hinge

Another butt hinge, this is used when it is necessary on occasions to be able to remove a hinged component such as a dressing table side mirror. The hinge separates into two halves quite easily. A good hinge is made of solid brass with a steel pin. Left hand and right hand versions are available.

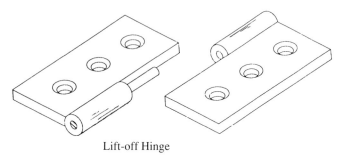
Lift-off Hinge

Rising butt hinge

A special hinge used for doors. As it opens one leaf rises. If this leaf is screwed to the door then as the door opens it will rise slightly. This is handy if you wish to protect an expensive floor covering or carpet. Left hand and right hand versions are available.

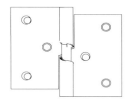
Rising Butt Hinge

Back flap hinge

This is a wide square version of the butt hinge. Made from brass or mild steel, the back flap hinge is used in drop leaf tables or bureau fronts.

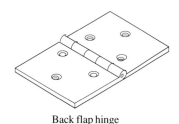
Back flap hinge

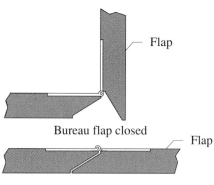
Bureau flap closed

Bureau flap opened

Table hinge or rule joint hinge

This is a version of the back flap hinge specially designed for mounting fold-down table flaps made with a rule joint. The hinge's longest leaf is screwed to the table flap because the screw holes are well away from the knuckle, allowing space for the ruled joint. Generally made from brass, the table hinge must be of strong construction.

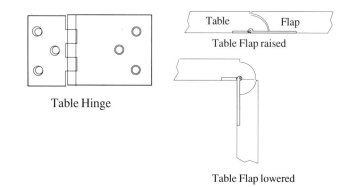
Table Hinge

Table Flap raised

Table Flap lowered

Flush hinge

A flush hinge is used for the same purpose as a butt hinge but for lightweight doors only. This type of hinge is easily fitted as it does not have to be recessed into the wood.

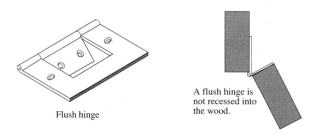
Flush hinge

A flush hinge is not recessed into the wood.

The cranked cabinet hinge

The cranked hinge is used for fine cabinetwork with lay-on doors. These are doors whose fronts stand proud of the frame, and also overlap the frame by a small amount. This makes door fitting easier. The narrow leaf of the hinge is screwed to the frame face and the wide leaf to the door. The knuckle is level with the door front.

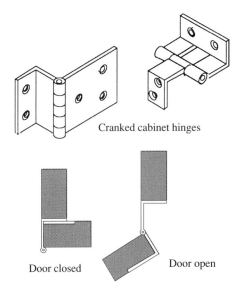

Cranked cabinet hinges

Door closed   Door open

T hinge

A heavy duty hinge, this gets its name from its shape. It is used on garage and shed doors, or garden gates. Usually made from mild steel which is black japanned or galvanised. The long strap can vary in length between 75mm and 600mm.

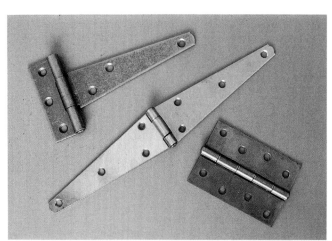

T and strap hinges

Strap hinge

Like the T hinge, this is used for heavy duty work. In order to be able to use this hinge the frame to which the gate or door is to be hung must be quite wide. The length is measured from the knuckle to the end of the strap and can vary between 75mm and 300mm.

Concealed cabinet hinge

Lay-on kitchen cupboard doors are usually hung using modern concealed hinges. These hinges are capable of adjustment so that a row of doors can be aligned accurately. They are designed to allow a door to be opened without colliding with another door butted next to it. Spring loaded versions keep the door closed.

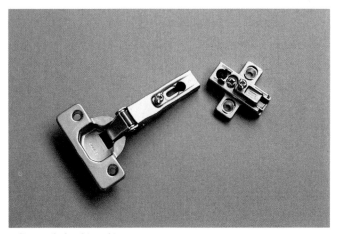

Concealed cabinet hinge

Centre hinge

Recessed into the edge of a door, lid or fall flap, this type of hinge is practically invisible when closed.

Centre hinge

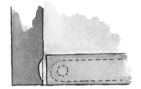

Centre-hinged door closed

Centre-hinged door open

Fitting hinges

Although the butt hinge is one of the most simple of hinges it is probably the most difficult to fit because both leaves have to be recessed, one into the door, the other into the frame. If the door hinges in particular are not fitted properly then the door may become 'hinge bound' or the hinges may eventually be pulled loose due to one hinge pulling against the other.

The most important thing to remember when fitting hinges is that the centre of the pin in the knuckle must be exactly in line with the face of the door. This will in fact leave half of the knuckle protruding beyond the front face of the door.

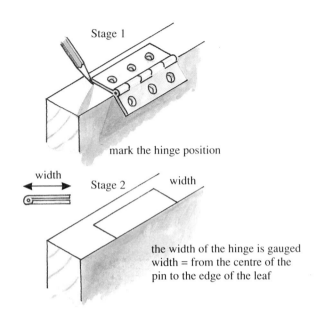

Stage 1

mark the hinge position

width

Stage 2 width

the width of the hinge is gauged
width = from the centre of the
pin to the edge of the leaf

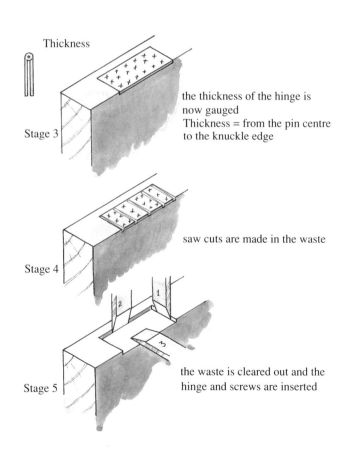

Thickness

Stage 3

the thickness of the hinge is now gauged
Thickness = from the pin centre to the knuckle edge

Stage 4

saw cuts are made in the waste

Stage 5

the waste is cleared out and the hinge and screws are inserted

The following procedure should be used when fitting butt hinges:

1. Lay the hinge in position on the door edge and mark its two ends.

2. Set the marking gauge to the width of the hinge. **Note that this is the distance from the centre of the pin to the edge of the leaf.**

3. Gauge this distance between the lines made on the door edge.

4. Now set the gauge to the thickness of the hinge. **Again, note that this is the distance from the centre of the pin to the knuckle edge.**

5. Gauge this on the door face.

6. Mark the waste.

7. Make sawcuts across the waste and then chop along the back edge of the recess with a chisel and mallet before paring out the waste. Take care not to go below the gauge lines.

8. Fit the hinge and insert the screws.

9. The same procedure is carried out with the other leaf in the frame.

Locks

Cupboard lock

Made from either brass or steel, the cupboard lock is screwed directly into the door. The bolt or ward fits into a mortise in the framing. It will work for right or left hand closing as the bolt will work in either direction.

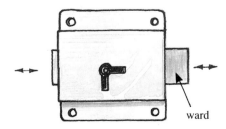

Cupboard lock

Cut door lock

Very like the previous lock, this lock is recessed into the door. Left hand and right hand versions are available as the ward has only a single movement. The cut door lock is often used to lock drawers.

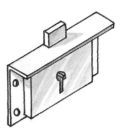

Cut door lock

Box lock

This lock comes in two parts: the lock and the keeper. The lock is fitted to the box, the keeper to the lid; both are recessed into the wood. When the lid is closed and the key turned the locking mechanism engages or catches the hooks in the keeper.

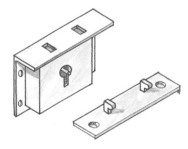

Box lock and keeper

Mortise lock

Commonly used in house doors, this lock is inserted completely into a mortise so that its front plate is flush with the door edge. A keeper is recessed into the frame to receive the ward. This is a very effective lock as it is completely hidden when the door is closed.

Mortise lock

Rim lock

Used on internal doors in houses, this lock is screwed to the back of the door while the keeper is screwed to the frame. More often seen in older houses, the rim lock is becoming less popular nowadays.

Rim lock

Sliding door lock

A special lock is required to secure overlapping sliding doors. The lock which is fitted to the outer door is operated by a push button that sends a bolt into a socket recessed in the inner door. A turn of the key withdraws the bolt. This type of lock is common on glass display cases.

Sliding door lock

Catches

In some cases a lock may be unnecessary or inconvenient. For cases like this a simple catch or bolt may be used.

Magnetic catch

A simple catch that works automatically. A small encased magnet is screwed to the inside of the frame. This magnet attracts a small metal striker plate fixed to the cupboard door. When they come in contact the magnetic force keeps the door closed.

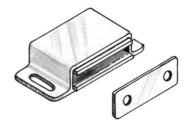

Magnetic catch

Ball catch

Another automatic catch, this consists of a spring-loaded steel ball trapped in a cylindrical brass case that is inserted in the edge of a cupboard door. When the door is closed the ball springs into a round recess in a metal striker plate screwed to the frame. Some catches have two spheres which grip a little clip on the frame.

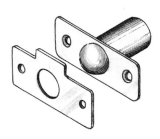

Ball catch

Barrel bolt

These come in large sizes (300mm) for garage and shed doors or small sizes (75mm) for cupboards and presses. They are particularly useful on a twin-door cupboard, one door being fitted with one or two barrel bolts, the bolt going into a hole in the frame, the door being fitted with a lock or catch.

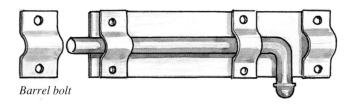

Barrel bolt

Spring catch

This is like a small version of the rim lock except that the ward is spring loaded and not operated with a key but rather with a handle.

Spring catch

Bullet catch

A light, small catch, this comes in two parts. The bullet is screwed into the frame, while the barrel is pushed into an aligned hole drilled in the door. This catch relies totally on friction for its strength. The sides of a bullet can be splayed further apart if a tighter fit is required or squeezed together if a looser fit is needed.

Activities

1. Make a diagram of a butt hinge and name its parts.

2. What is the function of a rising butt hinge? How does it work?

3. Make a diagram of a cranked cabinet hinge and describe briefly where and how it is fitted.

4. A heavy gate or door needs a heavy duty hinge. Suggest two suitable types of hinge. Make a neat sketch of each.

5. Write a brief note on a rule joint hinge.

6. Describe with the aid of sketches the fitting of butt hinges on a door.

7. Compare a mortise lock with a rim lock.

8. Make a diagram of a box lock and describe how and where it is fitted.

9. Sketch a ball catch and describe how it works.

10. What is a dead lock?

11. Draw a diagram of a piano hinge and explain its uses. How do you think it got its name?

12. Try to design a lock that would be suitable for sliding doors.

13. By doing some research find out what the following items are, and make a diagram of each:

    a) escutcheon plate;

    b) gate latch;

    c) hasp lock.

14. Make a diagram of a bullet catch and try to suggest how it got its name.

15. Suggest a suitable lock or catch for a first aid kit. Give reasons for your answer.

16. Try to design your own type of catch.

15

Woodfinishing

Woodfinishes are applied to enhance the appearance of wood and to provide protection from moisture, abrasion, heat, insect and fungal attack, etc. Therefore it is important to consider how a piece will be used and where it will be sited before selecting a finish.

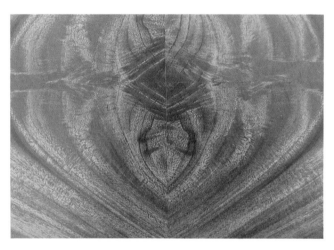
Polishing enhances the appearance of wood

Method

Use the smoothing plane to remove deep marks from flat surfaces, working with the grain.

Where there is a knot or 'wild' grain use a scraper or cabinet scraper. This is more effective on hardwoods than softwoods.

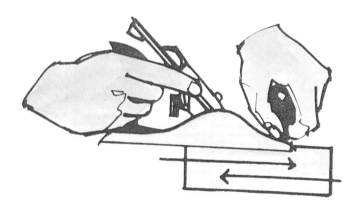
Planing

Scraping

Surface preparation

While wood finishes enhance the beauty of wood, they also highlight any imperfection such as marks or scratches. Therefore it is important that the surface of the wood should be smooth and clean before the application of a finish. The first part of finishing is the correct preparation of the wood surface.

Using a scraper

Use of abrasives

When wood is relatively smooth it should be sanded, using abrasive paper. Start with a coarse or medium grade, working progressively to a fine grade to achieve a smooth surface. For hardwoods start with a 150 grit and finish with 280 grit; use 120–240 grit on softwoods.

Sanding by hand

Divide the sheet of abrasive paper into four quarters. When sanding flat surfaces, use a cork sanding block with abrasive paper wrapped

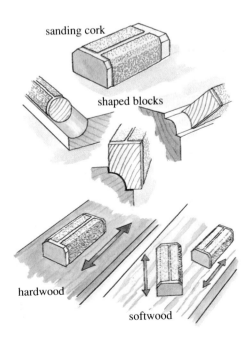

sanding cork

shaped blocks

hardwood

softwood

Using sandpaper

around it. Wood blocks with a cork or rubber strip will also give good results. For shaped and moulded work wrap the abrasives around a shaped block. When sanding hardwood always work with the grain. On softwoods begin by sanding at a slight angle to the grain, finishing off with the grain.

Note: When sanding, brush away the dust intermittently to avoid clogging the abrasive.

Using a power sander

When using a power sander, i.e. an orbital sander, grits slightly coarser than that used for hand sanding may be used. The palm (pad) sander is easier to use on small work. Always start the sander before placing it on the work, and remove it before switching off, to avoid leaving fine ring marks. It is not necessary to apply pressure to the sander as its own weight will supply sufficient pressure to the abrasive.

Electric palm sander

Health and safety

- Wear a dust mask when there is excessive dust.
- Use power sanders with dust collecting bags.
- Provide plenty of ventilation.

Types of abrasive

Glass paper: powdered glass glued to a yellow/brown paper. Cheap abrasive suitable for use on softwoods. 1½ and 0 (medium and fine) grades are the most popular.

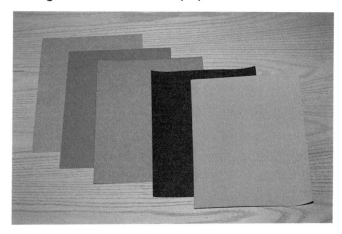

Abrasive paper

Garnet paper: crushed natural mineral, orange/red in colour. Much better paper than glass paper. Suitable for use on hardwood and softwood.

Aluminium oxide paper: aluminium oxide coatings resin bonded to a strong paper background. Available in different colours. Very hard with long-lasting qualities. Used on power sanders.

Silicon carbide paper: waterproof silicon carbide paper (known as wet and dry paper), is widely used on metals. Dark grey to black in colour and bonded to a waterproof paper. Used dry on wood. Also used in cutting down finishes, grits 60–1,200.

Lubrisil silicon carbide paper is light grey in colour. It has a dry lubricant to prevent clogging. Used for cutting (rubbing) down finishes between coats, grits 80–320.

Comparable grading table

	grit.	grain size		
	Aluminium oxide, Silicon carbide	Garnet	Glass	
Extra fine	600			
	500			
Very fine	400			
	360			
	320	9/0		
Fine	280	8/0		
	240	7/0	Flour	
	220	6/0	00	
Medium	180	5/0		
	150	4/0	0	
	120	3/0	1	
Coarse	100	2/0	1½	
	80	1/0	F2	F = Fine
Very coarse	60	½	M2	M = Middle
	50	1	S2	S = Strong
Extra Coarse	40	1½		
	36	2		
	30			
	24			
	12			

Grading of abrasives

Filling holes and defects

Proprietory stoppers are available in small tins in a range of colours, for filling holes and defects. Use a colour which matches the colour of the wood.

Using a shaped dowel or spatula, apply the stopper to the hole and work it in. Leave it a little above the surface and when it has hardened sand it level.

If the work is to be painted, standard decorator's filler can be used. This should be applied after the primer coat.

Filler

Removing a dent

If wood is dented, i.e. the fibres are not broken, this may be corrected using a damp cloth and a hot iron.

Place a damp cloth over the dent, apply a hot iron for a few seconds. When the dent is raised (swelled) sand it level with the surface.

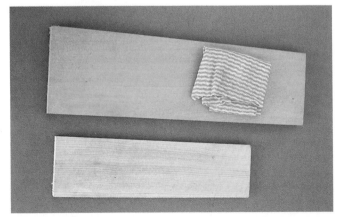
Removing a dent

Staining

Wood is stained for a number of reasons: to enhance its appearance; to emphasise the grain; to match different coloured woods and to blend new wood with old wood.

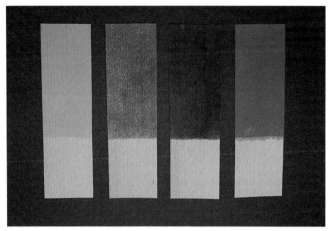
Samples of stained wood

Health and safety

- Do not smoke, drink or eat when using stains. Work in a well-ventilated area, preferably with an extractor fan.

- Wear a respirator if working in a confined area, wear protective gloves and clothing. Wear eye protection when handling chemical stain. Store in a cool place, in properly labelled containers.

- Wash hands after use.

Types of stain

There are many types of stain, most of which are available ready mixed. Water-based stains are favoured by most because they are lightfast, have good penetration, are easy to apply and are compatible with any finish. A disadvantage is that it raises the grain. For this reason it is necessary to dampen the wood, allow it to dry and sand it smooth, before applying water stain.

Recently developed solvent stains have most of the properties of water stain, without the disadvantage of raising the grain.

Stains and dyes

Application of stain

Stain should be applied to raw wood. It is best applied with a cloth to flat surfaces and by brush to mouldings and carved wood. Pour the stain into an open container. Soak the cloth with stain and apply a generous amount to the wood. Before it begins to dry, wipe off any surplus with a dry cloth, working with the grain. Leave for the required time before applying the finish.

Stains			
Type	Solvent	Characteristics	Use
Water	Water	Good penetration, lightfast cheap. Easy to apply. Its one disadvantage is that it raises the grain. Can be finished with any surface coating.	Furniture, general woodwork
Spirit	Methylated spirits	Dries out quickly, therefore difficult to apply over large areas. Tends to fade. Wide range of colours available. Does not raise the grain.	Furniture, touching up finishes. Tinting French polish.
Oil	White spirits turpentine	Widely available in ready mixed cans. Easy to apply. Colours can be inter-mixed. Can bleed through some finishes, e.g. lacquers and finishes with similar solvents. Slow drying. Some oil stains are lightfast.	Furniture, general woodwork.
Naptha	Naptha thinner	Sometimes called an oil stain, as white spirits is one of its ingredients. Easy to apply. Tends to fade.	As oil stain.
Chemical	Water	The colour is produced by a chemical reation with the wood's natural chemicals e.g. tannic acid.	
Bi-chromate of potash		*Poisonous* Made from crystals dissolved in water.	Colouring mahogany, oak, chestnut.
Ammonia .880 (35% pure ammonia)		Used to fume oak.	Oak furniture.
Solvent	Cellulose or similar thinner	Modern stain, lightfast, easy to apply by brush, cloth or spray. Dries very quickly, allowing finishes to be applied after 1 hour. Available in a wide range of colours. Non-grain raising	Used by furniture manufacturers and manufacturers of wooden fittings.

- Read the labels carefully and follow the manufacturer's instructions.
- Take proper precautions when handling these materials.

wiping off surplus

Applying stain

Grainfilling

Proprietory grainfillers are used to fill the grain of open-grained woods, and when a high-class finish is required. Available in a range of colours: transparent, oak, mahogany, etc.

wiping off surplus

coarse cloth

Applying grainfiller (use gloves or barrier cream)

Application

The grainfiller (not to be confused with stopping), should be applied after staining, as stain will not take over grainfiller. It should be applied with a coarse cloth, working the cloth in a circular motion. Rub it well into the grain, leave for a few minutes and wipe off the surplus, rubbing across the grain. Using a clean cloth burnish lightly with the grain.

Applied finishes (application)

Woodfinishes should be applied in a warm, dry, dust free atmosphere.

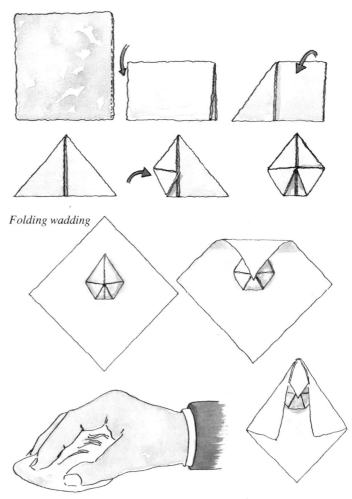

Folding wadding

Folding cotton cloth

Polished artifact

French polish

A very attractive finish, emphasising the natural beauty and grain of the wood. It can be coloured to give the desired tone. Full-strength polish is diluted with methylated spirits before application. The ratio is usually 75 per cent polish to 25 per cent methylated spirits for the early application, increasing the proportion of methylated spirits gradually and finishing with 25 per cent polish to 75 per cent methylated spirits.

French polish can be applied by two methods: *a*) traditional; *b*) brush.

a) Traditional:

The polish is applied with a 'rubber' or pad. A rubber is made from wadding wrapped in a piece of cotton or linen.

1. To make a rubber, take a piece of wadding 200 x 200mm and fold as shown.

2. Now place the folded wadding on a piece of cotton 250 x 250mm, fold as shown and twist into the palm of your hand.

3. To charge (soak) the rubber with polish, pour the diluted polish from a bottle into the back of the rubber. Refold the cotton as described and flatten the base of the rubber by patting it on a piece of wood. Test and see if there is the correct amount of polish on the face of the rubber.

4. Dust off the wood to be polished. Start applying the polish with the rubber using straight strokes working with the grain. Apply about five or six very thin coats. Leave to dry for six hours.

5. Cut down (sand lightly) the hardened polish with 320 'Lubrisil' silicon carbide paper. Then apply another five or six coats using circular or figure of eight motion, finishing with straight strokes. Leave to dry for six hours.

Oiling the rubber

Pad patterns

6. Cut down the polish again and apply another five or six coats of well diluted polish using straight strokes.

A little white oil may be used on the face of the rubber to help it move more freely. To apply the oil to the rubber, dip the tip of one finger into the oil, and spread it on the face of the rubber. If oil is used it must be removed from the surface of the polish or it will leave a streaky appearance. Apply a rubber with a high proportion of methylated spirits and use straight strokes to remove the oil from the surface.

0000 steel wool may be used instead of silicon carbide paper to cut down the polish.

The rubber should be stored in an airtight container to keep it moist for further use.

b) Brush:

Takes less time than the traditional method. Use a squirrel-haired mop or a fine-bristled brush. Dilute the polish with methylated spirits in the ratio of 60 per cent polish to 40 per cent methylated spirits, and add one tablespoon of French chalk to half a litre of polish. Shake well before use.

1. Apply a coat of polish, working with the grain. Leave for two hours.

2. Cut down with 320 'Lubrisil' silicon carbide paper. Brush on a second coat, leave overnight.

3. Cut down the polish, dust off.

4. Pad on one or two coats of polish, or alternatively apply a coat of wax polish.

Brush method

204

Wax

Gives a nice lustre to wood. One of the easiest finishes to apply, it can be used on raw wood or over other finishes. There are many proprietory waxes on the market, some containing solvents which evaporate very quickly and are more suitable for application over an existing finish. Beeswax and pure turpentine work very well on raw wood.

Waxes

To apply a paste wax to raw wood, use a soft cloth, e.g. mutton cloth. Take up some wax on the cloth and, using a circular motion, rub the wax into the wood.

Leave a few minutes and buff, using a soft cloth, in the direction of the grain. Leave a few hours and repeat the process. Finally apply a light coat with the grain and buff well.

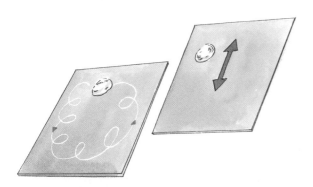

Wax application

Applying wax to a sealed surface

To give greater protection to the wood it can be sealed with a brush-on coat of French polish or sanding sealer. When this is dry cut it down and apply two coats of wax as described earlier. 0000 steel wool may be used to apply wax to a sealed surface, but always buff finish with a soft cloth.

To apply liquid wax, brush it on and rub it into the wood with a cloth and buff as with paste wax.

Oil

Suitable for interior or exterior use. It is easy to apply and has the advantage that the finish can be revived by an application of oil at anytime, even after many years. Apply a generous coating with a cloth, using a circular motion and rubbing well in to the wood. Wipe off any surplus oil with a clean cloth. Leave for six hours or overnight and repeat the process. Danish and teak oil require two or three applications.

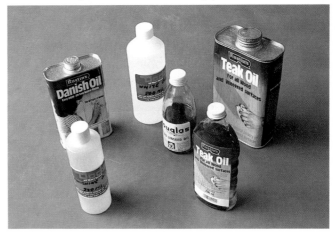

Oils

Varnish

The most commonly used of the clear finishes. It is used on doors, windows, boats, etc.

Before applying varnish the wood should be wiped down with a cloth dampened with methylated spirits or white spirits to remove dust and grease. Varnish may be applied with a brush or cloth. The first coat should be thinned with 10–15 per cent of turpentine or white spirits. Brush the varnish into the wood, working in different directions and finish off with strokes in the direction of the grain. Leave to dry for four to twelve hours, cut down and apply a second coat, using full-strength varnish. When dry apply a third coat if required.

Varnishes

When loading a brush with varnish dip about 10mm of the bristles into the varnish. Remove excess varnish by lightly rubbing the bristles on the inside of the tin, using an upward motion.

Loading the brush

Health and safety

- Wear gloves.

- Ensure proper ventilation.

- Read and follow the manufacturer's instructions carefully.

Paint

Suitable for internal and external use. It is an opaque liquid that hides the grain and any imperfections in the wood. It forms a smooth, coloured surface which is easily cleaned. There are various types of paint available, in a wide range of colours. Some paints have been developed for particular applications, i.e. heat-resisting paint for radiators. Paint is applied in a particular sequence, although this varies slightly with different types. Attention should be given to the manufacturer's instructions.

Aerosol paints are available in a wide range of colours. There are also non-toxic types on the market.

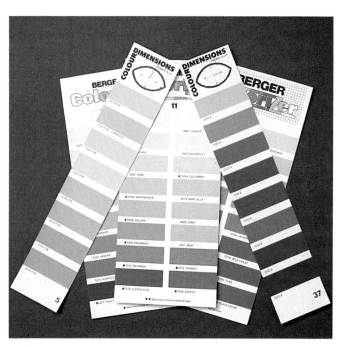

Different colours

Method of application (brush)

The brush is worked as it is for varnish.

1. Where there are knots in the wood they should be coated with knotting (shellac).

2. Apply a primer: aluminium primer for wood, white sealer for fibreboards.

3. Fill any holes or imperfections with stopping or decorator's filler. Rub down the primer and filler with 240 grit paper and dust off.

4. Apply one or two undercoats and rub down when dry.

5. Apply top (final) coat.

Each coat should be left to dry for the length of time indicated on the container. Most paints can be sprayed.

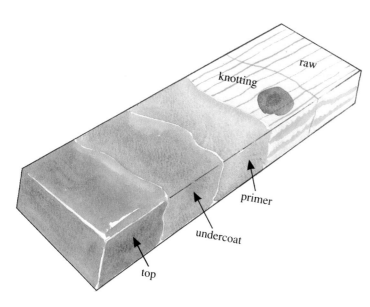

Stages in painting

Care of paint and varnish brushes

When finished painting, brush off remaining paint or varnish from the bristles using waste paper. Agitate the brush in a container of compatible solvent. Wash off solvent with water and detergent. Allow the brush to dry before storing it. Dispose of any solvent or paint-soaked paper or cloth carefully.

Lacquer

Lacquers are widely used in the furniture industry, and by manufacturers of wooden artifacts. A very good-quality finish can be achieved in a short time, due to the speed at which the lacquer dries and hardens.

The wood can be stained and grainfilled if desired.

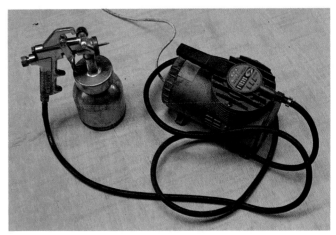

Spraygun and compressor

Spray application

1. A basecoat (sealer coat) is applied and cut down with 320 'Lubrisil' silicon carbide paper, when dry (30 minutes).

2. A coat of lacquer is then applied and allowed to dry.

3. A second coat of lacquer is applied.

Note: Tinted lacquers may be used to tone the colour of the wood. Lacquers are available in matt, satin and gloss finishes.

Matt = 25% sheen, satin = 60% sheen, gloss = 100% sheen.

Aerosol lacquers are available but are very slow drying.

Health and safety

- Materials are highly flammable (low flashpoint). Materials should be stored in a cool place. No naked flames, no smoking.

- Wear respirator.

- Do not eat or drink in the spraying area.

- Never spray at any part of the body.

- Take the necessary precautions when using polyurethane lacquers, refer to the manufacturer's instructions.

- Wash hands after use.

- Always follow the manufacturer's instructions carefully.

Essential equipment

- Spray gun.

- Air supply (compressor).

- Spray booth (extraction system).

- Respirator.

  Clean equipment thoroughly after use.

WOODFINISHES				
TYPE	MAIN CONSTITUENTS	SOLVENT	CHARACTERISTICS	USE
French Polish Button polish Transparent polish etc.	Shellac Methylated spirits	Methylated spirits	Attractive finish. Vulnerable to heat, water and alcohol. Spirit soluble aniline dyes are use to give various colours. Easily repaired	Hardwood. High class furniture
Wax	Beeswax Curnuba wax Turpentine	Turpentine	Satin finish, easy to repair, can be damaged by heat and moisture, becomes soiled with handling	To enhance polished surfaces. Turned work
Oil Teak & Danish	Tung oil drier	Turpentine White spirits	Water, heat and alcohol resistant, easily applied and restored	Exterior woodwork, furniture
Linseed oil	Linseed oil	Turpentine White spirits	Not as hard as tung oil. Slow drying	Restoration work
'Edible' oil	Vegetable oil		Non-toxic	Salad bowls etc.
Varnish Oil varnish	Resins — gums, Oil (tung, linseed) Turpentine Terebene (drier)	Turpentine White spirits	Slow drying. Traditional varnish	Furniture, joinery
Yacht varnish	Alkyds, resins	White spirit	Slow drying, high resistance to water, including saltwater	Boats, exposed wood
Polyurethane varnish	Polyurethane	White spirit	Tough and durable, resistant to alkyds, acids alcohol etc. Two part variety is very hard wearing. May give off dangerous fumes. Take proper precautions	Bars, kitchen furniture, floors

contd....

209

		WOODFINISHES (contd.)		
TYPE	MAIN CONSTITUENTS	SOLVENT	CHARACTERISTICS	USE
Microporous varnish	Organic and synthetic resins and oils	White spirits	Modern development for exterior use. Allows the wood to 'breathe'	External woodwork
Coloured (tinted) varnish	As above with a dye added	White spirits	Adds colour to the wood. Helps to counteract the effect of ultra violet rays	
Lacquer Pre-catalysed lacquer	Synthetic resin, nitrocellulose, catalyst	Compatible thinner	Modern finish. Highly inflammable. Spray application, quick drying. Oil stains tend to bleed through. Limited shelf life	Furniture
Acid-catalysed lacquer (Two-pack)	Synthetic resin, nitrocellulose, Acid-catalyst packed separately	Compatible thinner	Very fast drying, resistant to heat, alcohol. Provides a hard wearing surface. Difficult to repair	Furniture eg. table tops, worktops
Polyurethane lacquer (Two-pack)	Polyurethane	Special thinner	Very hard wearing. High resistance to acid, alkali, alcohol, heat and water. May give off toxic fumes. Take proper precautions	Where a hard wearing surface is required
Paint Oil paint (oleo-resinous)	Pigments, resins solvent, oil	Turpentine White spirits	Easily cleaned, moderately hard wearing	Interior or exterior use
Polyurethane paint	Polyurethane pigments etc.	White spirits	Very hard wearing, resistant to alcohol, acid and abrasion	Interior or exterior use
Acrylic paint	Acrylic pigments etc.	Water	Lightfast. Applied in one or two coats	Interior or exterior use
Cellulose paint	Cellulose pigment, thinner	Cellulose thinner	Highly flammable. Spray application	Man-made boards

Activities

1. What is a cabinet scraper?
2. When should you wear a dust mask?
3. Why are stoppers used in woodfinishing?
4. Why is stain used on wood?
5. Why is it necessary to use grainfillers?
6. What are the constituents of French polish?
7. State the advantages of using an oil finish.
8. Give an example of where an oil finish would be used.
9. Where are varnishes used?
10. Where would you use polyurethane varnish?
11. Where is yacht varnish used?
12. What is the main characteristic of microporous varnish?
13. Where is knotting used?
14. What is white spirit used for?
15. Why is it necessary to apply a finish to wood?
16. Describe how you would prepare wood for finishing.
17. Name three types of abrasive paper and describe two of them.
18. Describe how you would sand the ovolo moulding shown on p. 253.
19. Describe how you would remove a dent from a piece of wood.
20. What precautions should be taken when using stain?
21. Name three types of stain and discuss the advantages and disadvantages of each.
22. Describe how stain is applied.
23. How is grainfiller applied?
24. Describe how you would French polish a piece of wood.
25. Name two waxes and describe how they are applied.
26. Discuss the advantages and disadvantages of wax finishes.
27. Describe how an oil finish is applied.
28. Describe the application of varnish.
29. What precaution should you take when applying varnish?
30. Name three types of paint and state where each may be used.
31. Describe the painting of raw wood with an oil based paint.
32. Discuss the care of brushes.
33. List the precautions to be taken when using woodfinishes.
34. Name the main constituents of the following finishes: teak oil, oil paint and lacquer.
35. Explain matt, satin and gloss finish.

16

Other materials

Metals

What is a metal?

This seems a very easy question to answer, but is it? We think of metals as being hard, strong, shiny and heavy. This is not always the case, however. Iron is a metal and it will fit into the above categories but what about mercury? Mercury is a metal which is used in some thermometers yet it is a liquid, it has no definite shape. Sodium is another metal, yet it is light enough to float in water. Magnesium is another metal, but it burns very easily. Clearly we need to give a much more precise definition of metals than that given above.

Sections

Domestic appliances

Car industry

Ship building

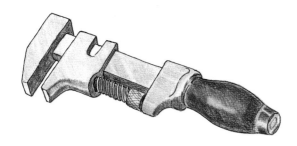

Tools

Doors

Packaging

Mercury, which is used in a thermometer, is the only metal which is liquid at room temperature

Properties of metals

1. They are solid: mercury is the only exception to this.

2. They are all good at conducting electricity.

3. They can all be given a shine (except mercury).

4. They are generally of high density. All metals are made up of atoms which are extremely small and cannot be seen by ordinary means. When we say that a metal has a high density we mean that these atoms are packed close together, leaving very few gaps.

5. You are able to bend or shape them when either hot or cold (except mercury).

6. They are good conductors of heat.

7. They expand when heated.

If we compare these properties to the properties of non-metals we should end up with a clear picture of what a metal is.

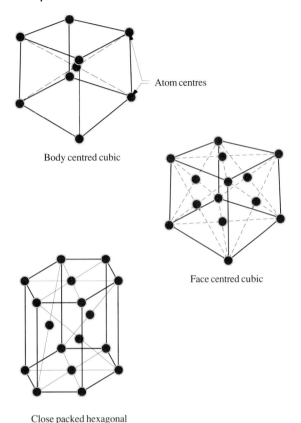

Body centred cubic

Face centred cubic

Close packed hexagonal

Metal atoms are packed closely together in one of these three patterns, which is repeated over and over again

Metal	Properties	Non-Metal
Very good	Conductivity (Electricity)	Very poor (except carbon)
Very good	Conductivity (Heat)	Poor
Easily bent twisted and shaped Molleable	Workability	Difficult to bend twist and shape Brittle
Shiny surface	Appearance	Dull surface

Properties of non-metals

1. They are brittle, they break or crack easily when bent or twisted.

2. They have no shine, they have a dull surface.

3. They are generally bad conductors of electricity.

4. They are generally bad conductors of heat, i.e. good insulators.

Unfortunately things are rarely as clear-cut as this. There are some elements which have metallic properties and non-metallic properties. These elements are referred to as **metaloids** or **semi-metals**, e.g. germanium, silicon.

The properties of metals and non-metals can be summed up in the following chart.

Classification of metals

Although there are many types of metals they can be classified into two main groups: ferrous and non-ferrous metals. Before we look at these, however, we must remember that a lot of metals that we are used to are in fact a combination of several metals. These are called **alloys**.

Ferrous metals

The latin *ferrum* means iron. Ferrous metals, therefore, are metals which are made up predominately of iron. Some examples of ferrous metals are cast iron, mild steel, tool steel. They are relatively cheap to produce and are used in thousands of everyday objects: cars, keys, cutlery, tins, etc.

Unfortunately most types of ferrous metals will rust if they are exposed to damp air or water, and will eventually become useless. For this reason they are usually coated with paint, some non-ferrous metal which will not rust, plastic, enamel, etc.

Steel is the most common type of ferrous metal available. Many types of steel are made, depending on where they are to be used and for what. They all contain different amounts of another element called carbon; 1.7 per cent carbon by weight being the usual maximum.

214

Poorly protected ferrous metals rust

Non-ferrous metals

All other types of metals are referred to as non-ferrous metals. These metals will not rust as they contain no iron. The five most commonly used non-ferrous metals are:

• aluminium; • copper; • lead; • zinc; • tin.

Making a copper bowl

USES	
Metal	Uses
Aluminium	Pots, pans, windows, doors, aerials, aeroplanes, drink cans, car parts, electric wires, boats
Copper	Electric wires, heating and plumbing pipes, ornaments, making brass and bronze
Zinc	Galvanising, batteries, making brass
Lead	Batteries, making solder, sealing between roofs and chimneys
Tin	Making bronze, making solder, coating, e.g. food tins

Finishing metal

Applied finishes

Finishes are applied to metal surfaces for two reasons:

a) to improve the appearance of the object,

b) to prevent it from corroding or rusting.

The problem of rust is a big one. How do you stop a steel gate from rusting away? Painting is one solution, but even this is not a permanent answer. Eventually the paint will crack or flake off allowing the steel below to rust. The best solution is to coat the item with a thin layer of zinc. This is done by dipping it into a molten bath of zinc and is called **galvanising**. Unfortunately galvanising is hardly a process which is carried out in the classroom.

Galvanising prevents rust

Painting, although not a permanent solution, is often sufficient. The best types to use against corrosion are:

a) those containing aluminium or zinc,

b) two-part epoxy resin paints.

215

Paints may be applied to metals by brush, spray or by dipping. Make sure that the surface is perfectly clean, rust and grease free. If better adhesion is required, score the surface of the metal lightly with wire wool or fine abrasive paper. Allow each coat of paint to dry thoroughly and also rub down gently between coats.

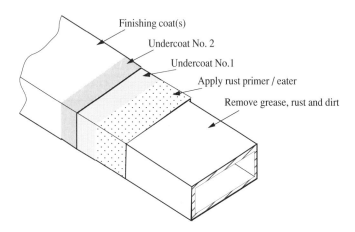

Painting metal.

Health and safety

- When brushing or spraying paint always work in a dust-free environment.

- Never spray indoors unless there is adequate ventilation.

Plastic coating

Plastic is another corrosion-resistant finish which can be done in the classroom. One method is by using the **fluidised bed system**. Plastic powder is fluidised by blowing air up through it. The metal to be coated is first heated and then dipped into the powder. The plastic powder will now stick to the metal giving it an overall coating.

A more simple method is low-temperature **enamelling**. The metal to be coated is cleaned and painted with a special gun. Powdered plastic is now sprinkled on the metal. The object is heated gently from below, using a candle under a wire gauze stand. The plastic melts, giving a uniform plastic coat.

paint on gum · shake on plastic powder

heat with a candle from below

Plastic coating

Decorative finishes

Metal is often finished purely for decorative purposes, particularly non-ferrous metals.

Scratch-brushing

One technique which does not involve special skills or equipment is scratch-brushing. This produces a satin texture by using a rotating stainless steel brush fitted to a bench grinder or an electric drill. The coarseness and speed of the brushes determine the depth and quality of the finish.

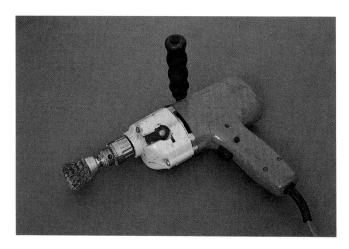

Drill with steel brush

Polishing

Start by removing scratches and marks, using a stiff brush in an electric drill coated with tripoli (an abrasive polish available from jewellers or craft suppliers).

Next, buff the metal to a high sheen using soft buffing mops, first with tripoli and then with jeweller's rouge or a suitable metal polish. The finish produced by this method is of very high quality.

Health and safety

- Always wear a face mask when polishing metal since the fine metal dust produced can be dangerous when breathed in.

Enamelling

The process of melting (fusing) coloured glass powder on the surface of a piece of metal by using heat. The best results are obtained by using a proper oven or kiln. However, enamelling can be done using a blow torch. The diagrams below explain the method fully.

Health and safety

- Always use tongs and gloves when handling hot metal.

Activities

1. What are the differences between ferrous and non-ferrous metals?

2. List five properties of metals.

3. What is the biggest disadvantage encountered when using ferrous metals? Describe in detail two ways by which this problem is overcome.

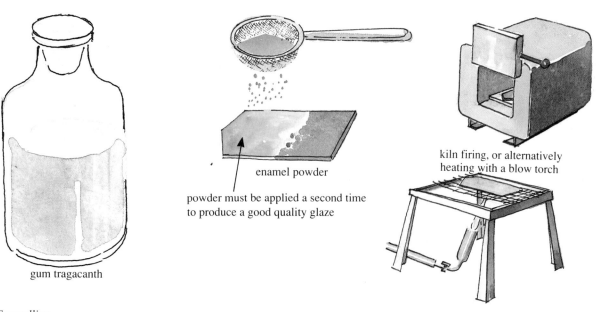

gum tragacanth

enamel powder

powder must be applied a second time to produce a good quality glaze

kiln firing, or alternatively heating with a blow torch

Enamelling

4. Non-ferrous metals are often seen in the home. Name three and give two everyday uses of each.

5. What is a metaloid? Give two examples.

6. Describe some safety precautions which must be taken when shaping and finishing metals.

7. The ancient Irish were a great metal-working nation. What types of metal would they have used most frequently? How would they have finished these?

8. Describe with the aid of diagrams the process of enamelling metal.

Plastics

Plastic is becoming more widely used every day. We all depend on plastic in some shape or form in our daily lives. When we say plastic we usually think of bags or buckets, containers or toys, but in fact there are so many things made from plastic nowadays it would be nearly impossible to list them all. Why is this? Plastic is such a versatile material that it can often be a cheap alternative to metal or wood. It can be moulded or cut into many intricate forms; it can be coloured; it can be made to resist heat, or to bend, it can resist corrosion, and so on.

Plastic household items

TABLE OF SOME COMMON PLASTICS GIVING PROPERTIES AND USES			
	Material	**Properties**	**Uses**
Thermoplastic	Polystyrene	(a) Expanded: light, good heat and sound insulation, easily crumbled (b) Conventional: brittle, water resistant, hard, light, no colour	Packaging and insulation Disposable plates cups, packaging, model, kits
	Polythene	(a) High density: fairly stiff, can be sterilised, waxy feel (b) Low density: soft and flexible, good electrical insulator, colours easily	Bottles, housware, buckets, pipes Bags, soft bottles, sheeting
	Polypropylene	Light, hard, will not break if bent continuously, easily joined, chemically resistant	Car parts, chairs, rope, nets, film
	Polyvinylchloride	Weather resistant, light, easily coloured, tough, good electrical insulator	Gutters, pipes, records, windows, shoe soles
	Nylon	Self-lubricating, resiliant to wear, heat resistant, creamy colour	Bearing, gear wheels, curtain rails stockings
	Acrylic ('perspex')	Rigid sheet or rod; comes in clear or brightly coloured sheets. It is fairly brittle and is easily scratched (usually protected with polythene membrane). May be joined using its solvent methylene chloride (dichloro-methane)	Car rear lamps, display cases, sheet glass substitute, modelling, etc.
Thermosetting	Urea-formaldehyde	Hard, brittle, strong, heat resistant, good insulator	Electric fittings, adhesives, knobs
	Polyester	Hard, brittle, heat resistant, good insulator	Fibreglass boats, car bodies, chairs

Before a plastic is used to make an object, it is important that we know for what purpose the object will be used. This is to ensure that the properties of the particular plastic used matches the job that it has to do. For example, the plastic used in a plastic fork must be strong and tough and be able to resist fairly high temperatures. The plastic used in a shopping bag must be cheap, strong and flexible.

With such a wide variety of uses how do we define a plastic? Any solid substance which can be moulded into a permanent shape during manufacture under heat or pressure is said to be a plastic.

Types of plastic

There are two types of plastics:

a) thermosetting plastics;

b) thermoplastics.

a) Thermosetting plastics

These materials are heated while they are being made into various objects. Once they cool and harden they cannot be softened again by heating. This is because the strands or chains of small particles (atoms) have formed cross-links with each other which will not break. This is an extremely useful type of plastic because it has great resistance to high temperatures. For this reason it is used in frying-pan handles, electric irons, ash trays, engine parts, etc. Some examples of thermosetting plastics are: urea formaldehyde used in gluing weather-resistant plywood, and polyester (terylene) used in some clothes.

b) Thermoplastics

These plastics can be repeatedly softened by heating and thus can be moulded and remoulded many times. One piece of plastic can be re-used many times to make many different items. Various types of thermoplastics become soft at different temperatures.

This family of plastics is very useful for disposable items because when their usefulness is over they can be made into something new. Some common uses of thermoplastics are dustbins, polystyrene foam, guttering, etc.

Thermoplastics and their uses	
Material	Uses
Polyethylene (polythene)	buckets, refuse bags, land drains, etc.
Polypropylene	chairs, car parts
Polyvinylchloride (PVC)	gutters, waste pipes
Polystyrene	house insulation, packaging
Acrylic	models, glass substitute

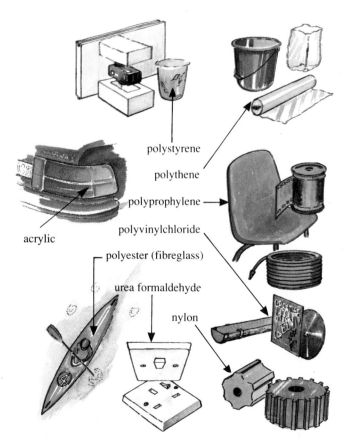

polystyrene

polythene

polyprophylene

acrylic

polyvinylchloride

polyester (fibreglass)

urea formaldehyde

nylon

(a) Two diagrammatic representations of the structure of thermosetting plastics

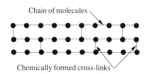

Chain of molecules

Chemically formed cross-links

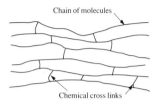

Chain of molecules

Chemical cross links

(b) Two diagrammatic representations of thermoplastics

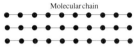

Molecular chain

no actual chemical link-up of chains

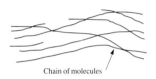

Chain of molecules

Secondary bond only force of attraction

Bending acrylic sheet

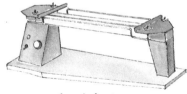

1. strip heater

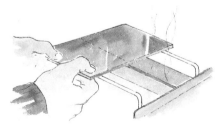

2. heating plastic sheet on 'bend-line'

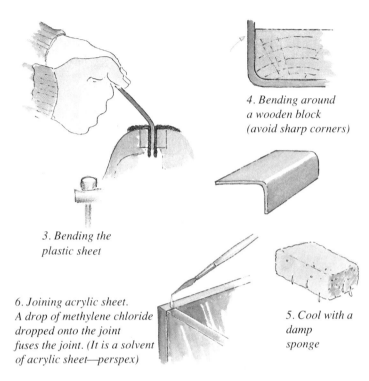

3. Bending the plastic sheet

4. Bending around a wooden block (avoid sharp corners)

5. Cool with a damp sponge

6. Joining acrylic sheet. A drop of methylene chloride dropped onto the joint fuses the joint. (It is a solvent of acrylic sheet—perspex)

Glass-reinforced plastics

Plastics are not always used in their pure state. They are often combined with other materials to give them different properties. One such material is glass fibre. By reinforcing the plastic/resin with fibres of glass we can get a strong, light material. This new material is called fibreglass, glass-reinforced plastic or simply GRP. The glass fibres make the fibreglass very strong, in fact strong enough to build boats, canoes, car parts, etc.

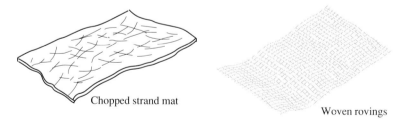

Chopped strand mat

Woven rovings

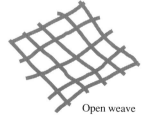

Open weave

Types of fibreglass reinforcement

220

Health and safety

There are several important safety features which must be observed when using plastics.

- When you cut them wear goggles because glass-like splinters can fly off.
- Never burn plastics as most of them release toxic fumes.
- When using chemicals always work in a well-ventilated area.
- If you get chemicals on your skin wash them off with water immediately.

Disposal of plastics

Unfortunately the disposal of plastic waste is becoming a worldwide problem. Plastic will not rot like wood, nor rust like iron, and as a result there is a steadily increasing amount of plastic waste in the world. How do we get rid of it? Burning gives off toxic gases and is harmful to the environment. One solution is to recycle plastics, particularly thermoplastics. In this way the same plastic is re-used again and again with very little wastage. The big problem here is collecting all the thrown-away plastic.

Activities

1. What is the difference between thermoplastics and thermosetting plastics?
2. Name three thermoplastics and state their properties and uses.
3. Name two thermosetting plastics and state their properties and uses.
4. Using sketches, describe how you would:

   (a) bend acrylic sheet

   (b) how it might be joined at a corner.
5. What do the letters GRP stand for, and why is this such a strong material?
6. What are some of the safety precautions needed when using and working plastics, and why?

Ceramics

Simple ceramics were one of the first materials used by ancient man. Mud or clay was shaped when wet into pottery, cooking utensils, bowls, etc. They were then baked in a fire to make them hard. Moulds were also made in this way for casting bronze weapons and implements.

The most common types of ceramics used today are **glass**, **tiles** and **cement**. All ceramics have the following properties:

1. Very high resistance to heat.
2. Brittle — a substance is brittle if cracks form and spread easily through it.
3. Very hard.
4. Do not conduct electricity.

Ceramics in general are difficult materials to work because of their brittleness and hardness. Shaping and cutting is best left to professionals. Of all ceramics, glass is probably the most widely used in furniture making. It is often used to cover highly decorative table tops, to protect the polish from stains and scratches. Cabinet doors and shelves can also be made from glass. In order to decorate the glass it can be bevelled, or engraved, or pictures and designs can be ground into it.

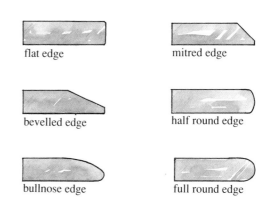

flat edge

mitred edge

bevelled edge

half round edge

bullnose edge

full round edge

Porcelain and china can often be used for door knobs and finger plates. In some cases where a table is to resist heat from a teapot, for example, ceramic tiles are set into the table top.

Joining ceramics

Both butt and lap joints can be formed between ceramic panels, using modern adhesives such as epoxy resin, silicon mastics or cyanoacreate. The latter can be used to form virtually invisible joints if the two surfaces are finished so that they match perfectly. Mitred joints are best ground by a glass merchant.

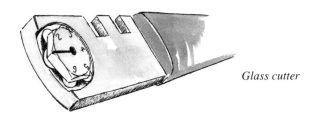

Glass cutter

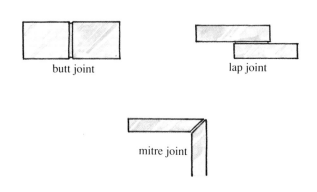

butt joint

lap joint

mitre joint

Health and safety

- Be very careful when handling ceramics of any type. Gloves would be recommended at all times. Dust particles from ceramics can be extremely dangerous, particularly if they get into your eyes or are swallowed. They can also give a nasty cut.

Working ceramics

As has been said previously, working ceramics is best left to professionals. This is because they cannot be sawn or filed or shaped like other materials because of their hardness and brittleness. Simple operations like cutting can, however, be carried out if great care is exercised.

To cut glass or tiles you must use a wheeled or a diamond cutter. These do not actually cut the material but rather score the surface. When pressure is subsequently applied to this scratch mark the material will (hopefully!) crack in the required place.

Once you have cut the tile or glass to the size wanted it is important that you round the sharp edges with a good quality emery paper.

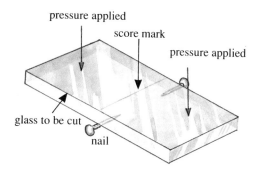

pressure applied

score mark

pressure applied

glass to be cut

nail

Cutting glass

Health and safety

- Remember to wear gloves.
- Ensure that all glass shards and dust are swept up and disposed of carefully.

Activities

1. What are some commonly used ceramic materials and what are their general properties?

2. How might you bond ceramic material?

3. Describe three types of joint suitable for ceramics.

4. What safety precautions would you take when cutting glass?

17

Woodcarving

Woodcarving is the craft of shaping wood into a variety of shapes. These can be purely functional or decorative or a combination of both. There are various forms of carving: incised; chip; relief; and carving in the round.

Tools for carving

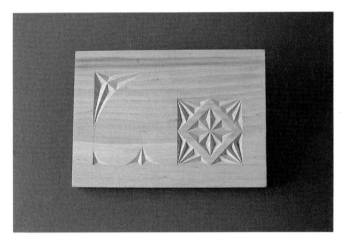

Beginning to carve

Tools

Special chisels and gouges are used for woodcarving. Standard woodworking chisels and gouges may be used for simple carvings, but for more advanced work it is necessary to use the special tools.

Woodcarving tools (mostly gouges) are made to a standard range of shapes and sizes and marked accordingly. They are identified by their size in millimetres, cross section (known as **sweep**) by number, and the shape of the blade. The shape of the blade can be straight, curved, spoonbent, backbent or fishtail.

Straight gouge (12mm No. 9)

Identification System						
	Straight	curved	spoon bent	back bent	fish tail	sizes available in mm
Chisel	1	21			F1	2 – 38
Skew chisel	2	22/23			F2	2 – 38
Gouge	3	12	24	33	F3	2 – 38
Gouge	4	13	25	34	F4	2 – 38
Gouge	5	14	26	35	F5	2 – 38
Gouge	6	15	27	36	F6	2 – 38
Gouge	7	16	28	37	F7	2 – 25
Gouge	8	17	29	38	F8	2 – 25
Gouge	9	18	30		F9	2 – 25
Gouge fluter	10	19	31		F10	2 – 25
Gouge veiner	11	20	32		F11	2 – 25
Parting or vee tool	39	40	43			2 – 16
Parting or vee tool	41	42	44			2 – 13
Parting or vee tool	45	46				2 – 25
Wing parting tool	47					6 – 13
Veining tool	48					2 – 6
Macaroni	49	50				6 – 16
Fluteroni	51		52			6 – 16

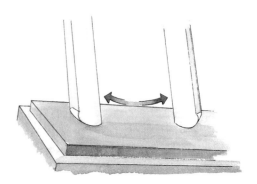

roll the gouge as it is being drawn on the oilstone

Honing a gouge

Variations of the gouges shown on the chart are available up to 50mm wide.

No. 1 tool is a square-edged straight chisel.

No. 2 is a skew-edged straight chisel.

Nos 3–11 are straight gouges, no. 3 has a shallow curve, progressing to no. 11 which has a deep curve. These are the most frequently used of the carving tools. No. 11 is also known as a veiner.

Nos 39, 41, 45 are vee tools or parting tools used for cutting V grooves and outlining.

All the other numbers refer to variations of the above tools (e.g. a no. 12 gouge has a no. 3 sweep with a curved blade).

Some specialised tools are made for particular applications.

Sharpening

Chisels are bevelled on both sides. Remove burr and polish bevel on a leather strop.

Gouges. The outside bevel is worked on the oilstone. Roll the gouge while it is being sharpened. The inside bevel is formed with a slipstone. Remove burr and polish bevel on a strop.

Parting tool. Sharpen each side as you would a chisel. This will form a hook where the two bevels meet. Remove the hook on the oilstone, remembering to roll the tool as you do so. Form a slight inner bevel with a V-shaped slipstone. Polish on a strop.

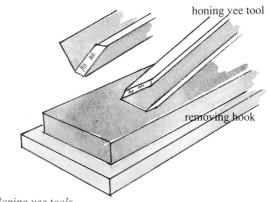

honing vee tool

removing hook

Honing vee tools

Carving mallets are traditionally made of wood and with a round head. The head is usually made from lignum vitae or beech, with ash or hickory handles.

Tools and equipment			
Mallet	Holdfast	Rifflers	Oilstones
Punches	Vice	Rasps	Slipstones
Carver's screw	Pivot vice	Coping saw	Strop

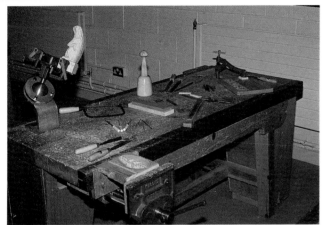
Tools and equipment for wood carving

Oilstones

Punches are used to texture the background of a carving. Available in various patterns.

Rifflers are miniature rasps. Useful for finishing intricate parts of a carving.

Woods

Most woods can be used for carving, but the close, straight-grained varieties are the most suitable (usually hardwoods). Lime is easily carved; sycamore, birch, chestnut, walnut, ash are also suitable. Beech is used for platters and eating utensils. Softwoods such as cedar and some pines may be used for carving. Medium-density

fibreboard (MDF) is easily worked in any direction. Birch plywood may be used for incised carving.

Woods for carving

Basic techniques

When carving wood, it should be held firmly in a vice; secured to the bench with a G cramp or holdfast; held with a carver's screw or woodblock screwed or glued to the work piece.

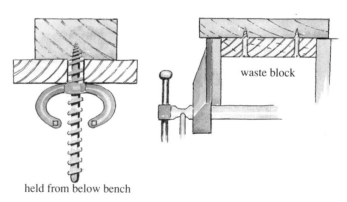
held from below bench   waste block
Carving screws

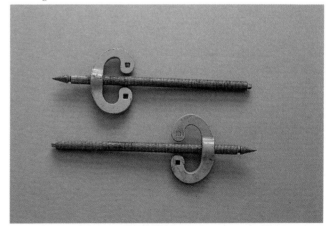

225

When you are using a tool rest your guiding arm on the work or bench to give you greater control. Hold the tool by gripping the handle firmly in one hand, index finger pointing down the handle. This hand is used to push the tool. Your other hand guides and controls the tool. When making a deep cut your guiding hand should be clasped over the blade. For light cuts hold the blade between the first two fingers and thumb. When using the mallet, grip the carving tool by the lower part of the handle and tap gently with the carving mallet.

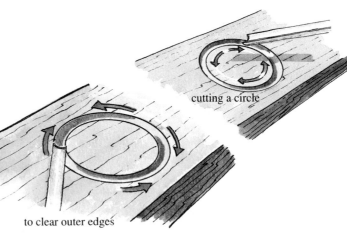

cutting a circle

to clear outer edges

Grip for deep cut

Grip for light cut

Cutting

Always work in the direction of the grain where possible. Working against the grain will leave a jagged surface. In carving it is often necessary to cut across the grain. When doing so work the tool at a slight angle to the grain, to give a cleaner cut.

When working a circle cut in four directions as shown.

Transferring designs to wood

Designs may be increased or reduced in size by using the grid method or using a reducing/enlarging photocopier.

Grid method: Place a sheet of clear plastic with a grid drawn on it over your original design (or draw a grid on the design). To reduce, transfer points *a*, *b*, *c*, etc. to a smaller grid. To enlarge, use a larger grid.

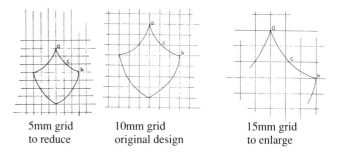

5mm grid   10mm grid   15mm grid
to reduce   original design   to enlarge

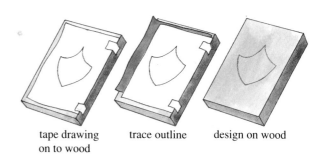

tape drawing   trace outline   design on wood
on to wood

A design is usually transferred to wood using carbon paper, or it can be pencilled on directly if the design is simple.

Method

1. Place the drawing on the wood in the desired position. The direction of the grain may need to be taken into account.

2. Tape or pin the design in place.

3. Slip a sheet of carbon paper under the drawing sheet and trace the design with a pointed instrument. Check all lines are traced on the wood before removing the drawing.

Incised carving

Consists of cutting along the outline of a design with a vee tool or veiner. Use a soft, straight-grained wood, e.g. lime.

sketch of finished piece

Incised carving

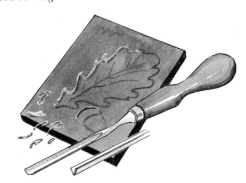

Method

1. Transfer the design to the wood as described earlier.

2. Secure the wood firmly to the bench.

3. Using a veiner or vee tool, cut along the outline of the design using reasonable pressure. Work in the direction of the grain where possible. Make continuous cuts (incisions) to leave a smooth outline.

4. When the complete design has been cut, sand off the pencil lines and apply a finish.

Note: to make the design stand out you can apply a woodstain.

Chip carving

One of the simplest forms of woodcarving. It is generally based on geometric shapes which are repeated again and again. The basic design is a triangular chip. The tools required are: a bevelled-edged chisel, a firmer chisel or special chop knives. Standard drawing instruments are used to set out the designs.

Example of chip carving

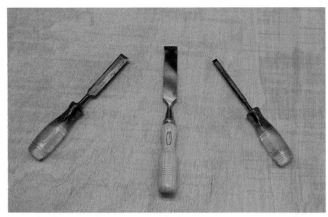

Firmer and bevel edged chisels for carving

The basic chip

Consists of three cuts: two stop cuts and a slicing cut.

1. Draw an equilateral triangle, 15mm side.

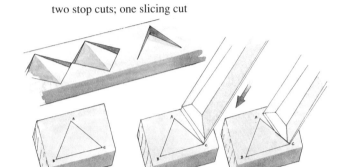

two stop cuts; one slicing cut

making stop cut

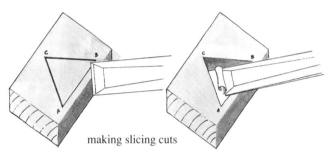

making slicing cuts

Stages in chip carving

2. Secure the wood to the bench.

3. Place a bevelled-edged chisel on side *ca*, with the edge at an angle to the surface of the wood. Tap the chisel with a mallet to a depth of 2–3 millimetres at point *a*. This is a stop cut.

4. Repeat the process on side *cb*.

5. Using a slicing cut remove the chip, working from side *ab*.

   To make a design using this chip set out a row of triangles. (The triangle need not necessarily be equilateral, any triangle can be used.)

   Remove the chip as described.

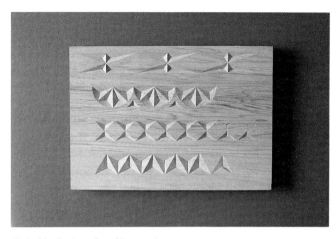

Suitable designs for chip carving

The six-cut chip

Consists of three stop cuts and three slicing cuts.

1. Set out an equilateral triangle and bisect the angles.

2. Secure the wood in the vice.

six-cut chip

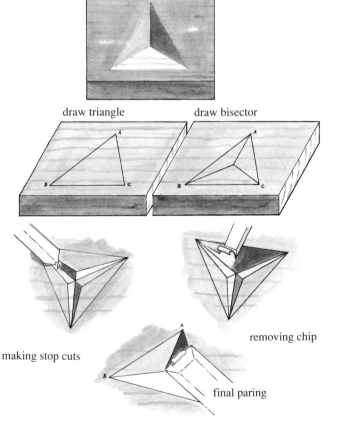

draw triangle   draw bisector

making stop cuts

removing chip

final paring

The six-cut chip

228

3. Push the vee tool from the apex of the triangle along the bisectors to a depth of 3mm at the centre.

4. Working from side *ac*, and using a slicing cut, remove the chip.

5. Repeat this from the other two sides. Clean up the three surfaces using fine slicing cuts.

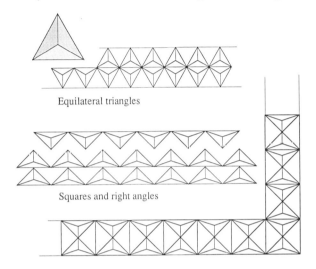

Equilateral triangles

Squares and right angles

Designs for chip carving

Relief carving

In relief carving the background is cut away to raise the design. **High relief** is raised at least 10mm above the background. **Low relief** is the simplest form and is worked to a depth of less than 10mm. Designs can be naturalistic, geometric, or completely abstract.

1. Draw out the design on paper to the required size. This will allow you to foresee problems and make necessary adjustments before starting to cut.

2. Transfer the design to the wood as described earlier.

3. Always secure the wood firmly to the bench. Turn the wood when necessary to maintain a comfortable working position.

Example of relief carving

Example 1

1. Transfer working drawing to the wood.

2. Mark a 3mm depth line around the edge of the wood.

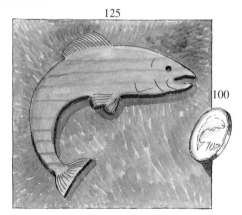

Carved salmon

3. Outlining: using a vee tool or deep gouge, cut around the outline of the design working about 2mm outside the line.

4. Setting in: to set in the tail use a straight chisel, for the body use a suitable gouge. Holding the tool in a vertical position trim the outline of the design. Use a mallet where necessary.

5. Grounding: using a sloping cut and working into the base of the outline pare away the background. Use a medium curved gouge. Continue until you have worked down to the depth line.

6. Shaping: round over the edge of the fish and put in the eye. Finish off the background with a gouge to leave a textured finish.

7. Apply a woodfinish to seal the wood.

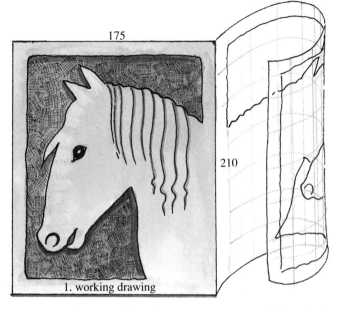

1. working drawing

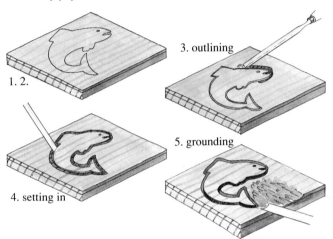

1. 2.

3. outlining

4. setting in

5. grounding

6. Sandpaper the design to a smooth finish if desired. Texture background with a punch.

7. Clean off and apply finish.

6. shaping

Stages in relief carving

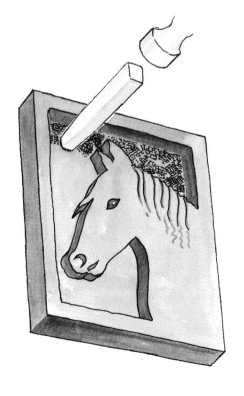

Example 2

1. Draw the design to the required size using the grid method. Transfer to wood.

2. Outline as described in example 1. Working depth 3mm.

3. Set in using appropriate tools.

4. Remove the background to a depth of 3mm.

5. Shaping: round over the edge of the outline. Incise the mane using a vee tool. Cut in the eye using a suitable gouge.

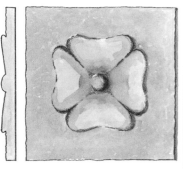

Floral pattern

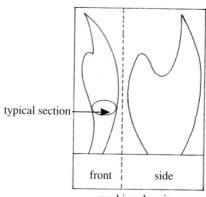

typical section →

front | side

working drawing

Carving in the round/Wood sculpture

Three-dimensional carving offers greater freedom to the carver, while making new demands, such as difficulty of holding the object, necessity to have a sense of proportion and the ability to visualise form.

A working drawing showing two views will usually be required. It may be helpful to make a model up in clay or plasticine.

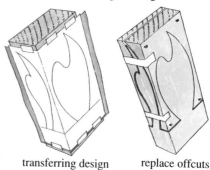

transferring design   replace offcuts

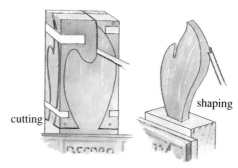

cutting   shaping

Remove the square at the bottom and fit to a base

Method

1. Having made a full-size working drawing showing a front and side view, transfer this to the wood using carbon paper.

2. Fold the drawing along the broken line and tape to the wood as shown.

3. Use a saw (e.g. coping, scroll or band saw) to remove the bulk of the waste. Cut along the side view first, leaving a square at the bottom (for holding in the vice).

4. Replace the offcuts and tape or pin them back in place. Cut along the outline of the face. (Replace one side only when using a coping saw.) It may be necessary to draw some of the lines on the roughly shaped block before going on to the next stage.

5. Using a flat gouge remove the corners. The section of the carving is oval throughout.

6. Complete the final shape working lightly with a flat gouge. The carving may be finished with a mottled gouge pattern or sanded to a smooth finish.

7. Remove the square at the bottom and fit to a suitable base.

Animal form

In this type of carving it would be helpful to have photographs or models of the subject, and to study the animal's shape or form.

231

Proceed as described previously, leaving a square block at the back of the animal for as long as possible to facilitate holding in the vice.

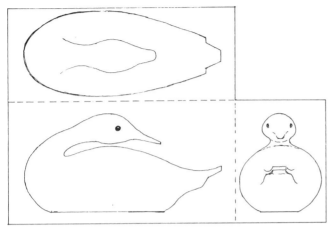

Working drawing

Incised technique

Lettering

Letters are either cut into the wood (**incised**) or raised by removing the background (**relief**). Different styles of lettering are used.

Always draw letters on paper first to ensure proper spacing and size.

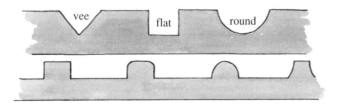

Example 1: V section: incised carving technique

1. Draw letters on paper and transfer to wood.

2. Using a vee tool make a cut along the centre of the letter, and along the bisector of each corner (stop cut).

3. Using a chisel (straight section) or a gouge (curved section) cut from the outline of the letter to the centre stop cut.

4. Work to the required depth.

5. Clean up the letter using very light cuts.

6. Seal wood.

Example 2: relief carving technique

1. Make a drawing and transfer to wood.

2. Outline using a vee tool or deep gouge.

3. Set in using appropriate tools.

4. Remove background to a depth of 3mm.

5. Clean up letters and background. Sandpaper where necessary.

6. Finish background with a frosted punch.

7. Apply a wood finish.

Relief carving of letters

Activities: see page 258 (Nos. 1–11)

232

Gloucester Old Style ™ 'Monotype' Gloucester Old Style 99 roman
ABCDEFGHIJKLMNOPQRSTUVW
abcdefghijklmnopqrstuvwxyz 123456789

Gloucester ™ 'Monotype' Gloucester 103 roman bold
ABCDEFGHIJKLMNOPQRSTUVW
abcdefghijklmnopqrstuvwxyz 123456

Gloucester ™ 'Monotype' Gloucester 243 roman bold extended
ABCDEFGHIJKLMNOPC
abcdefghijklmnopqrstuv

Gloucester ™ 'Monotype' Gloucester 198 roman bold condensed
ABCDEFGHIJKLMNOPQRSTUVWXYZ
abcdefghijklmnopqrstuvwxyz 123456789

Gloucester ™ 'Monotype' Gloucester 395 roman bold extra condensed
ABCDEFGHIJKLMNOPQRSTUVWXYZ
abcdefghijklmnopqrstuvwxyz 1234567890 .,:;!?"-()-

Goudy Modern ™ 'Monotype' Goudy Modern 249 roman
ABCDEFGHIJKLMNOPQRSTUVWXY
abcdefghijklmnopqrstuvwxyz 12345678

Goudy Modern ™ 'Monotype' Goudy Modern 249 italic
ABCDEFGHIJKLMNOPQRSTUVW
abcdefghijklmnopqrstuvwxyz 12345678

Goudy Text ™ 'Monotype' Goudy Text 292 roman
ABCDEFGHIJKLMNOPQRST
abcdefghijklmnopqrstuvwxyz 1234567890 .,:;!?"·(

Goudy ™ 'Monotype' Goudy 441 roman bold
ABCDEFGHIJKLMNOPQRSTU
abcdefghijklmnopqrstuvwxyz 1234

Goudy 'Catalogue' ™ 'Monotype' Goudy Catalogue 268 roman
ABCDEFGHIJKLMNOPQRSTUV
abcdefghijklmnopqrstuvwxyz 12345

Goudy Catalogue ™ 'Monotype' Goudy Catalogue 268 italic
ABCDEFGHIJKLMNOPQRSTUV
abcdefghijklmnopqrstuvwxyz 123456

Goudy ™ 'Monotype' Goudy 214 roman extra bold
ABCDEFGHIJKLMNOPQRST
abcdefghijklmnopqrstuvwx

Lettering styles

Examples of carving

233

18

Woodturning

What is woodturning?

Woodturning is the process by which a lathe is used to make round or cylindrical shapes in wood.

Pole lathe, seventeenth century

Woodturning is not just a machine process; to turn out a bowl or a table leg successfully requires much practice and an ability to appreciate a pleasing shape and sound craftsmanship. This chapter deals with faceplate turning and turning between centres.

Where did woodturning start?

The earliest known picture of a lathe occurs on a tomb relief of about 300 BC. Turning was known in the Middle East much earlier than this, because carvings on stone from about 1400 BC show stool legs and the feet of bedheads from the New Kingdom in Egypt.

In the Middle Ages the 'pole' lathe was invented. The cord was tied to a flexible wooden stick fixed to a ceiling or wall, and, after passing round the work, was attached to a treadle hinged to the floor. The turner would place his foot on the treadle and depress the cord. This pulled the stick downwards and caused the wood to revolve. In this way the wood was made to spin forwards and backwards, and the turner had to time the application of the tools to the work only on the revolutions towards him.

Other types of lathes from different eras were:

a) early crank and fly-wheel lathe;

b) great wheel lathe;

c) treadle lathe;

d) jeweller's bench lathe.

Lathe terminology

While woodturning lathes vary from manufacturer to manufacturer, it is required that all must be similar.

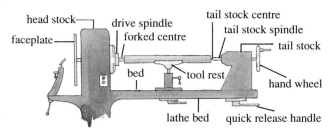

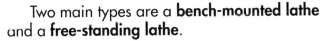

Parts of a lathe

Two main types are a **bench-mounted lathe** and a **free-standing lathe**.

- If you wish to turn a piece of square section wood, draw diagonals on the ends to find the centres as shown

- Plane wood to octagonal shape

- Knock the forked centre into position

- Place forked centre onto the lathe

- Slide the tailstock, with tail centre up to the work

- Lock the tailstock in position

- Turn the handwheel to push the tailstock centre into the work

- Position tool rest as close to the work as possible, setting in at centre height

- Spin the work by hand just to make sure it does not catch on the tool rest

Bench-mounted lathe

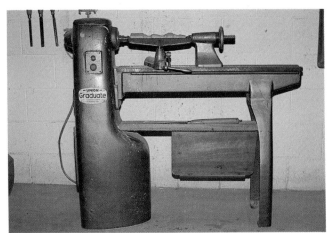

Free-standing lathe

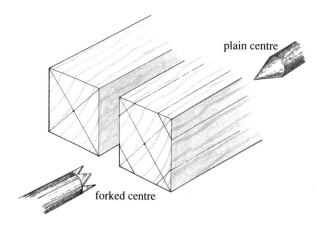

Finding the centre and rough shaping

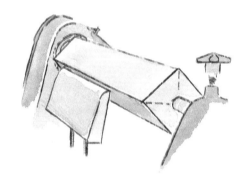

Making the centre. Using the mallet, tap firmly on forked centre into the centre point of end grain

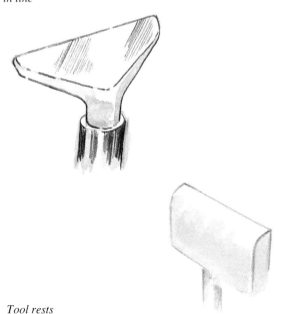

The top of the tool rest and the edge of the turning piece should be in line

Tool rests

Timber suitable for woodturning

Nearly every species of wood can be turned, but obviously some are more suitable than others.

Beech: fine even texture, pinkish buff.

Chestnut: for high quality work, bears a resemblance to oak.

Elm: lovely effects in bowl turning. Light brown in heartwood, yellowish white in softwood. Not to be used with carbon steel blades.

Sycamore: 'Sweet is sycamore as a nut'; very popular wood of old. It was used to make dairy and kitchen implements such as churns, rolling pins and bowls. Whitish with a close-fleck grain.

Applications of turning

Walnut: favourite of the woodturners of the Queen Anne period. Pale buff to dark brown.

Scots pine: an ideal wood to practise on. Matures to rich honey colour.

Ash: despite its coarse texture, ash turns very well. Ideal for such things as handles for tools, farm and garden implements and sporting equipment. Pale grey tinged with pink; heartwood light brown.

Basic set of turning tools

There is no great need to have a full complement of turning tools, early on. Begin with the basic tools and then as your skill develops you can use the less well-known and more advanced tools.

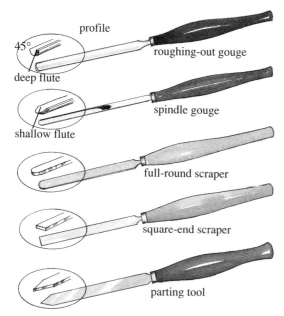

Basic turning tools

These specially designed cutting tools are fitted with short, stocky blades and long handles that provide the leverage required to control the tools.

1. Roughing-out gouge: 25mm. Used for turning square or octagonal work to a cylinder.

2. Spindle gouge: 12mm. Takes over from roughing-out gouge for between-centre turning.

3. Scrapers: Used for working inside bowls, etc. Blade width 12–25mm. All kinds of profiles are available, e.g. full round scrapers, domed scraper, square-end scraper.

4. Square-end chisel and skew-end chisels, also include beading tools. For finishing between-centre work. Recommended size blade width: 18mm.

5. Parting tools. Designed for cutting through the work and removing it from the lathe. Strictly speaking these are chisels. Recommended size: 3mm.

The **correct standing position** is vitally important. It is as important as the way you hold the cutting tool. Begin by practising turning softwood until you get used to the feel of the tools and have developed a sensitive touch.

Work at elbow height where possible

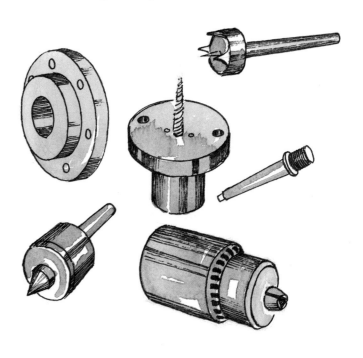

Basic accessories

1. The top of the tool rest and the edge of turning piece should be in line.

roughing-out gouge

2. When turning wood between centres hold the turning tool with its handle in line with your body and your elbow tucked into your side. Move the blade with your other hand from side to side along the rest. Use a skew chisel to smooth the work.

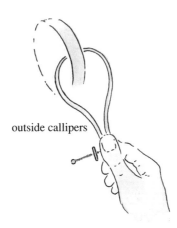

outside callipers

3. Using callipers, check the diameter required.

Summary

There are two categories of woodturning:

a) turning between centres;

b) faceplate turning.

Bowl turning

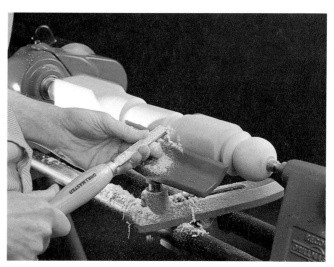

Spindle turning

Tools for turning between centres:

roughing-out gouges; spindle gouges, chisels, parting tools.

Tools for faceplate turning:

bowl gouges, scrapers.

Different types of turning

Examples of faceplate turning

Plan of round nosed scraper in use

Faceplate turning

One of the most popular aspects of woodwork. It requires a great display of skill because in turning a thin delicate bowl make one false move and the piece is destroyed.

A round-nosed scraper is used for cleaning up the inside of hollow ware such as goblets, vases, egg cups, and the inside of bowls.

Faceplate turning

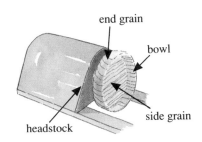

end grain

bowl

headstock

side grain

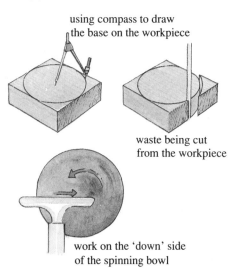

using compass to draw the base on the workpiece

waste being cut from the workpiece

work on the 'down' side of the spinning bowl

Bowl turned from burl

Sanding in the lathe

Burnishing in the lathe

Health and safety

- Ensure that the mains electricity is switched off before attempting to set up the machine or when the lathe is not in use

- Always protect your eyes with goggles or protective glasses

- Make sure that the elements to be turned are secure in the lathe and that there are no serious splits or cracks. See also that the centre piece is actually in the centre otherwise it will vibrate

- The piece to be turned should be well secured to the endplate

- Do not wear loose clothing or ties when turning, serious accidents can occur if clothing gets caught up in the lathe. Long hair should be in a net or tied back

- The lathe should be away from traffic and generally should be beside a wall. The chisels should be carefully handled and be held firmly

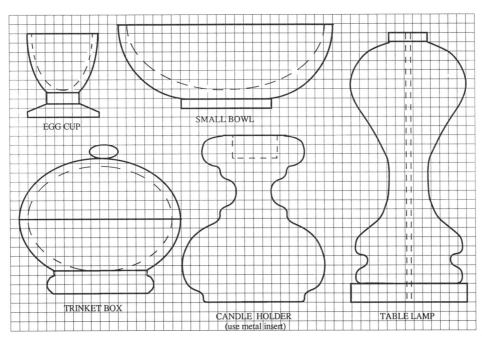

EGG CUP

SMALL BOWL

TRINKET BOX

CANDLE HOLDER
(use metal insert)

TABLE LAMP

Examples of Turning Exercises

19

Veneering and marquetry

Veneers

Veneers are very thin sheets of wood (called leaves). They can be cut by different methods to bring out the best features of wood. It is an economical way of using rare woods. Veneers may be bonded to solid wood, but are usually used in conjunction with manufactured boards. When bonded to manufactured boards using a modern adhesive, veneers can be superior to solid wood.

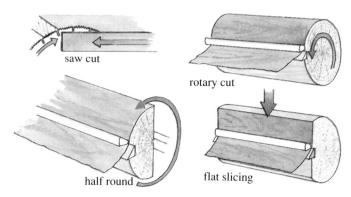

saw cut

rotary cut

half round

flat slicing

The log is taken from the forest, debarked, trimmed and softened by placing in a steam bath for a number of hours or days, depending on the species of wood. The log is then cut into veneer using one of the following methods.

a) Flat slicing

The log is either squared or cut in half and mounted on a horizontal or vertical table. As the table moves a knife slices off a veneer.

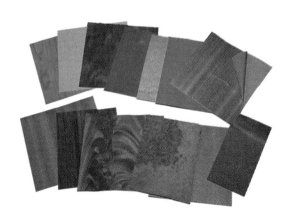

A range of veneer samples

Veneers are used in the manufacture of manmade boards, e.g. plywood.

b) Rotary cutting

The log is fixed in a lathe and rotated against a knife.

c) Half round cutting

The log or half log is mounted off centre into the lathe.

Manufacturing veneer

Although saw-cut veneer is available most veneers are sliced by knife to thickness of 0.6 to 0.8mm.

Drying

The veneers are passed through a drier and stacked in multiples of four in the order they came from the slicer.

Types of veneer

Veneers are available in a wide range of woods with various grain patterns.

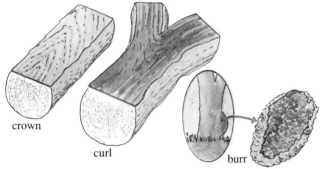

crown

curl

burr

Microwood veneer is a very thin veneer on a paper backing. It is very easily cut in any direction and is also available as a self-adhesive veneer.

Veneering and marquetry

Veneering is the bonding of thin sheets of wood to a groundwork (e.g. MDF). Using motifs, bandings and figured grain veneer, beautiful patterns can be achieved.

Marquetry is the creative use of veneer to form decorative patterns.

Tools and equipment

- Cutting mat (rubber) or board (plywood, hardboard).
- Straight edges (wood), one 400 x 50 x 8mm and one 200 x 35 x 6mm.
- Knives; hobby knife, scalpel with no. 10A and no. 11 blades.
- Veneer hammer.
- Masking tape (good quality) or veneer tape.

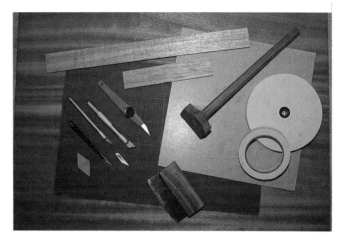

Tools and equipment for veneering

Lines (stringing) are narrow strips of veneer, usually black or white in colour and 1.5 to 3mm wide.

Bandings are made up of coloured woods to a variety of patterns. Made by bonding various sections of wood together to form a repetitive pattern. Available in one-metre lengths, 4 to 12mm wide and 1mm thick.

Motifs are made from a number of coloured veneers. They can be made to any design, but traditionally designs such as the urn, shell and floral patterns are used.

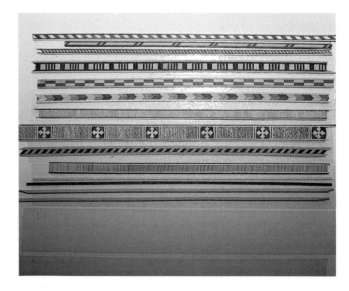

Bandings and lines

Groundwork is the name given to the material onto which the veneer is bonded. Solid wood or manufactured boards may be used. The most suitable manufactured board is medium-density fibreboard (MDF) or plywood. Hardboard may be used for small-sized work.

Flattening veneer

Groundwork

Veneering

Veneers should be handled carefully. They should be stored in an area which is cool and away from direct sunlight, ideally on a shelf in an enclosed press.

The veneer press can be used for flattening

Flattening

Flattening of veneers is necessary if the veneers are buckled. To do this dampen both sides of the veneer with a sponge and water. (Remember dampen, don't wet, the veneer.) Then press the veneer between two flat boards. Cramp the boards together or apply weights for one or two days.

When flattening a number of leaves of veneer place a sheet of paper between them to absorb the moisture.

Cutting

To cut veneer use a knife and a wooden straight edge, on a cutting mat or board. The blade of the knife must be sharp. When cutting, hold the straight edge firmly with one hand and work the knife against one edge. Hold the knife firmly but do not use excessive pressure. Make sure that the fingers of your other hand are not in front of the cutting edge of the knife. Make a number of light cuts until you have cut through the veneer. (A veneer saw is used in the same way.)

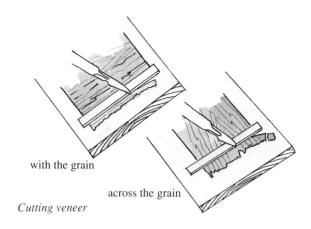

with the grain

across the grain

Cutting veneer

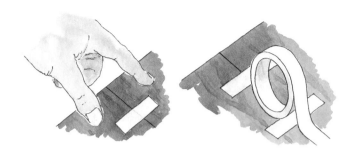

Taping the joints

Matching

Veneers often need to be joined to give the
required width or a particular pattern. When
joining, the edges must be cut straight to give a
good joint. Straight-grained veneer can be
matched quite easily. With figured grain it is
important to match the grain of each piece.

book matching

quartered

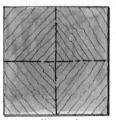

diamond

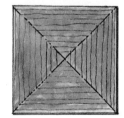

diagonal

Matching veneers

Jointing, Taping

When jointing, the edges of the veneer must be
cut straight.

To tape the joint pull the veneers together
with your fingers and thumb, and tape across
the grain. Repeat this at about 150mm intervals
along the joint. Then fix a piece of tape along
the length of the joint.

Borders, Crossbandings

Crossbanding: cut cross-grained strips to the
required width. Place the tape along the edges
of the centre panel, with about 10mm of tape
projecting. Turn over the panel and fix the
crossbanding to the tape. Overlap the banding
at the corners. Before cutting the mitres place the
tape on the banding to protect the short grain as
shown. Now using the straight edge and knife,
cut the mitres and tape the joints.

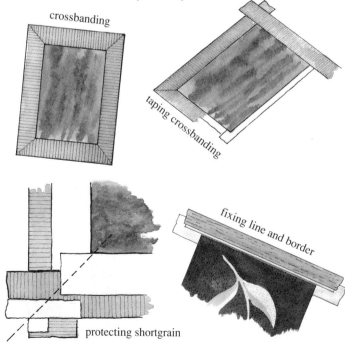

crossbanding

taping crossbanding

protecting shortgrain

fixing line and border

Bands and borders

245

Lined border

Lines: to make a lined border, tape the centre panel as above, turn it over and fix the line to the tape. Then fix the border to the tape. Allow them to overlap at the corners, cut and tape the mitres.

Use the same method to make up the pattern for the sides of a box.

Motifs: to fix a motif in a panel, temporarily tape it in position. Score around it with a knife. Remove the motif and cut through the veneer. Take out the piece of veneer and replace it with the motif. Tape the joint.

See page 251 on fixing to the groundwork.

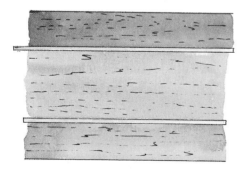

Pattern for side of box

Motif example

Marquetry

Marquetry is the technique of using veneer to form decorative patterns or designs. It makes use of the colour, texture and grain pattern of wood. Very intricate patterns are cut with a fretsaw, but most marquetry patterns are cut with a knife.

Example of marquetry

The process

Overlay method

In this method one veneer is laid on top of another.

Then cut through both veneers and interchange the pieces. Since both veneers are cut at once they must be a perfect fit for each other.

Example 1: Apple

Select suitable veneers: in this case beech, mahogany and teak.

a) Draw the outline on a sheet of paper and tape this to the cutting mat.

b) Tape beech veneer in position (background).

c) Tape mahogany veneer in position (apple).

d) Trace design onto one of the veneers (in this case the beech veneer) using carbon paper.

e) Cut around the outline of the apple ignoring the stem. Rotate the cutting mat to maintain a comfortable cutting position. Use a scalpel knife with a no. 11 blade. Continue to make light cuts until you have cut through both veneers.

f) Place the mahogany apple in the beech background and tape the joints.

g) Remove mahogany, position teak veneer and tape.

h) Cut out the stem.

i) Fit the teak stem in the background and tape.

j) Reverse side of pattern ready for adhesive for fixing to groundwork. A border may be added if desired.

247

Note: Where there is a short grain, e.g. stem, tape this area before cutting and then cut through tape.

Window method

In this method only one veneer is cut each time. The main advantage of this method is that it allows the grain to be positioned exactly, to give the best effect.

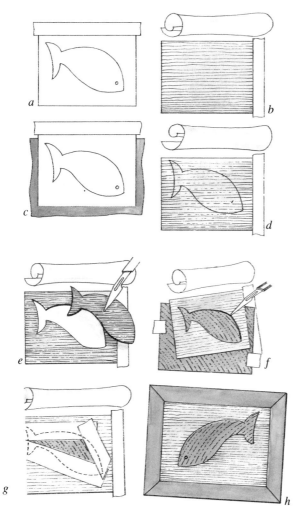

Example 2: Fish

a) Tape drawing onto cutting board.

b) Position and tape background veneer to cutting board.

c) Trace design onto veneer using a pointed dowel and black carbon paper.

d) Cut around the outline, moving the cutting board to maintain a comfortable cutting position.

e) Remove the fish shape.

f) Position the second veneer which should have a curved grain under the fish shape ('window') so the grain gives the best effect. Tape veneer and cut using the edge of the window as the template.

g) Insert the fish in the background and tape in position. To locate the eye flip back the drawing.

h) Add a border to complete the pattern.

Layered marquetry

This process involves building up one veneer on top another, to give a stepped effect.

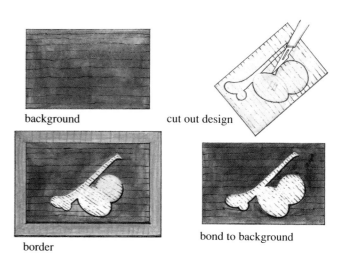

Layered marquetry panel

Select a background veneer, then select another veneer and on this draw a design. Now cut out this design and bond it to the background veneer. To add a border bond the background to a larger piece of veneer.

Microwood veneer is ideal for this process, particularly the self-adhesive type.

Fretsaw cutting

Very intricate shapes must be cut with a saw. A hand fretsaw or an electrically powered fretsaw (scroll saw) can be used. It will take some time to develop the ability to use the hand fretsaw. A number of veneers are cut at the same time in a pack. The pieces are then interchanged to form the required pattern.

Scroll saw in use

Fretsaw in use

Example 3: Outline of a leaf

Select appropriate veneers, two woods, e.g. walnut and sycamore. Place these two veneers between two backing veneers. Draw or trace the design onto the top veneer (backing veneer). Tape the pack together. Cut through the four

veneers with a saw. Remove the tape and tape the walnut leaf into the sycamore background.

Note: A piece of 4mm plywood may be used instead of the bottom backing veneer.

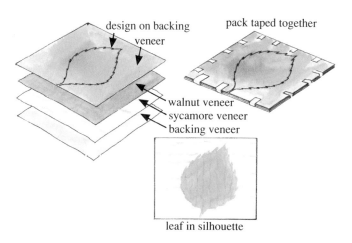

Parquetry

Similar to marquetry except that it is based on geometric shapes. All lines are cut using the straight edge and knife. Jigs are often used for repetitive shapes. Straight-grained veneers are the most suitable.

Chessboard: parquetry example

Example 4: Chessboard (400 × 400mm)

Select two contrasting veneers approximately 400mm long.

a) Trim one edge straight.

b) Using the jig and 40mm spacers, cut four strips of one colour veneer and five strips of the other. Place the strips to one side in the order in which they are cut.

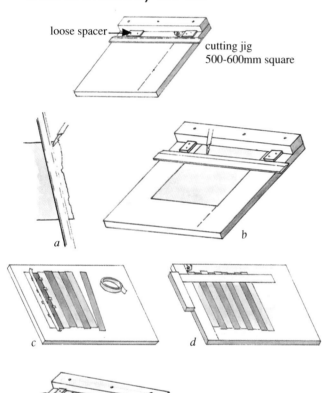

a *b* *c* *d* *e*

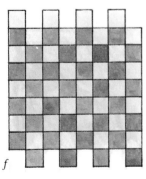

f

The process

g

c) Tape alternate coloured strips, firstly across the joint and then along the joint.

d) Trim one end square.

e) Cut eight strips across the joint lines.

f) Tape the joints as before, but stagger the squares, to form the chequered pattern. Remove the surplus squares from either side.

g) Tape around the edges of the pattern, reverse the side and fit a line and banding. Cut and tape mitres.

h) The reverse side is now ready for the adhesive to bond it to the groundwork.

Example 5: Cube pattern

To make this pattern cut strips with the grain to the required width, e.g. 15mm, using the cutting jig. Then cut these strips into diamonds on the jig shown below. Assemble and tape the cubes as shown on page 251. For the best effect use three slightly different shades of veneer for each face of the cube.

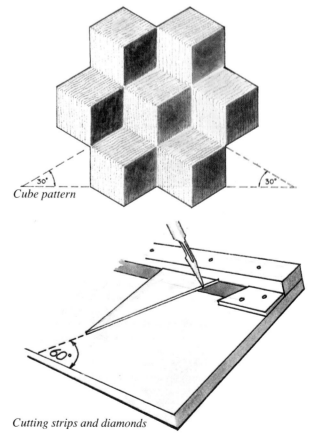

Cube pattern

Cutting strips and diamonds

250

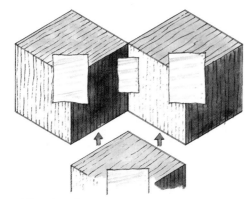

Assembling the cubes

Other patterns

Fixing to groundwork

Veneer is always bonded to groundwork. The groundwork can be solid wood or manufactured

Face and backing veneers

boards. The surface should be smooth. Any defects will show through the veneer.

When veneer is bonded to the face of the groundwork it has a tendency to 'pull' it out of shape. Therefore it is necessary to bond another veneer (backing veneer) to the back of the groundwork. This is known as **counter veneering**.

Adhesives

The adhesives used for veneering are contact/impact adhesive; glu-film; cascamite; PVA; animal glue. They have various methods of application.

Contact/impact adhesive

Use a brush-on impact adhesive, e.g. Evo-stick 613 and cleaner Evo-stick 191S.

a) Brush on a coat of adhesive to the veneer and groundwork. Leave for a few minutes until it is touch dry.

b) Place a sheet of paper over the groundwork leaving about 5mm at one edge exposed.

c) Position the veneer on the groundwork, press it down on the exposed adhesive.

d) Now remove the paper and press down the veneer. Work from the centre outward with a veneer hammer, applying pressure.

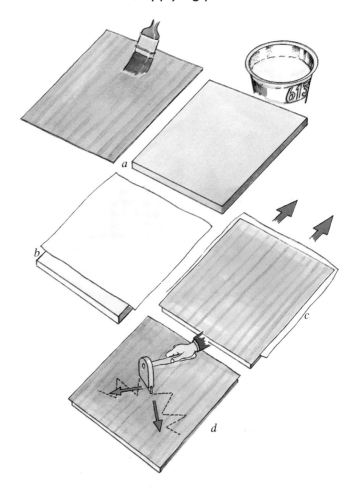

Glu-film

Peel off the backing paper from the film of glue, and position it on the groundwork. Place the veneer on top of it and the backing on top of the veneer. Using a medium-hot iron press down on the paper. Work slowly over the whole area applying final pressure with a roller or veneer hammer.

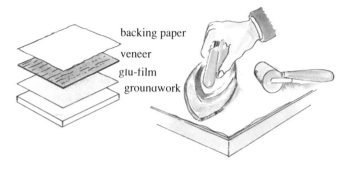

Veneer Press

Cascamite, PVA

These adhesives are applied to the groundwork only. When the veneer is positioned on the groundwork it must be kept under pressure for a number of hours until the adhesive has set. This is done by using cauls or presses:

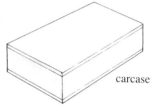

carcase

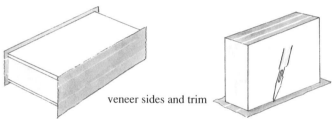

veneer sides and trim

Veneering a box

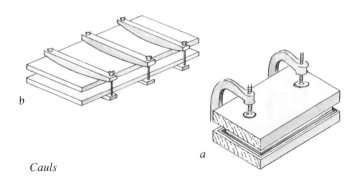

Cauls

veneer ends and trim

a) simple caul and G cramps;

b) cauls, slightly curved bearers and threaded bars or G cramps;

c) a simple veneer press.

Note: Place a few leaves of newspaper between the cauls or press plates and the veneer, to ensure even pressure on the veneer and to protect the cauls from glue.

Two examples of veneered boxes

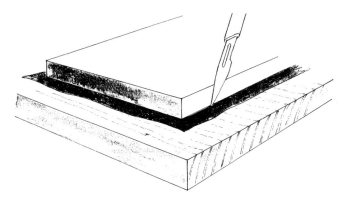

Trimming the veneer

Finishing

Remove tape carefully, sand carefully, especially at the edges and corners. Apply any woodfinish depending on type of finish required.

clean off veneer
with cabinet scraper

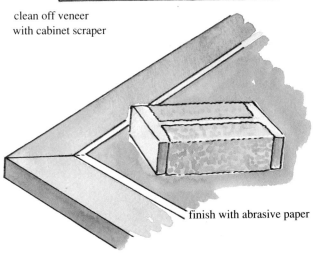

finish with abrasive paper

Finishing

A country scene

Positive and negative marquetry

For Activities, see page 258

20

Inlay, fretwork and laminating

Inlay

Inlaying is the setting in of decorative wood such as boxwood into the surface of solid or veneered wood. Other materials such as ivory, brass or plastic may also be used.

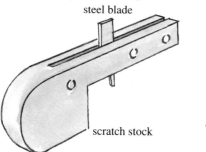

Basic inlay tools

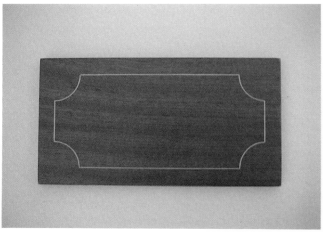

Inlaid panel

Inlaying with boxwood

a) Use a scratch stock to cut the straight grooves.

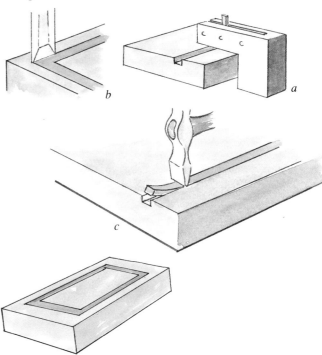

b) Finish corners using a chisel.

c) Apply adhesive to groove and push in the inlay with the back of a cross pein hammer.

Use the same procedure to inlay banding.

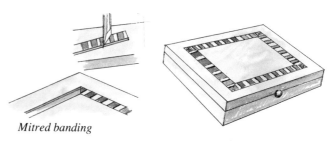

Mitred banding

Mitre the ends of the banding or inlay with a sharp chisel.

For curved work use a template as a guide and a chisel to cut the groove.

Corner treatment

Inlaying to an edge

Remove rebate with a cutting gouge. Apply adhesive to rebate and hold inlay in place with masking tape until the adhesive has set.

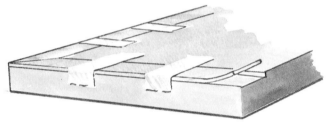

Edge inlay

Setting in a motif

Position a motif and temporarily tape in place. Score around the edge of the motif with a knife (alternatively mark with a sharp pencil). Remove waste using chisels and hand router, to a depth slightly less than the thickness of the motif.

Apply adhesive to recess and fit motif. Keep under pressure until adhesive has set.

Remove paper from motif and sand level with the background.

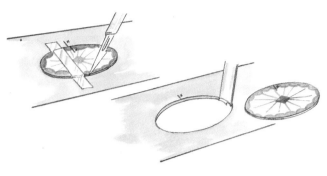

Setting in a motif

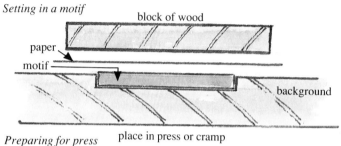

Preparing for press   place in press or cramp

Fretwork/Scrollwork

Traditionally fretwork was applied to furniture. Patterns were cut out of wood 3 to 5mm thick with a fine-bladed fretsaw, and then glued to the rails, legs, etc. of furniture.

Fretwork side panel

Method

Fretwork can be cut by hand, fretsaw or powered fretsaw (scroll saw). Where the pattern is pierced a hole is bored in the wood to allow the blade to be passed through.

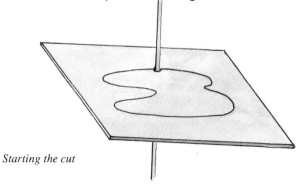

Starting the cut

255

Variations of fretwork or scrollwork

A variety of shapes and patterns can be cut with a fret/scroll saw.

Examples of fretwork

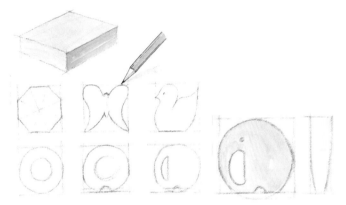

Designing a paperweight

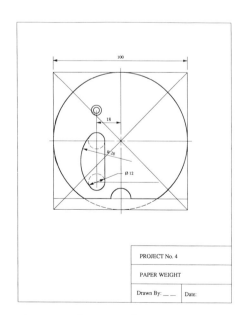

Measured drawing of paperweight

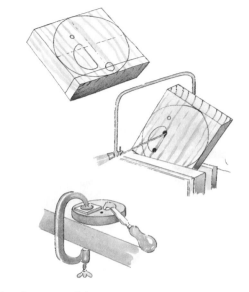

Making the paperweight

Ready for finishing

Pyrography

Pyrography is the art of decorating wood by burning designs into its surface.

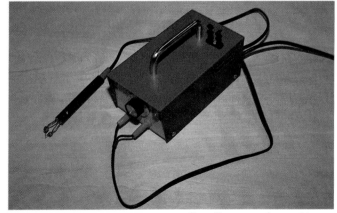

Pencil pyrography machine

Equipment

There are two main types of pyrography machines, the **poker** type and the **pencil** type.

The poker type is very similar to a soldering iron, with a range of different tips.

The pencil type (shown) consists of a control box and a pencil with a wire tip. The temperature of the tip can be adjusted at the control box. This machine runs on low voltage. This type allows greater freedom of design.

Designs

Patterns based on animal and plant life are very popular, though almost any design may be used.

Pyrography designs

Materials

Light-coloured woods are the most suitable, e.g. lime, sycamore, cherry, beech, chestnut, birch, etc. Wood should be sanded to a smooth finish before starting the work, and should be sealed with a clear finish when completed.

Colour

Colour may be added to a design by using stains, dyes, watercolours or oil paints.

Health and safety

- Do not touch the heated tip and switch off the equipment when not in use.

- Read the section on woodfinishes before using stains, dyes, paints, etc.

Mouldings

Mouldings are used as a form of decoration on woodwork. They can be formed by hand or powered tools.

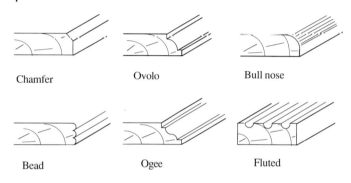

Types of moulding

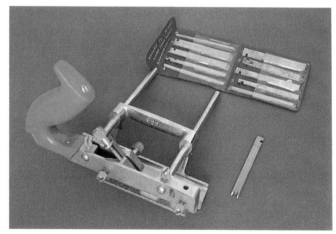

Combination plane and cutter

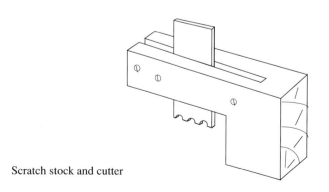

Scratch stock and cutter

257

Moulding a panel with router

There is a wide range of cutter profiles available

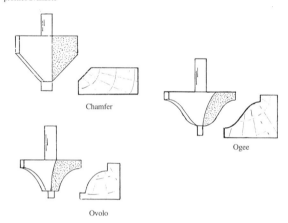

Chamfer

Ogee

Ovolo

Router cutter profiles

Activities (Chapters 17–20)

1. Name two woods suitable for carving.
2. Describe incised carving.
3. Describe chip carving.
4. Describe relief carving.
5. Where is a punch used in woodcarving?
6. What thickness is veneer?
7. What is 'banding'?
8. Name two materials suitable for groundwork.
9. What is meant by 'matching' veneer?
10. When is it necessary to use a fretsaw to cut veneer?
11. State the difference between marquetry and parquetry.
12. Name an adhesive suitable for bonding veneer.
13. Describe 'inlaying'.
14. What is pyrography?
15. What precautions should be taken when using pyrography?
16. Describe the following carving tools: no. 1, no. 3, no. 39.
17. Describe the sharpening of a vee tool.
18. Describe how you would transfer a design to the wood.
19. Sketch a design suitable for chip carving.
20. Draw a simple pattern for relief carving.
21. Make a working drawing for a nameplate.
22. Describe the manufacture of veneer.
23. Sketch the grain pattern of crown, curl and burr veneer, and state the part of the tree they are cut from.
24. Describe how veneer is 'flattened'.
25. Draw a pattern for marquetry and describe how it is transferred to the veneer.
26. Draw a pattern for parquetry.
27. Describe one method of bonding veneer to groundwork, and state why this is necessary.
28. Describe how you would inlay a motif into solid wood.
29. Make a working drawing of a simple fretwork project.
30. Describe how you would process a three-beaded moulding to the edge of a piece of wood.

Bending wood

When bends or curves are required in wood they can be achieved by cutting a curve from solid timber, steambending or laminating thin pieces of wood together.

Woods for bending

Most woods can be bent but the following are the most suitable: ash, beech, elm, sycamore, walnut. Use straight-grained sections.

Cutting a curve from solid timber

Select a piece of wood where the grain follows the curve. Mark out curve and cut to outline. This method is suitable for shallow curves.

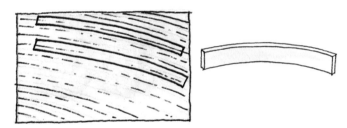

Grain selection

Steambending

To bend wood in its solid form it is necessary to steam it. This process softens the wood fibres, making it easier to bend. The outside surface of the bend will need to be supported during bending.

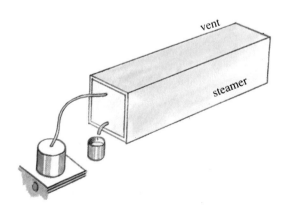

Simple steaming method

Equipment

Steamer: an insulated pipe, sealed at both ends, set at a slight incline to allow condensed water to run off, will satisfy requirements. Steam can be fed from a boiler at the lower end, with a small hole acting as a vent at the upper end.

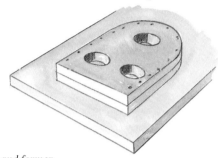

Strap and former

Strap: a metal strap with handgrips and stops is used to support the wood during bending.

Former: the former can be made from solid wood or manufactured board. The curve on the former should be slightly less than the required curve, as the wood will 'spring' a little when the cramps are removed. Cut holes in the former to take cramps if required.

Method

Place the wood in the steamer for 40 to 50 minutes for each 25mm of thickness. Then remove wood and place it in the former. With the strap supporting the wood pull it around the former and cramp it in position. When cool remove the cramps. The wood will retain its new shape.

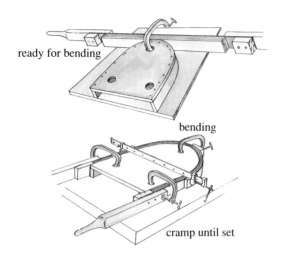

ready for bending

bending

cramp until set

Using the jig

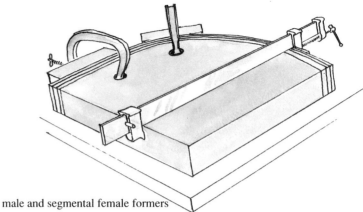

male and segmental female formers

Health and safety

- Use thick gloves when handling wood taken from the steamer.

Laminating

Lamination consists of bonding thin strips or sheets of wood together while bent around a former.

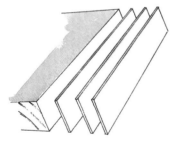

Cutting the laminates

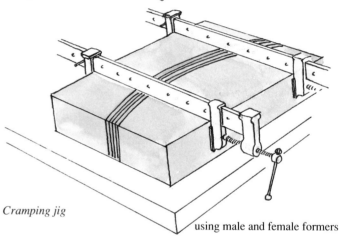

Cramping jig

using male and female formers

Panels

When curved panels are being formed layers of up to 3 to 4mm plywood or veneers are used. The plys or veneers are glued, placed between two formers and cramped.

Method

Cut suitable wood into 3mm-thick strips. Mark the wood before cutting to facilitate realignment of the strips. Realign strips as they come from the board. (This will make cleaning up easier, give a better appearance and avoid a build up of stresses.) Apply adhesive and place in formers. Cramp in position and allow adhesive to set.

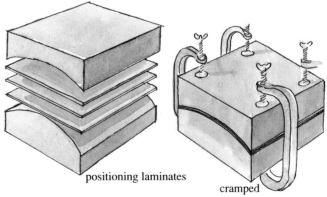

positioning laminates

cramped

Making laminated panel

21

Electronics

Introduction

Look around you and see the range of electronic devices we take for granted. We rely on videos, televisions, calculators, microwave ovens, computers and many others to make our lives easier and more enjoyable, at home, at school and at work.

Devices which use electronics

All these are relatively new inventions, being practically unheard of a few short decades ago. In fact, it seems that future historians will refer to this period as the **Electronic Age**, in the same way as we refer to the Ice Age and the Bronze Age.

But what is electronics?

If you remove the back from a television or a radio you are faced with an amazing array of wires and strange-looking components. However, despite this apparent complexity, all electronic devices are essentially simple in concept and operation. The systems approach describes it as follows:

e.g. smoke from a burning chip pan enters a smoke detector, breaking a light beam (*input*); this is *processed* by a circuit and an alarm bell sounds (*output*).

Example of electronic component

All electronic devices depend on controlling the behaviour of tiny atomic particles, called **electrons**, by passing them through circuits made up of a number of **components** arranged in a particular way.

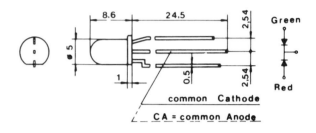

Electronic circuit diagram

Electric current and its sources

Everything around us is made up of atoms, tiny particles invisible under even the most powerful microscope. Atoms in turn are made up of smaller particles, each of which has an electrical charge. **Protons** (+ve charge) and **neutrons** (0 charge) make up the nucleus of the atoms, around which the electrons (-ve charge) rotate. Under certain conditions we can get these electrons to move from one atom to another, so creating an electric **current**.

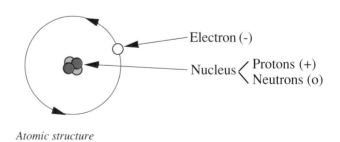

Atomic structure

In the early days of electrical study it was assumed that current would flow from positive to negative. This is now known to be incorrect; electrons flow from areas of negative charge to those of positive charge. However, the description of current flow as being from positive to negative is still used and is called **conventional current**.

For most of our work we will use **cells** or **batteries** to provide a flow of electrons. In a cell or battery chemicals react together to produce an excess of electrons at the negative (-ve) terminal and a shortage at the other, positive (+ve), terminal. If an electrical **conductor** is connected between the two terminals, an electric current will flow. We could think of a battery as an electron pump, pushing electrons around the circuit.

In order for electrons to flow in a circuit there must be a potential difference (PD) between the terminals. This PD is measured in volts (V). A single cell usually has a *potential difference* of 1.5v. If a larger voltage is required, several cells can be connected 'in series' to provide 3v, 4.5v, 6v, etc.

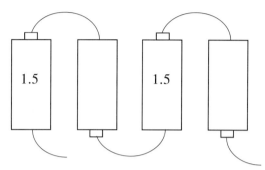

Four 1.5v cells wired in series to give 6.0v

The amount of current a battery can deliver is measured in **ampere hours**, i.e. the number of amperes that can be drawn in one hour. A battery rated at 1 amp/hour will supply 1 amp for 1 hour, 0.5 amps for 2 hours, 0.2 amps for 5 hours etc.

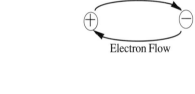

Conventional Current

Electron Flow

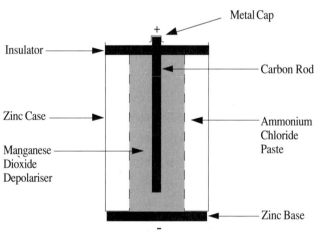

Dry Cell

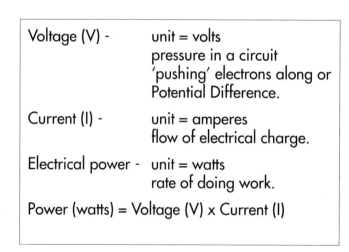

Voltage (V) -	unit = volts pressure in a circuit 'pushing' electrons along or Potential Difference.
Current (I) -	unit = amperes flow of electrical charge.
Electrical power -	unit = watts rate of doing work.
Power (watts) = Voltage (V) x Current (I)	

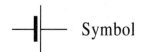

Symbol

Components

Switches

Included in circuits to 'make' or 'break' the circuit. While there is a wide variety of different switch types in various shapes and sizes, their mode of operation usually consists of one of the following:

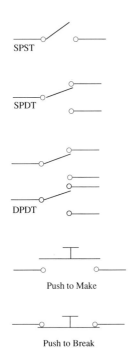

SPST

SPDT

DPDT

Push to Make

Push to Break

a) Single Pole Single Throw (SPST)

Simplest type of switch, in which a moving pole comes in contact with a fixed contact, so closing the circuit.

b) Single Pole Double Throw (SPDT)

A single moving pole may make a connection with one contact in one position, so causing one circuit to operate. In another different position the contact may close a different circuit, e.g. a flashlight having a mainbeam and a flashing beacon controlled by the same switch.

c) Double Pole Double Throw (DPDT)

Two moving poles switch between two sets of contacts. This could be used to switch two different circuits at the same time, e.g. motor and flashing lights on a model fire engine, or to achieve the reversing of a motor by changing the polarity of its circuit.

The type of switch used will depend very much on the design of the circuit and the article it is to be used in. Examples of those available are given here.

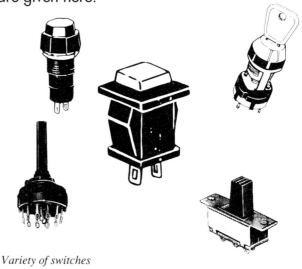

Variety of switches

Resistors

Control and direct the flow of current in a circuit. The two most commonly used types are *a)* fixed and *b)* variable.

Resistor — note coloured bands giving its value

264

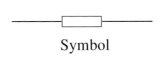

Symbol

a) Fixed resistors

These are relatively cheap and easy to use. The type most commonly used in electronics consists of a ceramic tube covered in carbon film and with a wire leg at each end. The composition and quantity of the carbon film determines the resistance, measured in **ohms** (Ω). The value of a resistor can be read from the four coloured bands at one end. Each colour has a different value: the first band gives the first digit, the second band the second digit and the third the multiplier as a power of ten. A fourth band, slightly separated from the other three, gives the maximum likely percentage variation to be found from the resistor's stated value:

silver $^+/_-$ 10%

gold $^+/_-$ 5%

e.g. orange orange brown silver

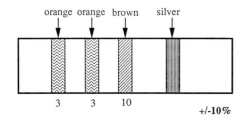

i.e. 330 Ω $^+/_-$ 33. Therefore this resistor could have an actual resistance between 297Ω and 363Ω.

If resistors are connected 'in series' in a circuit then the total resistance is given by the formula:

$$\frac{1}{Rtot} = \frac{1}{R_1} + \frac{1}{R_2} + \; - - - \; \frac{1}{R_z}$$

R1   R2

Resistors in Series

e.g.

Rtot = 450 Ω + 1.1 kΩ = 1.55 kΩ

450Ω 1.1kΩ

If resistors are connected 'in parallel' the total resistance is less than that of any single resistor because the current has more than one path to follow. The formula for resistance in a series circuit is:

$$Rtot = \frac{1}{R1} + \frac{1}{R2} + \; - - - \; \frac{1}{R2}$$

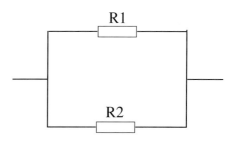

Resistors in Parallel

e.g.

$$\frac{1}{Rtot} = \frac{1}{450} + \frac{1}{900} = \frac{1}{300}$$

$$\Rightarrow \quad Rtot = 300\Omega$$

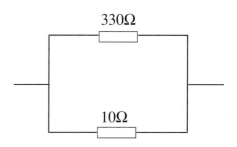

Black	0
Brown	1
Red	2
Orange	3
Yellow	4
Green	5
Blue	6
Violet	7
Grey	8
White	9

Value chart for bands

Variable resistor (use two connections only, centre and one other)

b) *Variable resistors:*

These allow the resistance to be adjusted between 0 ohms and the maximum resistance of each individual resistor. The most common type consists of a horseshoe-shaped carbon track with a contact at each end. A wiper, which is moved by rotating a spindle, is in contact with the track and has its own contact. By connecting one contact at the end of the track to one side of the circuit, and the wiper contact to the other, resistance can be varied by adjusting the amount of carbon track between the two contacts. (This type of variable resistor is also

known as a potentiometer, as by using all three contacts it can be used as a potential divider.)

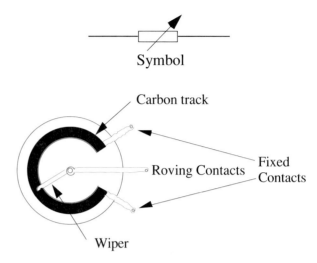

Symbol

Another type of variable resistance is a preset or trimpot. Its resistance is set using a screwdriver to the 'exact' value and left in place.

Preset resistor

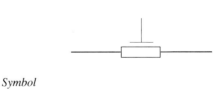

Symbol

266

Light-dependent resistor (LDR)

Manufactured from cadium sulphide (CdS), a material whose resistance varies with light intensity. In darkness it has a very high resistance (10mΩ), and in bright light it has a very low resistance (1kΩ). The most commonly used LDR in electronics is called an ORP 12, which has a very fast reaction time.

Light dependent resistor (ORP 12)

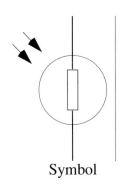

Symbol

Thermistor

Its resistance alters with changes in temperature and makes it suitable for use in fire-alarms, fridge control, etc. There are two varieties of thermistor:

a) NTC (negative temperature coefficient):

Their resistance falls with increases in temperature.

b) PTC (positive temperature coefficient):

Their resistance increases with increases in temperature.

NTC thermistors are probably more useful in the type of situations we will encounter.

Disc-type thermistors

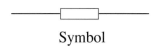

Symbol

Ohms law

Called after Professor George Ohm who did most of the research into it. Simply put, it describes the relationship between voltage (V), current (I), and resistance (R).

$$V = I \times R \; or \; R = \frac{V}{I} \; or \; I = \frac{V}{R}$$

By writing it in a triangle it is easy to see how to find one quantity when the other two are known. Simply place your finger over the unknown quantity and the arrangement of the other two gives the correct formula.

e.g.

a) If a 6v battery is powering a circuit with a total resistance of 330 ohms, what current is flowing?

$$I = \frac{V}{R} \qquad I = \frac{6v}{330\,ohms} = 0.018A$$

(more easily expressed as milliamps (mA) i.e. 18 mA)

b) If you want to restrict the flow of current in a circuit to 0.5A in order to control the loudness of a buzzer and you are using a 6v battery, what resistance should you use?

$$R = VI = \frac{6v}{0.5A} = 12\Omega$$

Diode

Made from a semiconducting material, such as silicon, with various impurities added in order to control the flow of electrons through it.

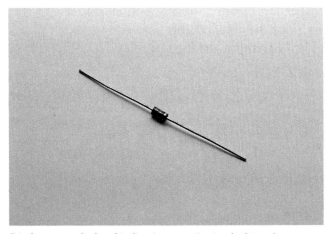

Diode — note the band indicating negative (cathode) end

Diodes are used as valves in a circuit, allowing current to flow in one direction only. The band on a diode must be placed on the negative (cathode) side of the circuit.

Symbol

A special type is the light emitting diode (LED), which is often used in circuits as an indicator, while at the same time fulfilling the diode's function. LEDs work on a low voltage (approx. 1.5v) so they need to be connected in series with a 'protective' resistor (usually about 330 ohms).

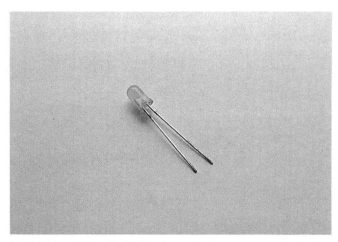

LED (light emitting diode). The longer is the negative (cathode) leg

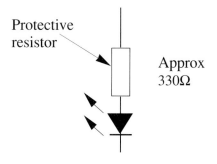

Protective resistor

Approx 330Ω

268

Capacitors

Used in circuits to store (charge) and release (discharge) current. The storage value of a capacitor is given in farads but electronics use capacitors with values in microfarads

$$\frac{1}{(1,000,000)}$$ (uf) or picofarads (1×10^{-12} f) (pf).

Most of the capacitors used in electronics are 'electrolytic' and must be connected in a circuit the correct way round i.e. cathode to cathode. Examples of capacitor circuits include time delay or extended signal applications.

Electrolytic capacitor — the negative leg is clearly marked

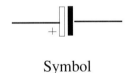

Symbol

Transistors

Prior to its invention in 1947 radios and other electronic devices were large and delicate because they relied on large glass valves. The transistor, being smaller and more reliable, allowed for, amongst other things, a reduction in the size of devices.

Transistor

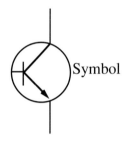

Symbol

Transistors are made from sandwiches of different types of silicon (either N-type or P-type silicon, depending on the impurities present). The way in which the sandwich of silicon is arranged dictates both the type of transistor created and the way it operates. Those most commonly used in our applications are NPN-type transistors.

Transistors can perform two functions in a circuit:

a) switching;

b) amplification.

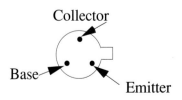

View from underneath

269

When connected correctly current is prevented from flowing through the **collector/emitter** circuit until a small base current (0.6v for BC108) switches it on.

The amplification factor of a transistor or **current gain** (hFE) varies depending on the type of transistor used. It can be calculated by the following equation:

$$\text{Current gain (hFE)} = \frac{\text{collector current (Ic)}}{\text{base current (Ib)}}$$

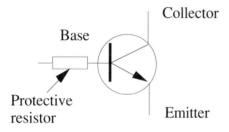

Like LEDs, transistors require a protective resistor

For the BC108 this is 100, i.e. a base current of 1mA triggers a collector/emitter current of 100mA.

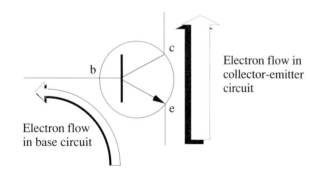

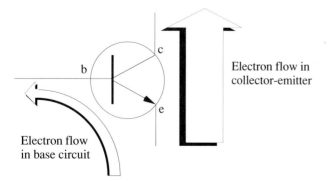

Potential divider and transistor circuits

Say that you have a device that requires a 3v power supply for a buzzer and a 6v supply for a motor. You could use two separate batteries. However, this would seldom be practicable and some means will have to be found whereby the voltage supplied by a single battery can be 'split'.

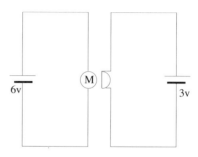

This can be achieved by using two (or more) resistors in series. If the voltage is measured across each resistor it will be found to be in proportion to the value of the resistors.

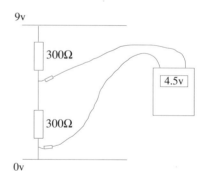

Note: by using all three contacts on a variable resistor the same effect can be achieved.

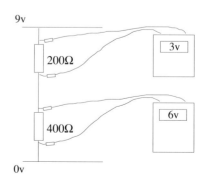

By combining the potential divider with a transistor we get a very useful and effective circuit that has many practical applications:

Circuit 1

To prove the operation of a transistor

In this circuit L2 lights but not L1 does not. However, if the bulb L1 is removed L2 goes out. This shows that there is a small current passing into the base of the transistor, keeping the emitter/collector circuit open.

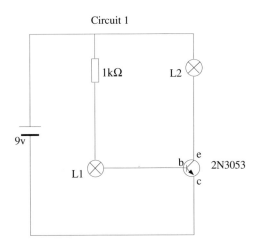

Circuit 1

Circuit 2

Light-sensing circuit

When light is falling on the LDR its resistance is low and there is not enough current flowing into the transistor's base to switch on the collector/emitter circuit. When the LDR is covered its resistance shoots up, the base current rises above the trigger voltage of 0.6v, and the collector/emitter circuit is completed. The output device will now operate.

Note: What would be the effect of switching the positions of the LDR and the 10kΩ resistor?

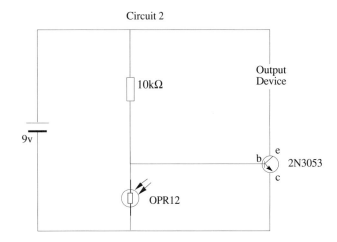

Circuit 2

Other useful PD/transistor circuits

Circuit 3

Heat-sensing circuit

When the themistor is cold its resistance is very high, higher than that of the variable resistor, therefore the voltage to the transistor is below 0.6v. When the thermistor heats up its resistance falls, the voltage to the transistor rises above 0.6v, switching on the collector/emitter circuit and the output device.

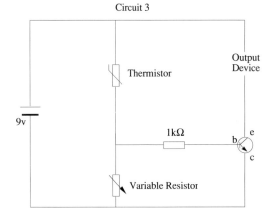

Circuit 3

Note: By changing the position of the thermistor and the variable resistor we get an output when it is cold.

Circuit 4

When the switch is closed the capacitor starts to charge. While this occurs the voltage across the capacitor starts to rise. When it reaches 0.6v the transistor's emitter/collector circuit is switched on and with it the output device. The time delay will depend on the size of the variable resistor and the capacitor.

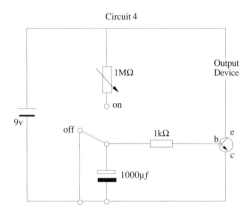

A simple way to establish the correct size of capacitor and resistor for the time delay required is to use the following chart.

1. Pick the timer delay you want (seconds).

2. Pick a capactor value that you have available (10 uf).

3. Draw a line through these two points on the chart. Where it hits the resistor line you can see the size of resistor to use for a 100-second delay using a 10 uf capacitor. In this case a 10 mΩ resistor would be required.

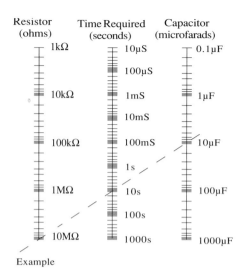

Circuit 5

Sometimes the current entering the base of a transistor is so low that, even if it does switch on the collector/emitter circuit, the amplification factor may not cause the output device to operate. This can be overcome by using a second transistor which takes the emitter current of the first transistor as its base current and amplifies it again. A typical gain for a Darlington Pair is in the order of 10 to the power of 4.

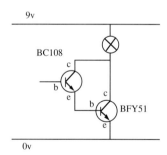

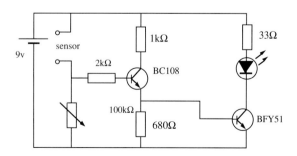

The LED lights up in the presence of even very low moisture levels

An example of this circuit's usefulness is in a simple moisture detector, where the amount of current flowing across the probes is unlikely to cause the output device to operate.

The LED lights up in the presence of even very low moisture levels.

Thyristor

Similar in many respects to the transistor, it too has three legs, **cathode**, **anode** and **gate**. If the gate receives a small voltage it turns on the full cathode/anode current and latches on, remaining on even when the gate voltage is removed. In order to switch it off a break must be made in the circuit. This latching effect makes it very useful in alarm-type applications.

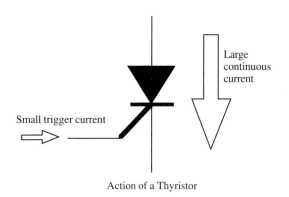

Action of a Thyristor

Relay

A device that allows two circuits to be separated, and for a circuit using very low voltages to switch on a circuit with much larger voltages. A typical example is the use of small DC voltages to switch on large AC devices. There are two parts to the relay, a switch and an electromagnet. When the electromagnet is activated by a current it becomes magnetic and attracts a pivoted plate which operates the switch. The switch can be of any type, SPDT, DPDT, etc. An example of its application might be the activation of a control panel by a car's headlights falling on it, and this, by means of a relay, operates the motor to raise the garage door.

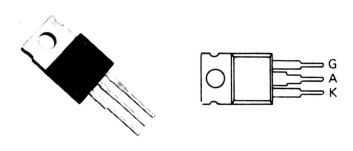

Thyristors

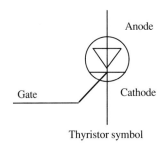

Thyristor symbol

Relay

273

Note: if a transistor is used in the relay switching circuit it must be protected from a backflow of voltage from the de-energising electromagnet by a 'clamping' diode.

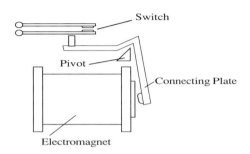

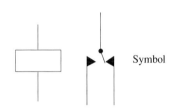

Symbol

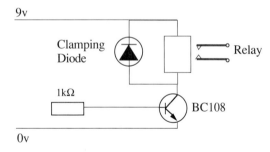

A small but powerful DC motor

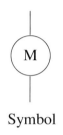

Symbol

In order to reverse a motor it is necessary to change the polarity of supply. The use of a DPDT switch is possibly the easiest way of achieving this. The rotational force of the motor is usually distributed by a system of pulleys or gears.

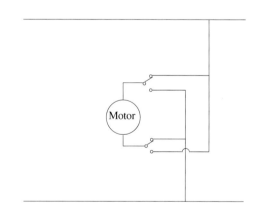

Circuit to achieve reversing of motor using DPDT switch

Motors

Small DC motors can be used as extremely useful outputs from many of the circuits described here or for circuits that you design yourself. Basically they consist of two permanent magnets set up at opposite sides of a casing and providing a fixed magnetic field. An *armature*, consisting of several electromagnets, rotates in the field of the permanent magnets and as their polarity opposes these the armature rotates. Because very strong permanent magnets have been developed we now have some very small but quite powerful DC motors.

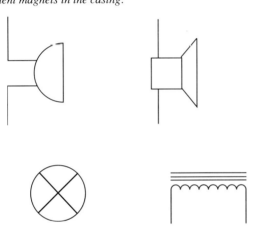

A disassembled motor. Note the electromagnets on the rotor and the permanent magnets in the casing.

Symbols

A number of miscellaneous components: from left to right a photovoltaic cell; b bulb and holder; c power supply unit; d buzzer; e battery dip; f miniature transformer; g loudspeaker

Integrated circuits or 'chips'

Up to now we have been looking at circuits built from separate or 'discrete' components. While serving well for such relatively small devices, their use in larger devices, such as computers, would make them too large and cumbersome. (Mark 1, the first commercial computer produced in 1950 by Ferranti, was 5m x 3m x 1m.)

Following the development of the transistor, further research discovered that several separate transistors could be placed on a single tiny piece of silicon. The first **integrated circuit** or **IC** was produced in 1958, and intense research and development has led to ICs with thousands of components incorporated in them. As a result, today's computers are a fraction of the size of the first models yet many times more powerful.

An old fashioned valve

The ICs or chips are tiny and may be extremely complex. In order for them to be handled and placed in circuits, they are embedded in a plastic case with metal contact legs wired with gold thread to the chip's connections.

An integrated circuit (chip) — and most of this is the casing!

How do they work?

Basically they operate through a series of **gates** built from the diodes, transistors and other components on the silicon chip. These gates—AND, OR, NOT, NOR, etc.—are arranged as adders and half adders to process the incoming binary (1 or 0) numbers and, as a result, provide specific outcomes.

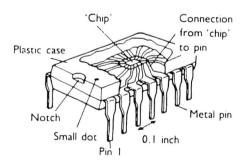

Half Adder

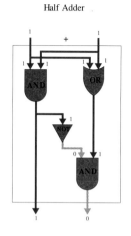

Full Adder

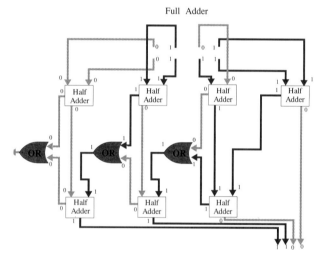

Some common integrated circuits

1. 555 Timer IC

The circuit on this chip consists of approximately 25 transistors, 16 resistors and 2 diodes in an eight-pin case. There are entire books written on this IC alone.

Two of its most common uses are as a **monostable** or **astable**.

a) **Monostable:** the circuit will switch on or off an output device for a set timed period.

276

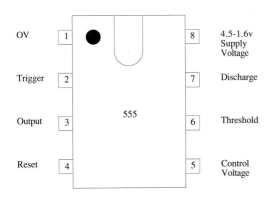

OV	1	8	4.5-1.6v Supply Voltage
Trigger	2	7	Discharge
Output	3	6	Threshold
Reset	4	5	Control Voltage

555

How it works:

i) Pressing the switch closes the circuit. The LED comes on;

ii) the capacitor starts to charge;

iii) when the supply voltage to the capacitor reaches 6v (from pins 6 and 7) the output returns to Ov;

iv) the LED goes out.

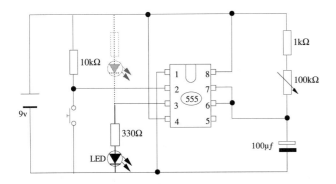

(In order to switch off the output for a timed period, move it to the position shown.)

The length of the timed period can be altered by selecting different capacitor/resistor combinations.

b) **Astable:** these circuits give a continuous on/off, on/off output such as might be used in a car alarm to flash the lights and/or cause the horn to sound.

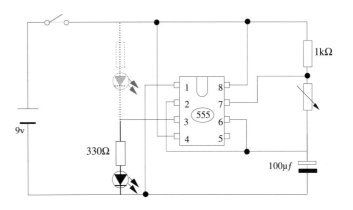

How it works:

i) Closing the switch starts the 555 working;

ii) the 555 turns the output on and off continuously. The interval is set by adjusting the 100K variable resistor.

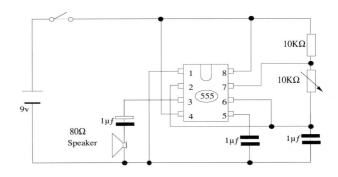

(A second output could be connected at the position shown so that the two LEDs could flash on/off alternatively.)

A modified circuit like this one, using small polyester capacitors and a speaker, will give a continuous noise.

2. LM3909 pulse generator

This is one of the easiest chips to use as it requires very few additional components to get it to work.

This simple circuit gives a flashing LED output or a continuous bleep to act as an indicator or warning, e.g. the flashing LED in the front of a car to say the alarm is on.

How it works:

i) Closing the switch starts the capacitor charging;

ii) the charged capacitor is switched in series with the battery;

iii) the capacitor is switched to be connected across the LED which lights up until the capacitor discharges. The sequence then restarts.

(The rate at which the LED flashes can be adjusted by changing the value of the capacitor.)

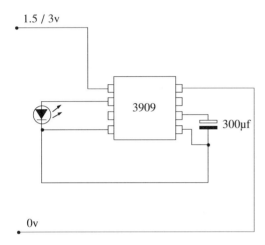

Breadboard or prototyping board

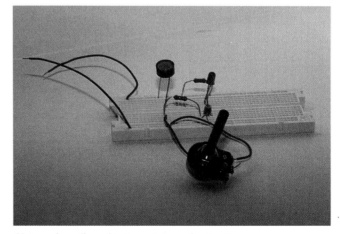

Tracking board

Building circuits

As in all design work, before the finished article is produced, it is often desirable to first make a prototype. This is even more relevant in the case of electronics where two out of three times the circuit will not work as intended the first time. Using a prototype or breadboard makes this task quite simple.

As shown, the sockets on the board are connected with copper tracks underneath the board. When components are inserted into the sockets and extra wire is looped over to form a complete circuit, the board is 'powered up' using the two rows of sockets running the length of the board. The channel down the board's centre allows ICs to be fitted to the board.

Using a breadboard to try out a simple circuit.

The completed circuit may be assembled on any of the following:

a) Matrix board:

Pins are inserted into pre-drilled holes in this plastic board and components soldered to them. Cheap but very untidy for anything other than simple circuits and there is no facility for fixing ICs.

A piece of matrix board. The pins are for soldering components and wires to.

b) Strip board

Similar to matrix board but with copper strips on its underside. Components are inserted through holes and soldered to these tracks. Breaks are made in the tracks to ensure a proper circuit. Easy to use but needs planning of component layout. Mounting sockets for ICs are available for fixing to the board.

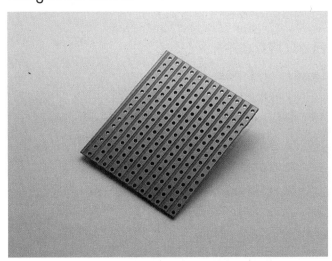

Strip board. The copper tracks provide the connections between components.

c) Printed circuit board (PCB)

Glass-reinforced plastic board coated with copper on one or both surfaces. The circuit connections and points for mounting components are drawn onto the copper face with a special pen. The board is then immersed in an acid bath and the excess copper is burnt off. It is widely used in industrial applications but could be used for relatively simple projects. Components are soldered to tracks through drilled holes.

Printed Circuit Board (PCB). Tracks are created by acid etching in a bath.

Health and safety

- Use only electrical solder with a non-corrosive flux core (flux helps solder to flow and stick properly).
- Make sure all surfaces are clean and free of grease.
- Apply solder to the heated component, not to the soldering iron.
- Allow joint to cool before allowing it to move.
- Use a heat sink to protect diodes and transistors.
- Use chip holders for integrated circuits, do not solder directly to IC pins.

Some other useful circuits

1. Flashing light

How it works:

The lamp flashes as each transistor is alternatively switched on and off due to the phased charging and discharging of the two capacitors. Changing the capacitor values and the two 10KΩ resistors will alter the flashing intervals.

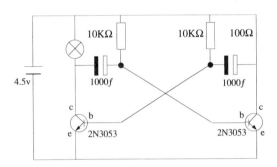

2. Intercom

How it works:

The microphone takes sound waves from the air and converts them into very small electric currents. These are boosted by the two-stage amplifier before being fed out through the loudspeaker again as sound.

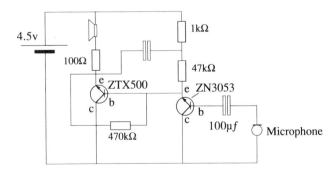

3. Simple radio

How it works:

A ferrite rod is wrapped in paper and wound with 2m of enamelled copper wire. The aerial should be at least 5m long. To tune the 'radio' the ferrite rod is moved in and out of the coil.

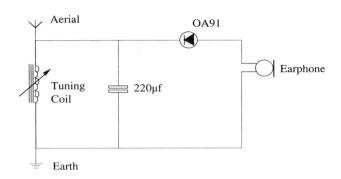

(In order to get good reception it must be well earthed, preferably connected to a metal water tap.)

The next step is to take the received signal and amplify it to improve its quality. This second radio circuit incorporates a simple transistor amplifier circuit.

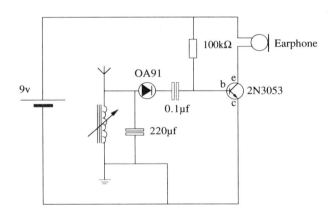

Activities

Design and make the following:

1. A letter box that will tell you when a letter has been delivered at a remote location.

2. A medicine storage chest with a light that comes on automatically on opening.

3. A desk storage tidy that incorporates an intercom.

4. A storage container for pegs that incorporates a rain alarm.

5. A model fire engine that has flashing lights and a forward and reverse direction of movement.

6. A portable chess game with a built-in move timer.

7. A magic candle.

8. A jewellery container with a tamper alarm.

9. How would you connect three 1.5v cells to give a total voltage of 4.5v?

10. Calculate the total resistance for a 330Ω, 17kΩ and 3mΩ resistor connected in a) parallel and b) series.

11. Explain what is meant by a potential divider and describe how you would use it to supply a motor with 6v and a buzzer with 3v from a 9v battery.

12. What is the difference between NTC and PTC thermistors?

13. Why does an LED need a resistor connected in series with it?

14. What is meant by the current gain (hFE) for a transistor?

15. Explain the operation of a transistor as a switch and as an amplifier.

16. Describe how a thyristor differs from a transistor.

17. If the current flowing in a circuit is 0.875A and the supply voltage is 9v, what is the circuit's resistance?

18. What is a Darlington Pair, and where might one be used?

22

Computer aided design drawing

In order to look in detail at computer aided design/drawing (CAD) we will first of all define computer graphics; secondly look at what equipment is required; thirdly look at CAD in general; and finally examine in some detail features which should be included in all good graphics programmes.

CAD work station

Computer graphics: What are they?

The following might be a good definition: 'Computer graphics is the science of producing graphical images with the aid of a computer.' The dictionary provides another definition: 'Diagrams, lines, pictures, maps or graphs used for illustration or demonstrations on the computer.' Clearly, computer graphics is about creating pictures by using a computer, even if these pictures end up on film or on paper.

Equipment

A computer system consists of two elements: the hardware and the software. The hardware is the electronic machinery that allows us to put information into the computer, that undertakes the calculations and manipulation of numbers, and that displays the information whether on screen or on paper. The software is the sequence of instructions driving the machine, the programme.

Most computers used in schools today are personal computers (PCs). Although these may be produced by many different companies the majority are based on one standard, i.e. they are IBM compatible, using the DOS system of operations. Others are BBC systems and, increasingly, the user-friendly Macintosh systems.

Computers work at varying speeds, and generally the faster a computer works the more expensive it will be. This speed is measured in **megahertz**. A speed of 8 megahertz or more would be considered suitable for graphic use.

The data required to run a programme or the information by which the computer operates must be stored in a permanent form unless it is to be lost every time the computer is switched off. This 'data' is stored on magnetic disks, either a floppy 5¼ inch or cassette 3½ inch which can be inserted or removed from the computer at will; or on a hard disk which is a larger disk permanently fixed inside the computer. It is a preferable to have a hard disk combined with either a 5¼ or 3½ inch disk drive.

Floppy disks (5.25 and 3.5 inch)

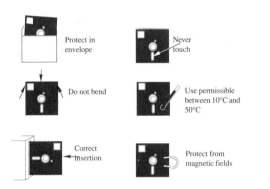

Protect in envelope

Never touch

Do not bend

Use permissible between 10°C and 50°C

Correct insertion

Protect from magnetic fields

Floppy disks must be treated with care

A computer's main memory is called **RAM** (Random Access Memory). The size of this memory is measured in units called **kilobytes** or K for short. A computer used for complex graphics needs 640K minimum. The more K the computer can handle the better.

Apart from computer's main 'thinking' parts it must have ways of letting the operator put information into it: **input devices**. Some of these are described below.

Keyboard

Familiar to everybody, the keyboard is the general purpose input device. It consists of the standard typewriter keys plus several extra function keys.

Mouse

Consists of a ball surrounded by a mouse box. When the mouse is moved across the table the electronics within it detect the type of ball movement and send this information back to the computer. The computer now moves a box or crosshair across the screen to match the mouse movements.

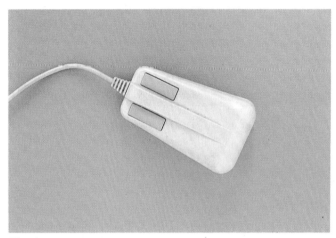
Two button mouse

Tracker ball

Used in a similar way to the mouse, the tracker ball has got a ball on top which is rotated by the fingers. It is in effect a mouse on its back.

Tracker ball control

Graphics tablet

Similar to the mouse, the graphics tablet has a crossed-hair targeting device which is used on a special drawing area, a tablet. It is extremely useful for tracing drawings into the computer.

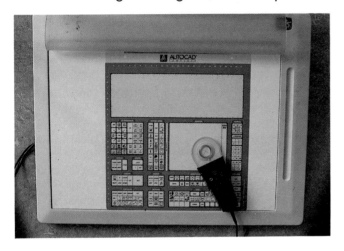

Graphics tablet

Scanner

It is possible to scan drawings and pictures using a light-sensitive scanner. A drawing can be entered into the computer in this way for further manipulation.

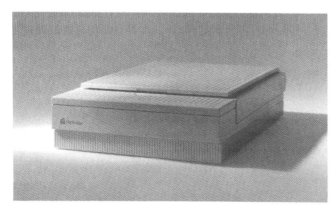

Scanner

It is essential that a computer have some of the above input devices, but it must also have **output devices** to allow the operator to get information out of it, such as:

Visual display unit/VDU/Monitor

The VDU behaves very like a television. The screen is made up of tiny squares or pixels. The smaller those are and the more of them on the screen the better the quality of graphics which can be achieved. Colour is very important for a graphics monitor.

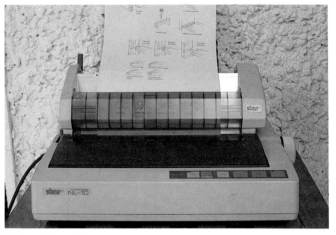

Dot matrix printer

Printer/Plotter

The information displayed on the computer screen, be it drawings, text, or a combination of both, can very easily be reproduced on paper if you have a printer or plotter. Plotters are preferred for graphic work.

The advantage of CAD

We can safely say that at present anything that can be drawn by hand can be drawn quicker and more accurately on a computer. The graphics produced will have a uniformly neat and precise appearance, regardless of who made them. Lines which should be parallel will be exactly so, corners will be exactly square, lines will meet exactly. Drawings will be accurate in another sense, with respect to distance. If, for example, you wish to draw a line 100mm long on a drawing board you may be accurate to ± 0.25mm. Using the computer accuracy will be ± 0.01mm.

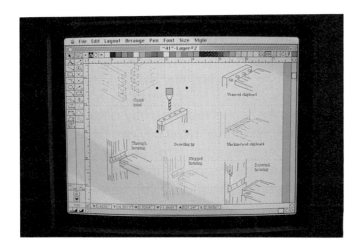

Tone of line in any drawing is very important, construction lines being light, outlines heavy, and dimensions somewhere in between. Using such techniques the finished drawing has more impact. Any drawing lacking such line tone will be both confusing and untidy. On a computer monitor this is not possible. We cannot vary line tone on a computer screen. There is a means, however, of making up for this deficiency: by using colours, up to 256 on some screens, an obtrusive colour like yellow could be used for construction lines, while block could be used for outlines.

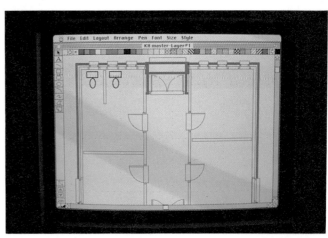

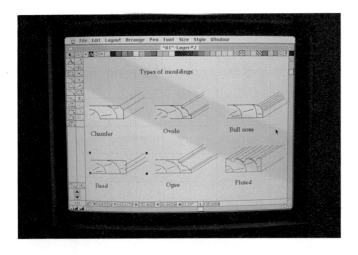

Computers are exceptionally well suited for design. At the initial design stages ideas are vague, are put down as sketches, modified, adapted and refined. Parts of a design may be kept while others are discarded. Using a computer this can be easily done. Parts of a drawing can be stored in a library while others can be wiped from the memory, or modified, stretched, shortened, twisted, etc. In fact on some occasions practically a whole drawing can be built up from library components. For example, it would be a time-consuming process to draw line by line every nut and bolt in an engine part. It is much easier to ask the computer to collect a nut and bolt of a certain type from its library and draw it at a certain place to the required scale. Furthermore lines can be drawn and erased thousands of times without any detrimental effect to the finished

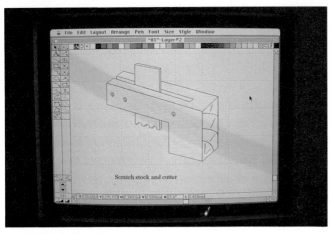

Examples of CAD drawings

product. If this was done on a drawing sheet you can imagine the result! The colour of lines, whether they are dotted, chained or solid can also be changed with ease on a computer.

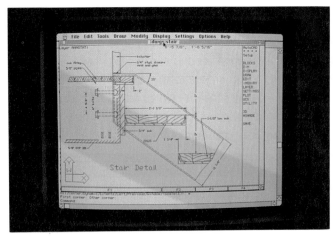

CAD working drawing

Graphical data

One big advantage of CAD, of course, is its speed. Drawings of high quality can be built up in a matter of minutes using library stored components. Repetitive items can be copied in a matter of seconds.

Using the computer as a design tool provides us with a very efficient method of storing our ideas. Each design or drawing can be stored under a suitable name on either a floppy disk or a hard disk, the computer filing each away in a directory.

Up until now we have been talking about two-dimensional drawings. Many powerful computer software packages can be used to actually draw in three dimensions. The computer can hold a 3D model in its memory which can subsequently be viewed from any angle: it can be rotated, enlarged, reduced, etc. Using this facility a designer can mirror exactly on screen what he/she has visualised in their mind. The design becomes dynamic: it can be viewed from every possible angle and perspective, it becomes almost real.

A designer faced with the problem of redesigning a car engine part may be faced with many different areas, e.g. fuel system, electrical system, cooling system. On a computer each system can be drawn on a separate 'layer' for clarity. Each layer can be worked in separately and they can all be combined to give the final result. Some programmes allow 30 or more layers to be used in any one drawing.

CNC router

Computer aided design/drawing is in many ways linked to **computer aided manufacture** (CAM). Computers may be linked up to robots, lathes and routers which can be used to mass produce the designs on the computer. This direct move from the design process to the manufacturing process can only be for the good. The computer sends information to the lathe, for example, in coded form. The lathe interprets this code and moves the cutting tool or spins the chuck accordingly. Possibly the greatest advantage of this is that identical objects can be produced time and time again very quickly, simply by using the same programmed codes.

Essential features

Having looked at the advantages of CAD it is time now to look at the essential elements of a computer graphics package.

Lines

These can be drawn in as solid, broken or centre lines. There are usually seven colours available, but up to 256 colours can be attained. Lines can be defined as having a starting point and an ending point. Alternatively they can be given a length and an angle or direction.

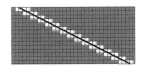

If you magnify any computer screen you will see that it is made up of tiny squares (pixels). These pixels produce a stair step effect with any sloped line. On good quality printers the pixels are so small that this stair step effect makes no difference.

Circles

Circles can be drawn using a wide range of information to suit different circumstances.

This information can be given as:

1. centre, radius,

2. centre, point and curve,

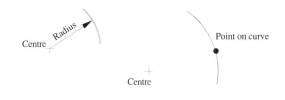

3. radius, circle to touch two lines,

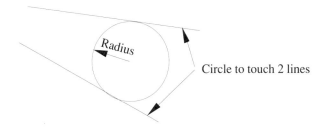

4. centre, tangent to line/arc/other circle,

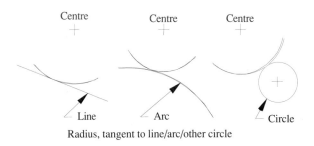

Radius, tangent to line/arc/other circle

5. radius, tangent to line/arc/other circle,

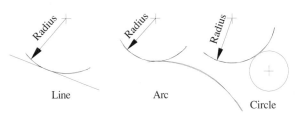

Radius, tangent to line/arc/other circle

6. three points in circumference,

7. radius, two points on circumference.

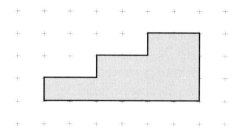

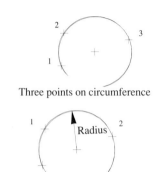

Three points on circumference

Radius, two points on circumference

Grid — a properly spaced grid can speed up the drawing of shapes based on rectangles

Arc

An arc is a part of a circle and as such can be specified in much the same way.

Ellipses

Ellipses are defined by giving the major and minor axes or by rotating a circle about its diameter.

Ellipses are specified by defining the length of the major and minor axes.

Grid

Here a grid of dots is drawn on the screen at a distance apart set by the person using the programme. They are not present on the final drawing but are there solely to aid in the build-up of the drawing, e.g. a grid of 1-metre squares would be very handy for anybody drawing the plans of houses.

Snap

This only allows the cursor to move at set distances. For example, we could have a grid of 10mm squares with a snap of 5mm. This will make the drawing of small objects very accurate.

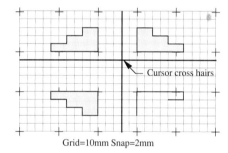

Grid=10mm Snap=2mm

Having a snap setting less than that of the grid means that the snap functions are a finer but invisible grid. The cursor cannot move to more snap points.

Zoom

This allows us to zoom in on a particular part of a drawing, enlarging it in the process, thus allowing more detail to be put in, or giving us a better view of the object.

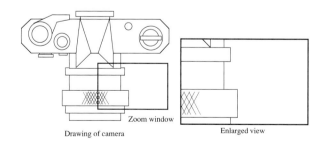

Drawing of camera   Enlarged view

Ortho

As was said before, 'ortho' means straight or at right angles. Using this facility lines on the monitor can only be drawn horizontally across the screen or vertically down it.

Translation/Dragging

It is often necessary to reposition an object by moving it sideways or up or down. This is a translation. The object can be dragged using the mouse or similar device into its new position.

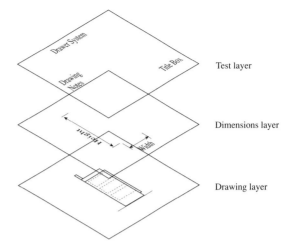

Test layer

Dimensions layer

Drawing layer

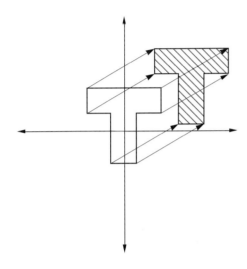

Objects can be translated / dragged or repositioned to anywhere on the screen

Hide

In a three-dimensional drawing the computer will generally ignore whether certain corners, edges or surfaces of the object can be seen or not. Consequently what is produced is a wire frame image. Under some circumstances this is not a problem but when objects are constructed from hundreds or even thousands of edges it is virtually impossible to discern their basic structure properties. The command 'hide' gets over this problem by removing all lines which should be not be seen.

A wire frame image. This is produced because all lines are shown, both those that would be visible and those that would not.

Layer

In order to build up complex drawings we need to put information on layers. A layer can be considered to be a transparent sheet on which we can put information. In a detailed working drawing one layer could contain the main drawing, another the dotted lines, another the dimensions and another the text.

Solid image: note shading and hidden lines removed

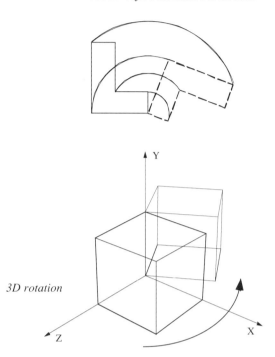

2D objects are rotated about points
while 3D objects are rotated about lines

3D rotation

Block

Any element that has to be drawn repeatedly can be called a block. As such it can be stored in a library of such shapes and can be retrieved and/or copied at will all over the drawing. This facility is very useful, as drawings having a lot of repetitive elements can be built up very quickly.

A repetitive element of a drawing like a nut and bolt can be blocked into the computer's library to be scaled and/or copied at will

Rotate

Lines, blocks, 3D objects and even whole drawings can be rotated to any angle.

Scale

It is possible to draw elements to different scales. This makes it possible to draw a standard-sized nut and bolt and then scale it to the required size, bigger or smaller, to suit your need. Thus a whole library of different nut sizes is unnecessary. Whole drawings can also be scaled using either reducing or enlarging scales. In this way the tiny circuits on the silicon chips can be drawn on the computer just as easily as building plans.

Mirror

Here an object is redrawn on the other side of a mirror line. Symmetrical objects can be drawn very quickly using this facility as only one half or one quarter need be drawn fully. The other side is produced using 'mirror'.

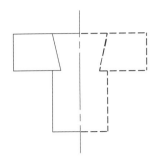

Half of this dovetail joint need only be drawn. The other half can be produced using a mirror.

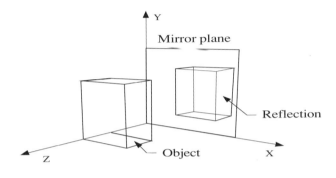

3D objects can be mirrored as well

Shading

Depth information and realism can be achieved in 3-dimensional drawings by using shade. Shading patterns can help to establish the contour or curve of surfaces while darker areas and shadows also help to identify the back of objects. In general shading patterns and shadows are difficult to achieve without expensive software.

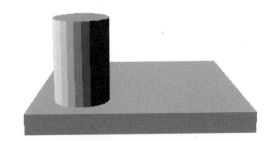

Shading

Extrusion

3D models can be formed by extruding 2D shapes. The model produced will have constant cross section. Extruding is a simple geometric process and is used in all 3D drawing packages.

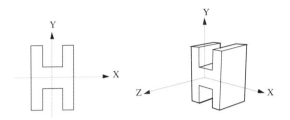

2D letter extruded to create a 3D model extrusion

Surfaces by revolution

Swept surfaces or surfaces of revolution provide a powerful 3D modelling technique for creating really complex objects. A curved or straight line is rotated about a fixed-axis line. To create a wine glass, for instance, all that is required is one contour which is swept around a vertical axis. A whole family of related objects can be produced in this way by varying the number of rotational steps in the final surface.

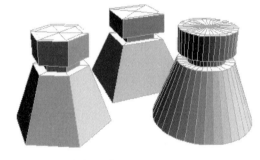

3 models produced along the same contours

Programmes

There are many excellent CAD programmes available providing features with very advanced geometry. Some of these cater for both 2D and 3D graphics. There are, however, many very versatile 2D graphics which are quite inexpensive. These are available for all computer systems, whether running on DOS (disk-operated system) or Macintosh or BBC. They will emulate most of the 2D features of the more expensive software but may be limited in areas of dimensionsing and text.

Remember that the computer is a very powerful design/drafting tool. It does not substitute, however, for sketching initial design ideas, and it definitely does not think for you. As the software and hardware continue to develop harness them to suit your needs. Be patient at first, proficiency only comes with lots of practice.

Activities

1. Explain the difference between hardware and software.

2. Describe using sketches five different ways that disks can be damaged.

3. Describe the difference between an input and an output device. List two of each.

4. Write an essay explaining your opinions on CAD, giving what you think are its advantages/disadvantages.

5. Why are more and more drawing offices using computers for drawing rather than drawing boards? Give five suggested reasons.

6. Explain CAM and where it could be used.

7. What is a pixel? If you magnify a sloped line on a screen you will see a stair-step effect. Why is this?

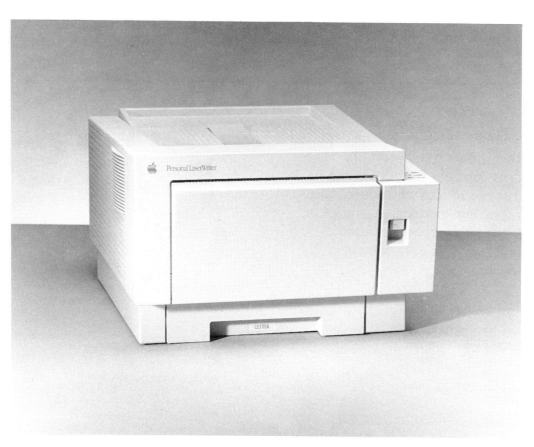

Laser printer

8. Describe five of the following CAD terms:

    a) zoom,

    b) grid,

    c) layer,

    d) hide,

    e) translation,

    f) mirror,

    g) surfaces by revolution,

    h) extruded solid.

9. What is the difference between snap and grid?

10. Use the computer to draw the following:

    a) a rectangle,

    b) a football pitch,

    c) a television,

    d) a house.

11. Why might drawings produced by computers be more accurate than those made on a drawing board?

12. When producing a 3D shape on the computer we first produce a wire frame image. Explain what you understand by a wire frame image.

13. Changing a 3D wire frame image into a true 3D drawing requires a lot of computer power and is a slow process even on a very powerful computer. Explain in your own words why this is the case.

14. Why is the computer so useful as a designing tool?

15. Make a multiview drawing of a simple project you have made or intend to make.

16. If your software package allows you to do so, place a) text; b) drawings; c) dimensions; on different layers.

17. From freehand sketches use the computer to make a working drawing of a small bookcase.

18. Plot your drawings on a plotter and print them on a printer.

19. Other than producing drawings, what additional uses might a computer have in design and manufacture?

23

Mechanisms

Introduction

You very probably came to school this morning in a car or on a bike. Both of these are **machines**, or a collection of **mechanisms** designed to perform a specific function. In the case of the car this function is to transport people and goods over varying distances at a range of speeds.

Common everyday machines, but by no means simple

However, if we were asked to define exactly what a mechanism *is* we might have some difficulty. This is because they are so much a part of our everyday life that we take them very much for granted and seldom, if ever, think about them.

What is a mechanism?

We might define it as:

'A device which employs simple mechanical principles to achieve specific outcomes.'

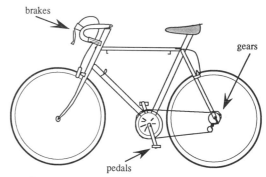

Some mechanisms on a bicycle

Such devices may be very simple, e.g. the lid of a jam jar, a zip on a skirt or a car jack, or they may be more complex, such as the gears on a bike, a large crane or the engine of a car. But no matter how involved and complicated they become, they have been designed either

a) to perform a specific function more easily, or

b) to perform some function that might be impossible to achieve without them.

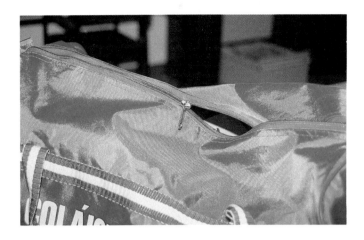

The engine of a car — an extremely complex mechanism

The gears on a bicycle — how hard cycling would be without them!

Simple examples that we take for granted

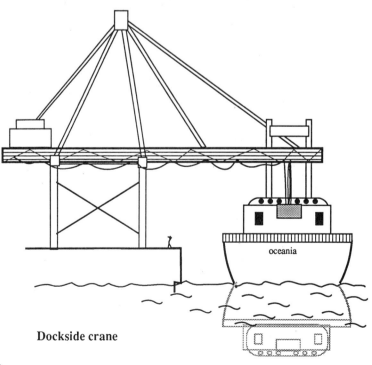

Dockside crane

Characteristics of mechanisms

If we study closely any number of mechanisms we will find that they show the following characteristics:

- All require an **input** to make them work, e.g. hand pulling a bike's brake lever.

OUTPUT — brake blocks gripping wheel rims

INPUT — Hand pulling brake lever

- An **output** of some form is generated, e.g. the brake pads grip the wheel rim, generating friction which stops the bike.
- They make the job easier to perform.
- Some form of **force** is involved.
- They involve some form of **motion**.

Forces

'A force is anything which causes change, or tends to cause change in the velocity of an object.'

Mechanisms attempt to do one or both of two things with forces:

a) convert it from one form to another, e.g. the use of a jack to lift a car. The rotational force applied by the crank is converted into a vertical, upward force;

Jacked-up car. Could you lift it alone?

b) achieve a large output force through the amplification of a smaller input force, e.g. turning a vice handle allows a much greater force to be exerted on the work in the vice.

The vice grips works firmly through the application of a small force

Extending the length of the spanner to remove those stubborn nuts!

In order for some machines to operate effectively the moments on both sides of the pivot point must be balanced, e.g. in cranes or weighing scales.

This amplification of forces has a lot to do with the idea of moments.

moment (Nm) = force (newtons) x distance (from fulcrum in metres)

e.g. a force of 20N applied to the vice handle 150mm from its pivot point gives a moment of

20 x .15 = 3Nm.

Increasing the distance from the pivot point at which the force is applied allows for greater output and moments without any increase in the input. For example, if the vice handle was increased in length to 1m the moment of the same 20N force would be 20Nm, nearly seven times as great. This idea of achieving a greater output or moment by increasing the distance of the effort from the load can be seen practically when a bar is fitted over a spanner to remove stubborn nuts.

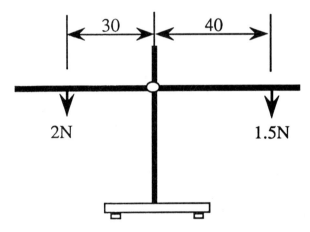

Moments balanced

Motion

There are four principal forms of motion:

a) **rotary:** the rotation of things in circles, e.g. cogs, wheels, etc.;

b) **linear:** movement in a straight line, e.g. the carriage in a typewriter or the daisywheel in a printer;

Rotary motion

Linear motion

c) **oscillating:** backwards and forwards motion in a fixed arc, e.g. a clock's pendulum;

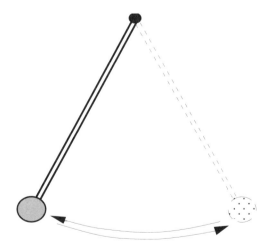

Oscillating motion

d) **reciprocating:** movement upwards and downwards in a straight line, e.g. a scroll saw blade, pistons in an internal combustion engine, etc.

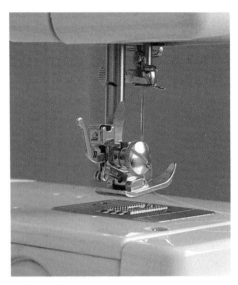

Reciprocating motion

A lot of mechanisms involve the changing of motion from one form to another, e.g. the rotation of the electric motor being converted into reciprocating motion in the scroll saw, or the oscillation of a clock's pendulum being converted into rotary motion in the clock's mechanism.

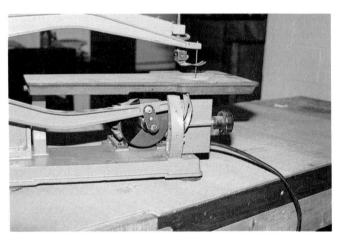

Rotation of wheel creates reciprocating motion in the scroll saw blade

Some of the simplest and most useful mechanisms known to mankind are:

a) levers;

b) linkages;

c) pulleys;

d) gears.

Levers

Very basic in concept and operation, they are probably the earliest mechanism discovered by people, being used to move heavy boulders and rocks from fields that otherwise they would not have been capable of shifting (see mechanical advantage).

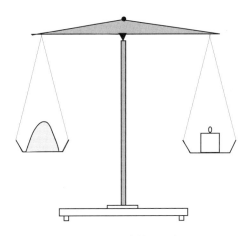

Balance type weighing scales

All levers consist essentially of a rigid beam pivoted at a point called the **fulcrum** and operate on the application of the principle of moments.

There are three classes of lever:

First class of lever

a) The fulcrum is located between the load and the effort. By increasing the distance between the fulcrum and the effort you can either

  i) move a larger load than would otherwise be possible; or

  ii) use a smaller effort to move the same load.

Examples: weighing scales, scissors, crowbar, etc.

Second class of lever:

b) The fulcrum is located at one end of the lever and the load is between it and the effort. Since both the load and the effort are on the same side, it is the difference between their respective moments that provides their effectiveness. In other words, the further the effort is from the load, and consequently the fulcrum, the easier the work becomes.

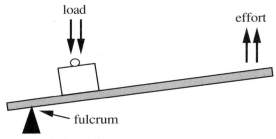

Second class of lever

Examples: wheelbarrow, bottle opener.

Third class of lever:

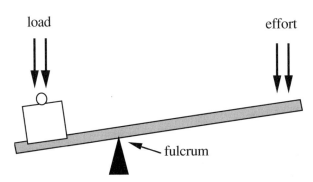

First class of lever

Bottle openers

c) The fulcrum is at one end of the lever and the effort is applied between it and the load. The closer the effort is to the load the easier it is to move, but the moments for the load will always be greater than those for the effort.

Examples: shovel (when lifting earth), tweezers.

Mechanical advantage

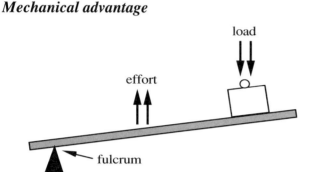

Third class of lever

We can see with levers that a large load can be moved through the application of a relatively small force or effort. In other words, the lever allows us to achieve a **mechanical advantage**.

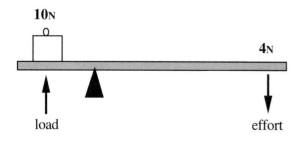

Mechanical advantage = $\dfrac{\text{load}}{\text{effort}}$

e.g. MA = $\dfrac{10}{4}$ = 2.5

In order to obtain this advantage, the effort must move through a greater distance (800 mm) than the load (240 mm). The ratio of these two distances is called the **velocity ratio**.

Velocity ratio = $\dfrac{\text{distance moved by effort}}{\text{distance moved by load}}$

e.g. VR = $\dfrac{800}{240}$ = 3.33

All mechanisms lose some of the input effort through friction, heat, etc. The **efficiency** of such mechanisms is given by

Efficiency = $\dfrac{\text{MA}}{\text{VR}}$

e.g. Efficiency = $\dfrac{2.5}{3.33}$ = 75%

Linkages

When a number of levers are connected together we get another mechanism, a linkage. Linkages allow us to change a force's direction, change its magnitude, or both. In addition, we can use linkages to make parts move parallel to each other. An example of a simple linkage is the mechanism whereby a pedal bin opens when you press down on the pedal. The pedal is attached to a lever which pushes up a rod at the back and this in turn pushes up the lid.

The direction of motion can be changed in a linkage by using a simple connecting lever. In addition, by adjusting the position of the fulcrum in the lever we can adjust the magnitude of the output motion.

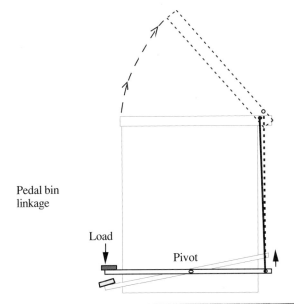

Pedal bin linkage

Load

Pivot

An old but effective linkage: downward pressure on footrest rotates wheel.

In order to get an output motion in the same direction as the input motion it is necessary to use two levers in the linkage.

In order to change the direction between input and output through 90° we need to use a **bell crank** linkage. The brakes on a bike operate on this bell crank principle.

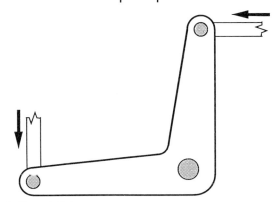

Bell crank linkage

We can also use linkages to make things move in a certain direction and keep a fixed distance between them, e.g. the linkage on a tool box that displays all the trays when the box is opened. Other useful examples of such **parallel linkages** can be seen in the lazy tongs, a pantograph copier or the safety gates on industrial elevators.

Parallel linkages assisting the opening of a tool box

Because a linkage consists of a number of connected levers it is possible to obtain a considerable mechanical advantage through their use.

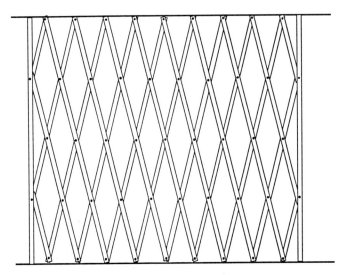

Parallel linkages (folding gate)

Pulleys

Have been in known existence for nearly 3,000 years. They consist of what are essentially grooved wheels, on which a rope or belt runs. The two principal uses they have today are:

a) lifting heavy loads;

b) transferring and increasing/decreasing rotary motion from one shaft to another.

a) Lifting:

You will often see pulleys being used on a building site to raise heavy loads. Effort is applied by pulling down on the rope and, while no mechanical advantage is achieved, it is easier and safer to pull down rather than up (unless the rope breaks!). In theory the effort required should be just greater than the load but in practice the effort will be much bigger than this as a large proportion of it will be expended in overcoming friction.

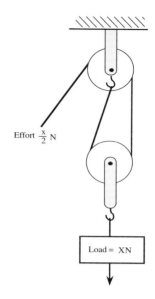

Getting a mechanical advantage with two pulleys

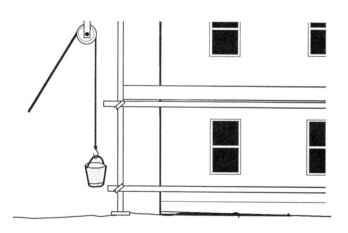

Use of pulley on a building site

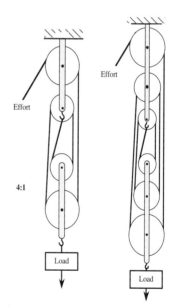

Mechanical advantages of 4:1 and 6:1

However, it is possible to achieve a mechanical advantage by using a system of two or more pulleys. The mechanical advantage is worked out by simply counting the number of pulleys the rope passes around. If the rope passes around four pulleys a mechanical advantage of 4 is achieved. Therefore only 1/4 of the original effort is required to raise the load. But four times as much rope must be pulled to achieve this.

b) Transferring motion

Pulleys are widely used in machines to transfer rotary motion from one spindle to another and often to change the speed at the same time. In fact up to quite recently all the machines in a workshop would have been driven by belts coming from a central shaft onto their own pulleys. A typical example of where this system is still used can be seen on the woodworking lathe or the pillar drill.

Belts and pulleys in drills gear box

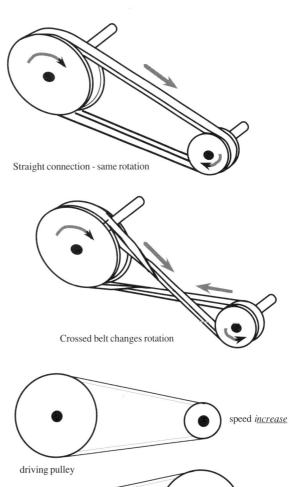

Straight connection - same rotation

Crossed belt changes rotation

speed *increase*

driving pulley

speed *decrease*

driving pulley

The bells and pulleys in the head of a pillar drill

In the early days pulleys would have been connected by ropes. Nowadays the most commonly used belt is a V-belt which fits snugly into the pulley's groove to avoid slippage. When the **driver** pulley is connected to the **driven** pulley without crossing the belt both will rotate in the same direction. Changes in speed are achieved by using different sizes of driver and driven pulleys. In general, a large driver pulley connected to a smaller driven pulley will give a high output speed. Lathes and drills have stepped cone pulleys where different combinations of driver and driven pulleys can be set for different speed settings.

Stepped cone pulleys for controlling the speed of the lathe

The **velocity ratio** for pulleys is given by

$$VR = \frac{\text{diameter of driven pulley}}{\text{diameter of driver pulley}}$$

The **output speed** can be worked out using

$$OS = \frac{\text{Input speed}}{VR}$$

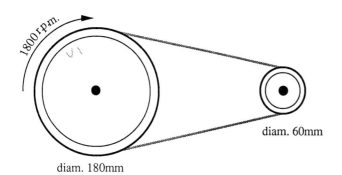

Calculate the rpm of the smaller pulley

e.g. if the driver pulley has a diameter of 180mm and an input speed of 1800rpm and the driven pulley is 60mm in diameter, calculate the output speed.

$$VR = \frac{60}{180} = \frac{1}{3} \text{ or } 1{:}3$$

$$OS = \frac{1800}{1{:}3} = 1800 \times \frac{3}{1} = 5400 \text{ rpm.}$$

Torque

Torque is the turning force of a system. Changing the speed alters the torque inversely, i.e. increasing the speed reduces torque, reducing the speed increases torque. A slower turning wheel is capable of producing larger forces than a faster turning one; e.g. a small motor rotating

at 3000 rpm can easily be stopped by catching between two fingers (be careful!). By reducing the speed through a pulley system the torque is increased.

Output torque = input torque x VR

e.g. a small motor produces a torque of 5Nm. It is used to power a model car using a driver pulley of 50mm diameter and a driven pulley of 10mm diameter.

$$VR = \frac{50}{10} = \frac{5}{1} = 5{:}1$$

Output torque = 5Nm x 5 = 25Nm.

Other variations on the pulley mechanism include round belts (used where driver and driven pulleys are at 90° to each other, e.g. vacuum cleaners), chains and sprockets, e.g. bicycles, and toothed belts, which reduce the tendency for slippage to occur, e.g. in graphics, plotters.

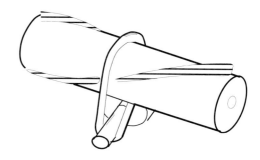

Round belt on vacuum cleaner

The chain and sprocket drive on a planing machine

Toothed belt on a typewriter carriage

Reverse rotation in two gears

Gears

One of the most common and useful types of mechanism we have. They are wheels with specially shaped teeth that enable them to connect or **mesh** smoothly with other gears in order to change the direction and/or magnitude of rotational forces. When a number of gears are connected together we get a **gear train**.

A simple gear train — note the direction of rotation

There are different types of gears that may be used to achieve different outcomes.

a) Spur:

These are used in light-duty applications to either reverse the rotational direction of the shafts or to reduce/increase their rotational speed. The drive shafts of spur gears are parallel to each other.

Unlike pulleys, where gears mesh together, the direction of rotation is reversed. When this is undesirable a third **idler** gear is included in the train to maintain the same direction in both the driven gear and the driver gear.

The use of an idler to maintain direction of rotation in a gear train

When spur gears are used to change the speed of rotation the velocity ratio can be calculated as follows:

$$VR = \frac{\text{no. teeth on driven gear}}{\text{no. teeth on driver gear}}$$

e.g driver gear has 12 teeth, driven gear has 48 teeth

$$VR = \frac{48}{12} = 4:1$$

i.e. four turns of the driver gear are necessary to obtain one revolution of the driven gear. In other words, the output speed is 1/4 the input speed. (*Note:* torque will have increased in the same proportion.)

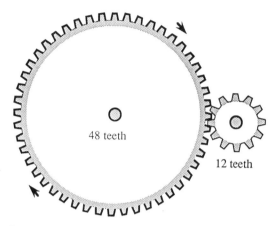

If an idler is being used in a gear train to maintain the direction of rotation it will have no effect on the velocity ratio between the two gears.

Compound gear trains, involving several sets of meshing gears, are often used to achieve large speed reductions/increases between input

Calculating velocity ratio for a compound gear train

and output shafts. To calculate the velocity ratio for the whole train we need to know the VR for each pair.

$$VR_{tot} = VR1 \times VR2 \times VR3$$

b) *Bevel*

These are used to connect two shafts that are at 90° to each other. They can also be used to achieve quite significant velocity ratios. Used in woodwork hand drills, food mixers, etc.

Use of bevel gears in a band and breast drill

c) *Worm*

These gears are also used to connect shafts at 90° to each other but with the specific function of achieving large speed reductions and torque increases. The worm gear has only a single continuous tooth therefore the velocity ratio is high

e.g. a worm wheel has 25 teeth, the velocity ratio is $\frac{25}{1}$, so that it would take 25 revolutions of the worm to give one revolution of the wheel.

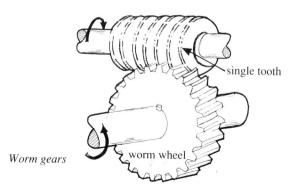

Worm gears

d) Helical

The teeth on a helical gear wheel are at an angle across the face of the wheel, being part of a helix. They give a more positive meshing affect, particularly at high speeds and are quieter than spur gears. Widely used in engine gearboxes for cars.

Helical gears

Changing the helical pattern of the teeth to a spiral allows them to transfer motion through 90°. These are known as crossed helical gears.

Crossed helical gears

e) Rack and pinion

These allow the conversion of rotary motion to linear motion or vice versa. They are used in the steering mechanism of many cars where the pinion is fitted to the steering wheel shaft and the rack to the front transverse axis. They are also used on mortise machines and pillar drills to bring the drilling head down onto the work.

Rack and pinion

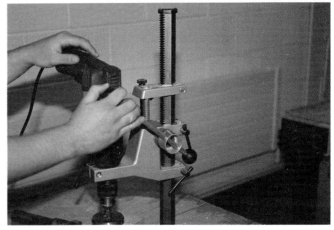

The use of a rack and pinion in a small drill stand for a portable drill

Friction

Friction is a serious enemy of all mechanisms and machines. It reduces their efficiency and means that the input must be increased to maintain the same output. It also leads to wearing of the moving parts, overheating, brittleness and eventual failure. Friction can be reduced by:

a) Lubrication

Lubricant is forced between the moving surfaces so that instead of two rough surfaces moving over each other they float on a film of oil or grease. While these are suitable for many locations, other lubricants are also used. For example, **graphite** is often used in precision instruments where grease would collect dust.

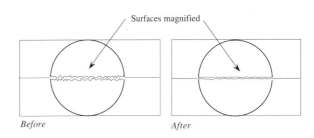

Action of a lubricant

b) Bearings

They are commonly used where shafts are involved to reduce the friction between the shaft and its mountings. There are three main types of bearings:

Plain

Also called **bushes**, they are usually made from a softer material than the shaft and kept well lubricated, having grooves machined in them to hold and dispense the lubricant effectively. Nylon is used in the manufacture of bearings for light loads such as in cassette recorders as it does not require lubrication. Bronze and bronze alloys are used for heavier loads such as small electric motors.

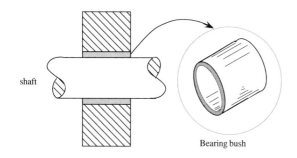

Plain bearing

Ball

Two circular grooved **races** have a number of spheres between them. These may be of plastic, brass or steel and are usually soaked in grease for lubrication. In order to reduce friction the ball bearings are separated from each other by **cages**. They are extremely useful and are widely used in motors, bicycles, toys, washing machines, etc.

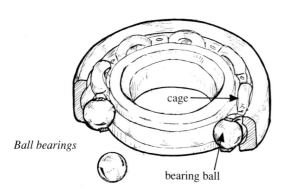

Ball bearings

Roller

These are similar to ball bearings but use steel rollers in place of spheres. This enables them to carry greater loads or to be fitted where space is limited. **Taper** roller bearings are widely used for the wheel bearings in many types of car.

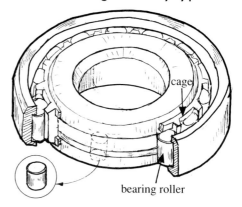

Roller bearing

Activities

1. Sketch four different articles that you use every day that make use of mechanisms.

2. Calculate X for each of the following:

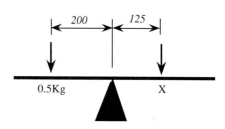

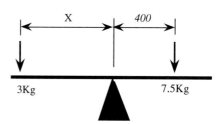

3. Describe the three classes of lever and give examples of each.

308

4. Explain what is meant by:

    a) mechanical advantage

    b) velocity ratio

    c) efficiency

5. If a load of 200kg is to be raised 25m using a system, as illustrated, of four pulleys, what is a) the effort required and b) the rope pulled in if the efficiency is 100%.

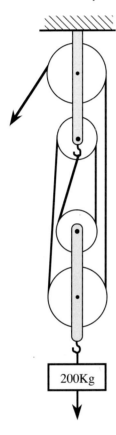

200Kg

6. If a driver pulley has a diameter of 210mm and an input speed of 450rpm, what will be the output speed for a 70mm driven pulley.

7. If a motor produces 10Nm of torque to a driver pulley 75mm in diameter and the output torque is 30Nm, what is the diameter of the driver pulley?

8. Why is an 'idler' gear used in a gear train?

9. Calculate the velocity ratio for this gear set.

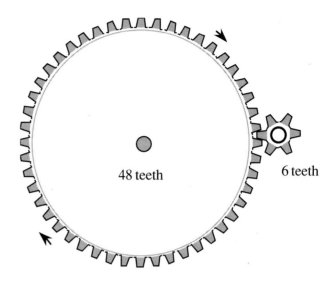

48 teeth   6 teeth

10. Explain how friction affects mechanisms and how it can be reduced.

11. Design and make a storage container for computer disks that can be opened with one finger.

12. Design and make a medicine cabinet with a self-closing door.

13. Design and make a folding study table.

14. Design and make a disc sanding machine.

15. Design and make a model crane that is capable of lifting 2kg.

16. Design and make an electric vehicle with more than one speed.